Cleaning Up Renaissance Italy

Cleaning Up Renaissance Italy

Environmental Ideals and Urban Practice in Genoa and Venice

JANE L. STEVENS CRAWSHAW

Great Clarendon Street, Oxford, OX2 6DP,
United Kingdom

Oxford University Press is a department of the University of Oxford.
It furthers the University's objective of excellence in research, scholarship,
and education by publishing worldwide. Oxford is a registered trade mark of
Oxford University Press in the UK and in certain other countries

© Jane L. Stevens Crawshaw 2023

The moral rights of the author have been asserted

All rights reserved. No part of this publication may be reproduced, stored in
a retrieval system, or transmitted, in any form or by any means, without the
prior permission in writing of Oxford University Press, or as expressly permitted
by law, by licence or under terms agreed with the appropriate reprographics
rights organization. Enquiries concerning reproduction outside the scope of the
above should be sent to the Rights Department, Oxford University Press, at the
address above

You must not circulate this work in any other form
and you must impose this same condition on any acquirer

Published in the United States of America by Oxford University Press
198 Madison Avenue, New York, NY 10016, United States of America

British Library Cataloguing in Publication Data
Data available

Library of Congress Control Number: 2023932357

ISBN 978–0–19–886743–2

DOI: 10.1093/oso/9780198867432.001.0001

Printed and bound in the UK by
Clays Ltd, Elcograf S.p.A.

Links to third party websites are provided by Oxford in good faith and
for information only. Oxford disclaims any responsibility for the materials
contained in any third party website referenced in this work.

For Ann and Richard Stevens

Acknowledgements

The pilot research for this book was funded by a Leverhulme/British Academy Small Grant in 2012–13. This provided the opportunity to hold a conference in Oxford in 2012 and I am very grateful to all attendees and speakers for their fascinating contributions. I had the privilege of continuing my research on this topic as part of an Early Career Fellowship funded by the Leverhulme Trust between 2012 and 2017. At the end of my ECR fellowship, I was appointed to a permanent post in the School of History, Philosophy and Culture at Oxford Brookes University. Throughout my time there I have received research support from the School itself and the completion of this book would not have been possible without a University Research Excellence Award in 2020. My colleagues at Oxford Brookes have been a source of insight, encouragement, and support, particularly Maya Corry, Tom Crook, Ian Holgate, Sally Holloway, Ioanna Iordanou, Erik Landis, Marika Leino, Glen O'Hara, Viviane Quirke, Charles Robertson, and Cassie Watson. Joanne Begiato, Alysa Levene, and Andrew Spicer have shared particular wisdom and friendship for which I remain indebted.

I have enjoyed conversations and collaborations with many scholars, including audiences at seminars and conferences. I remain grateful to Alex Bamji, Janna Coomans, Julia DeLancey, Filippo de Vivo, Guy Geltner, Federica Gigante, Lydia Hamlett, John Henderson, Mary Laven, Marie-Louise Leonard, Elaine Leong, Giuseppe Marcocci, Carole Rawcliffe, Gervase Rosser, Rosa Salzburg, Sharon Strocchia, Emanuela Vai, and Claire Weeda for their advice and feedback. Marie-Louise provided generous assistance in early 2021 when the COVID-19 pandemic prohibited my return to the city. The material for chapter one was developed as part of a stimulating Global City project led by Emma Hart.

The archivists and staff at the Archivio Storico del Comune, in Genoa, and the Archivio di Stato in Venice were courteous and generously shared their professional expertise. Anna and Federico Re provided hospitality and friendship in Genoa, not only to me but also to my family. They made the city soon feel like a home away from home and seeing Genoa through their eyes was an unexpected delight of this project.

Cathryn Steele and Stephanie Ireland provided excellent support at Oxford University Press. The anonymous readers' reports were of considerable value and I am grateful to the scholars who engaged so constructively with the peer review process.

I began my research project on Renaissance cleanliness around the same time that our first child was born. Since that time, I have learned a great deal about dirt and hygiene, as well as sickness and health, both past and present. My two children have been a source of unimaginable joy during the research and writing of this book. My husband has been steadfast in his love and support: 'a fountain in a waste | a well of water in a country dry, or anything that's honest and good | an eye that makes the whole world bright'.[1]

I had always planned to dedicate this book to my parents but could never have anticipated how much they would deserve it. They have constantly put the well-being and needs of my young family above their own. I will always owe them more than I can express.

---

[1] Edwin Muir, 'The Confirmation' in Gaby Morgan (ed.), *A Year of Scottish Poems* (London: Pan Macmillan, 2020).

Contents

List of Illustrations	xi
List of Abbreviations	xiii
Introduction	1
1. Constructing Ideals and Practices in Renaissance Port Cities	26

PART ONE: THE EBBS AND FLOWS OF DAILY LIFE

2. Channelling Health: The Flow of the Streets	51
3. Preserving Purity: The Symbolic and Practical Regulation of Water	78
4. Stemming the Tide: Innovation and Purgation	105

PART TWO: BODIES: CONCEPTS OF BALANCE AND BLAME

5. Working with Waste: Space, Reuse, and the Urban Body	133
6. Dealing with Disasters: Environments, People, and Piety	158
Conclusion: Corruptible Cities	184
Bibliography	187
Index	205

List of Illustrations

I.1 Jacopo Tintoretto, *The Last Judgement* (1562–64). Venice, Church of the Madonna dell'Orto. Oil on canvas. cm 1450 × 590. © 2020. Cameraphoto/ Scala, Florence and reproduced with kind permission of the Ufficio Beni Culturali del Patriarcato di Venezia [Prot 12.22.2702]. 2

I.2 Map of Venice from Tommaso Porcacchi, *L'isole piu famose del mondo* (1572), © Wellcome Collection. Attribution 4.0 International (CC BY 4.0). 16

I.3 Genoa city and port, 1597. Painting by Cristoforo Grassi, copy of an older picture from the end of the 1400s, it shows the naval parade commemorating the Battle of Otranto, 1481. Genoa, Museo Navale di Pegli. © 2020. DeAgostini Picture Library/Scala, Florence. 21

1.1 Painting of an Ideal City (*c.*1480–4). © The Walters Art Museum, Baltimore (CC0 license). 27

1.2 Sixteenth-century Venetian glass tile showing Doge Andrea Gritti from the collection of the British Museum. © The Trustees of the British Museum. 44

4.1 Painting showing the dredging of the Genoese port in 1545: View of Genoa Port. Genoa, Museo Navale di Pegli. © 2014. DeAgostini Picture Library/Scala, Florence. 107

4.2 Painting showing the dredging of the Genoese port in 1575, Dyonis Martens, 'Escavazione del fondo marino del Mondraccio a Genova'. Tempera su tela del 1575. Genoa, Galata Museo del Mare. © 2020. A. Dagli Orti/Scala, Florence. 108

4.3 Painting showing the dredging of the Genoese port in 1597: Genoa harbour. Unknown artist. Genoa, Museo Navale di Pegli. © 2014. DeAgostini Picture Library/Scala, Florence. 109

6.1 Tile panel, earthenware; The Virgin and Child between Saint Sebastian and Saint Roch. Central Italy, probably Pesaro; about 1500–1510 © Victoria and Albert Museum, London. 159

List of Abbreviations

Antichi scrittori	R. Cessi and N. Spada (eds), *Antichi scrittori d'idraulica veneta* (Venice: Premiate Officine grafiche Carlo Ferrari, 1952)
ASCG	Archivio Storico del Comune, Genoa
ASV	Archivio di Stato, Venice
b.	*busta* (archive bundle)
BMC	The Biblioteca del Museo Correr, Venice
BMV	The Biblioteca Marciana, Venice
Cini	Fondazione Giorgio Cini, Venice
Comun	The archive of the Venetian Provveditori del Comun which had responsibility for the regulation of public space
Paschetti	Bartolomeo Paschetti, *Del conservare la sanità, et del vivere de'Genovesi* (Genoa, 1602)
PdC	The archive of the Genoese Padri del Comune which had wide-ranging responsibilities for infrastructure, public space, and the port
r	recto
reg.	*registro* (register)
Rompiasio	Caniato, Giovanni (ed.), *Metodo in pratica di sommario o sia compilazione delle leggi, terminazioni et ordini appartenenti agl'illustrissimi et eccellentissimi Collegio e Magistrato alle acque, opera dell'avvocato fiscale Giulio Rompiasio* (Venice: Ministero per I beni culturali e ambientali-Archivio di Stato, 1988).
Sanità	The archive of the Provveditori alla Sanità in Venice (Health Office)
SEA	The archive of the Venetian Savi ed esecutori alle acque (Water Office), responsible for the maintenance of bodies of water within and surrounding Venice
Secreta MMN	The series *Secreta, Materia miste notabili* in the Venetian State Archive
Senato Terra	Copies of the proposals put to vote in the Venetian Senate (the main decision-making council in Venice)
v	verso

Who can forget those moments when something that seems inanimate turns out to be vitally, even dangerously alive?

Amitav Ghosh, *The Great Derangement*

They ... found the long Bridge of Beruna in front of them. Before they had begun to cross it, however, up out of the water came a great wet, bearded head, larger than a man's, crowned with rushes. It looked at Aslan and out of its mouth a deep voice came.

'Hail, Lord,' it said. 'Loose my chains.'
'Who on earth is that*?' whispered Susan.*
'I think it's the river-god, but hush,' said Lucy.
'Bacchus,' said Aslan. 'Deliver him from his chains.'
'That means the bridge, I expect,' thought Lucy.
And so it did.

C. S. Lewis, *Prince Caspian*

Introduction

The Venetian Church of the Madonna of the Garden (the *Madonna dell'Orto*) lies at the northern edge of the district of Cannaregio, close to where the built environment meets the lagoon. A magnificent painting dominates the wall of the church's chancel. Jacopo Tintoretto's *Last Judgement* (*c.*1562) is a distinctive, Venetian variation on a common Catholic-Reformation theme [Image I.1]. Here, the moment of judgement arrives as a cascading flood. The waters sweep away the living and the dead. Angels lift the faithful from the waves. Divine temporality and the dynamics of salvation are realized through the forces of the natural world.

This is a powerful image for a city which was renowned for its distinctive construction 'in the middle of the sea'.[1] Venice's location has attracted the awe and affection of observers for centuries but it also inflicts a heavy physical toll on the city's infrastructure, from the intense strain of floods to the incremental changes wrought by humidity and the movement of the tides.[2] In the period in which Tintoretto's painting was created, the condition of the natural environment was imbued with additional force and meaning.[3] The environment was believed to reflect and shape moral conditions and concerns. What the topographical singularity of Venice made evident was true of cities across the early modern world: in order to understand the strengths and challenges of a place—political, economic, religious, social and medical—it was essential to recognize the particularities of the environment.[4]

---

[1] John Evelyn cited in Jill Steward and Alexander Cowan, 'Introduction' in *The city and the senses: urban culture since 1500* (London: Routledge, 2016), p. 4.

[2] Elizabeth Crouzet Pavan's *'Sopra le acque salse': Espaces urbains, pouvoir et société à Venise à la fin du Moyen Age* (2 vols, Rome: Istituto storico italiano per il Medio Evo, 1992) considered the ways in which the environment shaped space and forms of government in medieval Venice. Ermanno Orlando's nuanced study of the lagoon focused upon political administration rather than health and the environment. *Altre Venezie: Il dogado veneziano nei secoli XIII e XIV (giurisdizione, territorio, giustizia e amministrazione)* (Venice: Istituto veneto di scienze, lettere ed arti, 2008). See also the *Antichi scrittori* volumes and Salvatore Ciriacono, 'Scrittori d'idraulica e politica delle acque' in Girolamo Arnaldi and Manlio Pastore Stocchi (eds), *Storia della cultura veneta. Dal primo Quattrocento al Concilio di Trento* vol 3/II (Vicenza: N. Pozza, 1980), pp. 500–5. An important work on the Venetian environment during the Renaissance is Karl Appuhn, *A forest on the sea: environmental expertise in Renaissance Venice* (Baltimore MA: Johns Hopkins University Press, 2009).

[3] Claire Weeda, 'Cleanliness, civility and the city in medieval ideals and scripts' in Carole Rawcliffe and Claire Weeda (eds), *Policing the environment in premodern Europe* (Amsterdam: Amsterdam University Press, 2019), pp. 39–68.

[4] As yet, Alexandra Walsham's exploration of the influential relationship between the Reformation and the landscape in Britain has not been matched for the Catholic Reformation. Alexandra Walsham, *The Reformation of the landscape: religion, identity, and memory in early modern Britain and Ireland* (Oxford: Oxford University Press, 2011).

Cleaning Up Renaissance Italy: Environmental Ideals and Urban Practice in Genoa and Venice. Jane L. Stevens Crawshaw, Oxford University Press. © Jane L. Stevens Crawshaw 2023. DOI: 10.1093/oso/9780198867432.003.0001

2 CLEANING UP RENAISSANCE ITALY

Image I.1 Jacopo Tintoretto, *The Last Judgement* (1562–64). Venice, Church of the Madonna dell'Orto. Oil on canvas. cm 1450 × 590. © 2020. Cameraphoto/Scala, Florence and reproduced with kind permission of the Ufficio Beni Culturali del Patriarcato di Venezia [Prot 12.22.2702].

INTRODUCTION 3

The ligatures that bound people to their broader settings during the premodern period were the correspondences between the constituent parts of the human body (the four humours) and those of the natural world (the four elements).[5] These connections lay at the heart of the Hippocratic corpus of medical ideas and had been infused with Christian theology.[6] It was widely believed that environments could alter the nature of the body, shaping temperaments, behaviours and health.[7] Seafaring men, for example, were said to be 'like the Element they belong to, much given to loudness and roaring'.[8] These associations prompted government activities to manage urban space and natural environments; crucially, they endowed such work with social and symbolic significance. Interventions such as the cleaning of streets, the dredging of ports or diversion of rivers, then, were often intended to have social or religious, as well as medical and environmental, effects.[9] It is these measures and their meanings which lie at the heart of this book, which explores the social and cultural history of environmental management in two Renaissance ports: Genoa and Venice.[10]

The relevance of this subject matter is illuminated in a second painting in Venice's church of the *Madonna dell'Orto*: Tintoretto's *Presentation of the Virgin at the Temple*. As the young Virgin Mary—embodying purity—ascends ornate steps towards the High Priest, her path is lined by people: young and old, rich and poor, male and female. In the vibrant, cosmopolitan ports of Genoa and Venice,

---

[5] Sandra Cavallo and Tessa Storey (eds), *Conserving health in early modern culture: bodies and environments in Italy and England* (Manchester: Manchester University Press, 2017) considers the non-naturals in a broader geographical and chronological context.

[6] Simona Cohen has reminded us that 'correspondences established between categories of Time (days, seasons, months, ages), space (cardinal points, signs of the zodiac and planets as celestial and temporal images), and matter (elements, humours) were conceived as evidence of the divine' in 'The early Renaissance personification of Time and changing concepts of temporality', *Renaissance Studies* 14:3 (2000), 306–7. The correspondences that connected the human body (the microcosm) with the macrocosm of the environment or created world also included associations with the body politic. Just as there were four humours and elements, there were four seasons and times of the day, four parts of the known world (Africa, the Americas, Asia, and Europe) as well as four cardinal virtues in Plato's Republic (wisdom, courage, moderation, and justice). There were further correspondences between the three principal organs of the body, three ages of man, and the Christian Trinity as well as seven ages of man and seven stages in world history.

[7] Nancy G. Siraisi, *Medieval and Renaissance medicine: an introduction to knowledge and practice* (Chicago IL: University of Chicago Press, 1990).

[8] Mandeville cited in Lotte van de Pol, *The burgher and the whore: prostitution in early modern Amsterdam* (Oxford: Oxford University Press, 2011), p. 157.

[9] These connections in a colonial context see the brief mention of the drainage project of *desagüe* in Mexico City discussed by Daniel Nemser, 'Triangulating blackness: Mexico City 1612', *Mexican Studies/Estudios Mexicanos* 33:3 (2017), 349.

[10] Similar correspondences could be fruitfully explored in relation to the economy. Regulation of marketplaces was often driven by public health considerations. See Dennis Romano, *Markets and marketplaces in medieval Italy c.1100–1440* (New Haven and London: Yale University Press, 2015). For valuable work on the impact of the concept of the marketplace on expressions of spirituality and salvation see the studies by Giacomo Todeschini including *Il Prezzo della salvezza: lessici medievali del pensiero economico* (Rome: Nuova Italia scientifica, 1994). Caroline Bruzelius refers to the imagery of Christ as a good merchant in *Preaching, building and burying: friars in the medieval city* (New Haven and London: Yale University Press, 2014), p. 127.

4 CLEANING UP RENAISSANCE ITALY

the stories of environmental management involve a broad cross-section of Renaissance society: from courtesans to street food sellers and architects to canal diggers. Although the sources on which this study rests are largely archival, produced by a miniscule proportion of the male population, they reveal something of the ideals and lived experiences of a far broader social cross-section in relation to health and the environment. In his reflection on cultural history as polyphonic history, Peter Burke portrayed the history of cleanliness as a 'meeting point' between studies of codes, cultures, metaphors and identities, along with the physical objects of bodies and environments.[11] It is thus explored in this book as a point of intersection between ideas, behaviours and regulation.

A last look at the church of the *Madonna dell'Orto* reveals a final idea relevant to the management of the environment and health: the dynamic intersection between the units of the locality and the state.[12] Many of the images on show in the church depicted or were produced by inhabitants of the parish, including members of the Tintoretto family and Paris Bordone.[13] These remain alongside representations of important civic figures, as well as Venetian saints, the portraits of whom were commissioned in 1622 by the city's Patriarch Giovanni Tiepolo.

This interplay between the circumstances of the locality and the intentions of centralizing institutions (including both the state and the Catholic Church) is also evident if we move 165 miles west, to a second church dedicated to Our Lady of the Garden (*Nostra Signora dell'Orto*) in the seaport of Chiavari on the Ligurian coast. Here, in the early decades of the seventeenth century, a cult developed amongst the poor inhabitants of a suburb. It gained such momentum that the ecclesiastical and political authorities eventually authorized and formalized the devotions.[14] Its history reminds us that layers of authority and identity coexisted in Renaissance territories. The concerns and priorities of people at local, civic and territorial level sometimes competed. Notions of order, piety or wellbeing could as readily result in tension as collaborative enterprise. Communities also used the structures of environmental management, amongst others, to resolve the challenges of urban life—both social and physical—as well as being subject to the oversight of the same.

---

[11] Peter Burke, 'Cultural history as polyphonic history', *ARBOR Ciencia, Pensamiento y Cultura* CLXXXVI 743 (2010), 479–86. See also the work of Mark Jenner including 'Doctoring the environment without doctors? Public cleanliness and environmental governance in early modern London', *Storia urbana* 112 (2006), 17–37.

[12] On Renaissance Italian states and key historiographical debates and developments see the introduction to Andrea Gamberini and Isabella Lazzarini, *The Italian Renaissance State* (Cambridge: Cambridge University Press, 2012). Michael J. Braddick, *State formation in early modern England c.1550–1700* (Cambridge: Cambridge University Press, 2000) provides a valuable series of perspectives on state formation of this period. For the vitality of the locality in Venice see the series of volumes coordinated by Gianmario Guidarelli entitled 'Churches of Venice. New research perspectives'.

[13] Tom Nichols, *Tintoretto: tradition and identity* (London: Reaktion, 2015).

[14] Jane Garnett and Gervase Rosser, *Spectacular miracles: transforming images in Italy from the Renaissance to the present* (London: Reaktion, 2013), p. 81.

INTRODUCTION 5

This book bridges the histories of urban and natural space, studying cities in their wider contexts and highlighting the importance of the environment for the wellbeing of early modern society.[15] The environmental ideals referred to in the title include those which relate to both built and natural settings. The reference to urban practices is not intended to suggest that the spatial unit of study here is limited by walls or other civic boundaries. Instead, the study is directed by what might be termed an urban gaze and dilates upon those environmental issues and concerns which were believed to be pertinent to the health and wellbeing of the city. The dynamics of ideal and practice in central squares and prominent streets are considered alongside spaces which were more hidden from view: dark, narrow alley ways and capacious subterranean drains.[16] These places formed a vital part of the infrastructure of health, which was so central to the experience of life in the Renaissance city, and through which urban centres were connected with their wider settings.[17]

This perspective highlights the notable importance of the locality and region in early modern environmental thinking, even at a time when History was being written and rewritten in the context of expanding understandings of the world.[18] In Genoa and Venice explanations of environmental changes rarely employed a frame of reference as broad as an ocean or continent.[19] Instead, environmental problems and solutions were situated in a more limited geographical area.[20] The

---

[15] For a discussion on the historiography of urban and environmental history of the early modern period see Martin Knoll, 'From "urban gap" to social metabolism: the early modern city in environmental history research' in Martin Knoll and Reinhold Reith (eds), *An environmental history of the early modern period: experiments and perspectives* (Zurich: Lit, 2014), pp. 45–50. Useful reflections on methodology and approach are also made in Georg Stöger, 'Environmental perspectives on pre-modern European cities—difficulties and possibilities' in Martin Knoll and Reinhold Reith (eds), *An environmental history*, pp. 51–5. Excellent introductions include Sverker Sörlin and Paul Warde (eds), *Nature's end: history and the environment* (Basingstoke: Palgrave Macmillan, 2009) and Paul Stock (ed.), *The uses of space in early modern History* (New York NY: Palgrave Macmillan, 2015). On the concept of 'space' for historians see Peter Arnade, Martha Howell, and Walter Simons, 'Fertile spaces: the productivity of urban space in northern Europe', *Journal of Interdisciplinary History* 32 (2002), 515–28.

[16] Fabrizio Nevola, *Street life in Renaissance Italy* (New Haven and London: Yale University Press, 2020) has explored this relationship between people and place in the built environment.

[17] This study argues for a broad definition of 'health infrastructure' and notes the ongoing debate in a contemporary context about an 'artificial divide between physical and human infrastructure' in Bhav Jain, Simar S. Bajaj, and Fatima Cody Stanford, 'All Infrastructure Is Health Infrastructure', *American Journal of Public Health* 112:1 (2022), 24–6.

[18] Giuseppe Marcocci, *The globe on paper: writing histories of the world in Renaissance Europe and the Americas* (Oxford: Oxford University Press, 2020). Lydia Barnett, *After the flood: imagining the global environment in early modern Europe* (Baltimore MA: Johns Hopkins University Press, 2019).

[19] Cornell Fleischer, 'A Mediterranean apocalypse: prophecies of empire in the fifteenth and sixteenth centuries', *Journal of the Economic and Social History of the Orient* 61:1–2, 18–90 on the interesting connections between Millenarian thought across the Mediterranean. Alison Bashford, David Armitage, and Sujit Sivasundaram (eds), *Oceanic histories* (Cambridge: Cambridge University Press, 2018).

[20] Future research would benefit from an exploration of those environmental features, such as rivers which traversed political boundaries in order to explore issues of localism and regionalism in greater depth.

6 CLEANING UP RENAISSANCE ITALY

themes explored in this book, therefore, require a specific form of 'connected history', which is distinctly situational and social.[21] Knowledge about health and the environment combined social, religious and ethnic stereotypes and prejudices with medical theory and empirical observation. This argument builds on insights from anthropology (particularly the widely-influential work of Mary Douglas [1921–2007]).[22] Her methodology for aligning human universals and cultural phenomena has paved the way for comparative approaches to health and wellbeing.[23]

When writers of the period referred to public health (as *salute 'commune'*, *'pubblica'* or *'universale'*), they understood this to encompass a broad, interconnected range of ideas and initiatives relating to behaviour, morality and salubrity, including both preventative and curative practices.[24] This language was frequently invoked in Venice, alongside that of 'comfort', 'utility' and 'benefit' to justify environmental interventions. In Genoa, however, strikingly similar measures were justified with reference to 'public comfort' (*commodo publico*) and the need to protect the city's port. The concept of public health was articulated less readily to justify government interventions and a greater role was acknowledged for individuals, particularly members of the elite, in sparking and sustaining activities. Here we see the 'informal world [of Italian Renaissance politics which] faced the institutions, forming with them the *unicum* of politics'.[25] The comparison between these two city-states helps to shift our focus away from the dominance of notions (or long histories) of public health in recent studies to recognize that efforts to preserve the health of cities might not require the frequent deployment of this term or its associated bureaucratic structures (represented so often in a Renaissance Italian context by government Health Offices).[26]

---

[21] For an important study of connected history see Sanjay Subrahmanyam, 'Connected histories: notes towards a reconfiguration of early modern Eurasia', *Modern Asian Studies* 31:3 (1997), 735–62.

[22] Mary Douglas, *Purity and danger: an analysis of concepts of pollution and taboo* (London: Routledge, 2002).

[23] For a stimulating discussion of Douglas's ideas and their impact see Mark Bradley, 'Approaches to pollution and propriety' in Mark Bradley (ed.), *Rome, pollution and propriety: dirt, disease and hygiene in the Eternal City from antiquity to modernity* (Cambridge: Cambridge University Press, 2012), pp. 11–40.

[24] See Sandra Cavallo and Tessa Storey, *Healthy living in late Renaissance Italy* (Oxford: Oxford University Press, 2014); Roberta Mucciarelli, 'Igiene, salute e pubblica decoro nel Medioevo' in Roberta Mucciarelli, Laura Vigni, and Donatella Fabbri (eds), *Vergognosa immunditia: igiene pubblica e privata a Siena dal medioevo all'età contemporanea* (Siena: NIE, 2000); John Henderson, *The Renaissance hospital: healing the body and healing the soul* (New Haven and London: Yale University Press, 2006); Laura McGough, *Gender, sexuality and syphilis in early modern Venice: the disease that came to stay* (Basingstoke: Palgrave Macmillan, 2011); Samuel K. Cohn Jr., *Cultures of plague: medical thinking at the end of the Renaissance* (Oxford: Oxford University Press, 2010) and Gauvin Bailey, Pamela Jones, Franco Mormando, and Thomas Worcester (eds), *Hope and healing: painting in Italy in a time of plague 1500–1800* (Worcester MA: Worcester Art Museum, 2005).

[25] Andrea Gamberini and Isabella Lazzarini (eds), *The Italian Renaissance State*, p. 4.

[26] Traditional accounts, such as the excellent work of Carlo Cipolla, recognized the early development of Italian health boards and their broad jurisdictional responsibilities. For example, Carlo Cipolla, *Public health and the medical profession in the Renaissance* (Cambridge: Cambridge University Press, 1976).

INTRODUCTION 7

Alternative concepts might also facilitate efforts to institute urban cleanliness and collective wellbeing. What emerges from this study of Genoa and Venice is the emphasis placed on environmental ideals to justify urban practices in relation to health.

An emphasis on the condition of places highlights the historically-contingent nature of the agency of space. As part of the 'spatial turn' in historical writing, scholars have responded to the work of Michel De Certeau and Henri Lefebvre, amongst others, to explore the dynamics of space in cities and on streets.[27] As yet, these studies have yet to be aligned fully with the mechanisms by which place was believed to exert agency over time.[28] For many centuries, and across many cultures, this impact was explained using the tenets of the Hippocratic Corpus.[29] In this enduring framework, people were directly shaped by (and, in turn, altered) their urban and natural environments. 'Private' issues of behaviour and cleanliness, therefore, were of public significance. A failure to follow health measures was more than an inconvenience or annoyance: the nature of neighbours and neighbourhoods could have physical and moral consequences.[30]

The focus here on the fifteenth and sixteenth centuries is not intended to suggest that these correspondences, implications or practices were new in the Renaissance.[31] There is significant continuity to be emphasized in the environmental and medical practices undertaken between the periods which precede and follow the one under consideration here.[32] Indeed, it is hardly surprising to find

[27] Beat Kümin and Cornelie Usborne, 'At home and in the workplace: a historical introduction to the "spatial turn"', *History and Theory* 52 (2013), 305–18. For the early modern period see Marc Boone and Martha Howell (eds), *The power of space in late medieval and early modern Europe: the cities of Italy, Northern France and the Low Countries* (Turnhout: Brepols, 2013) and Georgia Clarke and Fabrizio Nevola (eds), 'The experience of the street in early modern Italy', *I Tatti Studies in the Italian Renaissance* 16:1/2 (2013).

[28] These associations have attracted less attention from early modern social and cultural historians than scholars of English literature or medical history. Exceptions include Sara Miglietti and John Morgan (eds), *Governing the environment in the early modern world: theory and practice* (London: Routledge, 2017) and Hannah Newton, ' "Nature concocts and expels": the agents and processes of recovery from disease in early modern England', *Social History of Medicine* 28:3 (2015), 465–86.

[29] Charles Estienne explained variations of soil with reference to humoural combinations—clays were cold and moist, sands hot and dry and all others were mix. See Paul Warde, *The invention of sustainability: nature and destiny c.1500–1870* (Cambridge: Cambridge University Press, 2018), p. 45. For the revival of Hippocratic ideas in the sixteenth century see David Cantor (ed.), *Reinventing Hippocrates* (Aldershot: Ashgate, 2002).

[30] See Barbara Rouse, 'Nuisance neighbours and persistent polluters: the urban code of behaviour in late medieval London' in Andrew Brown and Jan Dumoly (eds), *Medieval urban culture* (Turnhout: Brepols, 2007), 75–92; Bronach C. Kane and Simon Sandall, *The experience of neighbourhood in medieval and early modern Europe* (London: Routledge, 2022); Paula Hohti Erichsen, *Artisans, objects, and everyday life in Renaissance Italy: the material culture of the middling class* (Amsterdam: Amsterdam University Press, 2020), pp. 70–1.

[31] Kathleen Davis, *Periodization and sovereignty: how ideas of feudalism and secularization govern the politics of time* (Philadelphia PA: University of Pennsylvania Press, 2008).

[32] For the preceding period see Guy Geltner, *The roads to health: infrastructure and urban wellbeing in medieval Italy* (Philadelphia PA: University of Pennsylvania Press, 2019) and 'Healthscaping a medieval city: Lucca's *curia viarum* and the future of public health history', *Urban History* 40:3 (2013), 395–415; Carole Rawcliffe, *Urban bodies: communal health in late medieval English towns and cities*

8 CLEANING UP RENAISSANCE ITALY

repetition in measures, given that cleaning is often ongoing and repetitive work. Whilst acknowledging important continuities, archival material reveals four things which were specific about the management of health and the environment during the Renaissance. First, this work was undertaken in a context of considerable epidemiological and environmental change. Europe entered what has been termed the Little Ice Age and scholars of epidemic disease have recognized that outbreaks of plague (and the new disease of the pox) intensified in frequency and severity.[33] These changes were not specific to Northern Italian cities but were combined in this context with the second notable change of this period: significant demographic growth and urbanization.

Genoa and Venice were amongst the most populous European cities during the fifteenth and sixteenth centuries. The size of the former increased from approximately 51,000 people in 1531 to 67,000 in 1579: a rise of a third over the course of fifty years. Venice's population in 1563 was estimated at just over 168,000, having risen from 115,000 at the turn of the sixteenth century, presenting a larger percentage increase than that of Genoa.[34] In neither city were the changes in population size linear. Successive periods of natural disaster prompted considerable fluctuations. Overall, however, both cities experienced demographic and urban growth during the sixteenth century. The identification of population density as a driver for the intensification of concerns about cleanliness is not a new idea.[35] It has not, however, been the traditional explanation for these measures in Renaissance Italy where developments have been more readily attributed to perceptions of an advanced form of the Italian Renaissance state or the shock caused by demographic crises such as recurrent outbreaks of plague.[36]

(Woodbridge: The Boydell Press, 2013). Janna Coomans, *Community, urban health and the environment in the late medieval Low Countries* (Cambridge: Cambridge University Press, 2021). See also contributions to Carole Rawcliffe and Claire Weeda (eds), *Policing the urban environment*. For responsibilities in medieval statutes see Miri Rubin 'Urban statutes and newcomers' in *Cities of strangers: making lives in medieval Europe* (Cambridge: Cambridge University Press, 2020), pp. 33–5. For the eighteenth century see the excellent work of Maria Pia Donato and Renato Sansa.

[33] On the little ice age see Wolfgang Behringer, *A cultural history of climate*, P. Camiller (trans) (Cambridge: Cambridge University Press, 2010). On the changing nature of plague in the premodern period see Jane Stevens Crawshaw, *Plague hospitals: public health for the city in early modern Venice* (Aldershot: Ashgate, 2012), pp. 9, 240, and 245. Guido Alfani, *Calamities and the economy in Renaissance Italy. The Grand Tour of the Horsemen of the Apocalypse* (Basingstoke: Palgrave Macmillan, 2013). John Henderson, *Florence under siege: surviving plague in an early modern city* (London and New Haven: Yale University Press, 2019).

[34] Daniele Beltrami, *Storia della popolazione di Venezia* (Padua: CEDAM, 1954) estimates 168,027 in 1563 but this fell to just over 120,000 following the plague of 1575–77 and then rose to 134,871 in 1581.

[35] For this argument in relation to the Dutch Republic see Sir William Temple, *Observations upon the United Provinces of the Netherlands* (1672) cited in Bas van Bavel and Oscar Gelderblom, 'The economic origins of cleanliness in the Dutch Golden Age', *Past and Present* 205:1 (2009), 42. This important article attributes the renowned cleanliness of the Dutch Golden Age to the economic forces, including hygiene measures essential to the dairy industry in a humid climate.

[36] Douglas Biow, *Culture of cleanliness in Renaissance Italy* (Ithica NY: Cornell University Press, 2006), pp. 11–13.

Population growth meant that both Genoa and Venice were sites of considerable urban development during the sixteenth century, with its attendant urban disruption. A number of initiatives that were designed to enhance urban contexts, including housing and infrastructure projects, placed a strain on cities by using significant quantities of water and generating waste on a large scale.[37] In Genoa, for example, the significant quantities of water required for the building trades was drawn from cisterns as well as local wells and even directly from the aqueduct.[38] Many Renaissance cities existed in a state of 'semi-perpetual incompletion' although projects could be completed with remarkable celerity.[39] New branches of government emerged to oversee the management of specific types of land use, natural resources and elements of the environment. In Genoa and Venice, the government bodies for health and the environment (which extended beyond Health Offices, as discussed below) also employed new mechanisms (notably systems of privileges) in order to encourage innovation and the development of new technology by citizens and foreigners alike to address the pressing environmental challenges of the day.

This volume, then, seeks to complicate the images which we have of the Renaissance—conventionally characterized as a time of extraordinary political and cultural achievement alongside intense urban problems.[40] A study of health and the environment allows historians to bridge the sometimes-conflicting characterizations of the governance and setting of these Northern Italian cities, since it is precisely because of the developed cultures of record-keeping that we know about urban and environmental issues.[41] This volume concentrates on community-level measures, rather than those related to the care of the home or the body, to highlight three concepts that influenced premodern social and environmental policies: balance, flow and cleanliness.[42]

---

[37] Katherine Rinne, *The waters of Rome: aqueducts, fountains and the birth of the Baroque city* (London and New Haven: Yale University Press, 2010), p. 37.

[38] Anna Boato and Anna Decri, 'Archive documents and building organisation', p. 383.

[39] ASCG, PdC, 3-40 (18 June 1470). Anna Boato and Anna Decri, 'Archive documents and building organization: an example from the modern age' in S. Huerta (ed.) *Proceedings of the first international congress on construction history* (Madrid, 2003), p. 382 refers to the reconstruction in stone of the Ponte Calvi in Genoa in just over five months during the fifteenth century.

[40] Peter Burke, *The European Renaissance: centres and peripheries* (Oxford: Blackwell, 1998), *Europe in the Renaissance: metamorphoses 1400–1600* (Zürich: Swiss National Museum, 2016) and John Jeffries Martin (ed.), *The Renaissance: Italy and abroad* (London: Routledge, 2003).

[41] Filippo de Vivo, Andrea Guidi, and Alessandro Silvestri (eds), 'Archival transformations in early modern Europe', *European History Quarterly* 46 (2016) and Liesbeth Corens, Kate Peters, and Alexandra Walsham (eds), 'The Social History of the Archive: record-keeping in early modern Europe', *Past and Present* 230 suppl. 11 (2016).

[42] On the distinction between the environment and landscape, whereby the latter acts as a repository of collective memory 'widely compared with a parchment and palimpsest a porous surface upon which each generation inscribes its own values and preoccupations without ever being able to erase entirely those of the preceding one' see Alexandra Walsham, *The reformation of the landscape*, p. 6. On the home and the body see Sandra Cavallo and Tessa Storey, *Healthy living in late Renaissance Italy*. For a discussion of the 'constellation of associations [between] purity, whiteness and liquidity' in the context of colonial Mexico see Daniel Nemser, 'Triangulating blackness', p. 359.

10 CLEANING UP RENAISSANCE ITALY

Balance, Flow, and Cleanliness in the Premodern European City

Environments lay at the heart of civic identity in premodern cities, often creating the distinctive context for origin stories and miracle narratives.[43] In Venice, the lagoon was seen to protect the city from foreign invasion (in stark contrast to the rest of the Italian peninsula) until the arrival of Napoleonic troops in 1797. In Genoa, alluding to the vital roles played by the port, the port area itself was described in 1460 as the 'foundation' and, later, 'the crown of this city'.[44] The surrounding breakwater was declared a pious work in 1245 and from 1469 all testators were asked to leave money in its favour.[45] In a supplication to the government in 1554 the city of Genoa without ships in the port was described as a 'body without a soul' (*corpo sensa anima*).[46] Both cities were tied closely to the water in practical and symbolic ways.

Early modern theories about the elements placed them in a specific hierarchy, in descending order of nobility: fire, air, water and earth. They were maintained in specific order 'together link'd with Adamantine Chains'.[47] The closer the association between water and civic identity, the more open to corruption it was considered to be. Yet in writings on both Genoa and Venice, as with many other ports, authors extolled the virtues of their bodies of water. Fynes Moryson [1566–1630] likened the water of the Venetian canals to 'the blood through the veines of a man's body'.[48] This has been widely cited in relation to the role played by the waterways in supplying nutriment (through trade). The celebration of these bodies of water derived from the confidence that any vulnerabilities in the natural environment could be offset by the quality of the body politic and its practices.[49]

Elements of the environment—like the flows of humours through the human body—were in constant movement: air and fire upwards and water and earth downwards, as well as processes of transmutation between them. Some studies in the history of medicine have underscored that the humoural body was perceived as much in terms of its liquids and flows as its organs and limbs.[50] Health

---

[43] For a succinct account of the origins of the city see Deborah Howard, *The architectural history of Venice* (New Haven and London: Yale University Press, 2002), pp. 2–3. See also Simon Schama, *The embarassment of riches: an interpretation of Dutch culture in the Golden Age* (London: Fontana, 1987).

[44] ASCG, PdC 1-71 (16 May 1460) and 13-10 (3 December 1528).

[45] Giorgio Doria and Paola Massa Piergiovanni (eds), *Il Sistema portuale della Repubblica di Genova: profili organizzativi e politica gestionale (secc XII–XVIII)* (Genoa: Nella sede della Società ligure di storia patria, 1988), p. 92.

[46] Supplication from Giuliano Nassano in ASCG, PdC, 22-83 (29 December 1554).

[47] Edmund Spenser, 'An Hymne in Honour of Love' from *Epithalamion* (1596).

[48] Fynes Moryson, *An Itinerary* (Amsterdam: Da Capo Press, 1971), p. 163. In the system of correspondences, it was air which corresponded with blood; water was the equivalent of phlegm—perhaps providing a less enticing simile.

[49] Carrie E. Beneš (ed.), *A companion to medieval Genoa* (Leiden: Brill, 2018).

[50] Katherine Craik has also emphasized that the ideal states of movement applied also to the emotions of the body (as e-motions) in Katherine A. Craik, 'Introduction' in Katherine A. Craik

INTRODUCTION   11

depended upon uninhibited flows around the body and separate pathways for distinct liquids.[51] Returning to this framework of medical understanding draws our attention beyond the identification of particular organs to an interest in the flows and channels between them.[52] If we recognize the correspondences between man and the built and natural environments, it takes us naturally to a concern with flows and channels of movement through the body of the city.[53]

In order to maintain the health of a city, it was imperative to regulate the quality and flow of the air. A healthy environment required that *'l'aere sia aperto'* (literally the air is open), as Venetian Health Office officials expressed.[54] The quality of the air was essential for the balance of the humours in the body.[55] As the Genoese doctor Bartolomeo Paschetti wrote, from the appropriate balance of humours followed good habits and morals (*le buone inclinazioni et i buoni habiti dell'animo*).[56] Conversely, restricted movement of elements, materials or people was a source of concern. Individual bodies, including those of the idle poor who failed to sweat because of a lack of exertion or women whose menstruation was not regular, might generate anxiety.[57] Putrefaction and disease could derive from stickiness, obstruction or stagnation within a body or city.[58] Balance and flow, therefore, were central to notions of healthy bodies, as well as lying at the root of good behaviour and morality.[59]

Environments were often distinguished in, as well as between, cities, which shaped the characterization of local neighbourhoods and their inhabitants. As Herman Roodenburg has expressed:

(ed.), *Shakespeare and emotion* (Cambridge: Cambridge University Press, 2020), p. 1. See also Barbara Duden, *The woman beneath the skin: a doctor's patients in eighteenth-century Germany* (Cambridge MA: Harvard University Press, 1998).

[51]   Carole Rawcliffe, *Urban bodies*, pp. 55–60.

[52]   Filippo de Vivo, 'Walking in sixteenth-century Venice: mobilising the early modern city', *I Tatti Studies in the Italian Renaissance* 19:1 (2016), 115–41.

[53]   Kimberley Skelton (ed.), *Early modern spaces in motion: design, experience and rhetoric* (Amsterdam: Amsterdam University Press, 2020) identifies a shift in ideas in the sixteenth century from bounded to continuous motion as a design principal. Medical ideas about flow were long-standing and endured through this period although they were given particular prominence in seventeenth-century iatromechanical medicine.

[54]   Rinaldo Fulin (ed.), *I diarii di Marin Sanudo* (58 vols, Venice, 1879–1903), vol 49 [1 October 1528–28 February 1529], p. 137. For Savona see *Statuti politici della citta di Savona: con le sue rifforme et additioni rimosse a suo luogo, tradotti in linguq volgure* (Genoa, 1610), pp. 86–7.

[55]   Joel Kaye, *A history of balance 1250–1375* (Cambridge: Cambridge University Press, 2014). It also informed many, broader aspects of early modern culture, including concerns about ostentation and neglect in clothing and fashion as discussed in Susan North, *Sweet and clean? Bodies and clothes in early modern England* (Oxford: Oxford University Press, 2020), p. 34.

[56]   Paschetti, p. 178.

[57]   Kevin Siena, *Rotten bodies: class and contagion in eighteenth-century Britain* (New Haven and London: Yale University Press, 2019), p. 43. On 'improper flows' see also Mary Fissell, Vernacular bodies: the politics of reproduction in early modern England' (Oxford: Oxford University Press, 2004).

[58]   Kevin Siena, *Rotten bodies* and Andrew Wear, *Knowledge and practice in early modern English medicine, 1550–1680* (Cambridge: Cambridge University Press, 2000), pp. 136–41.

[59]   Douglas Biow, *The culture of cleanliness*. Kathy Stuart, *Defiled trades and social outcasts: honor and ritual pollution in early modern Germany* (Cambridge: Cambridge University Press, 1999). Katherine Rinne, *The waters of Rome*, p. 7.

12 CLEANING UP RENAISSANCE ITALY

in its physical structures (flat or hilly, having spacious or narrow streets and plazas, few or many waterways) each town had its own auditory, olfactory or tactile identity, often already varying from neighborhood to neighborhood, even from street to street.[60]

The doctor Paschetti dedicated five pages to his discussion of the quality of the air in different districts of Genoa based largely upon their elevation and orientation.[61] He also provided advice as to where residents might best take their exercise at different times of the year in order to preserve their health.[62] Observers recognized the variation across as well as between urban centres.

This book, then, melds social, urban and environmental history to provide a distinct framework for understanding environmental management and societal wellbeing in this period. It demonstrates the concern of Renaissance governments for the physical cleanliness of urban and natural environments and illustrates that problems in the environment were, in part, actively combatted because of the intricate relationship which linked people and place. Social harmony and stability could affect urban and natural environments but were also believed to be achievable through interventions in the same. Such initiatives were designed to deal with dirt and waste with their various physical and moral manifestations.[63] The management of these concerns formed part of a well-instituted government through both regular maintenance activities and exceptional interventions in times of need.

The State of Genoa and Venice

As a Venetian Senate decree maintained in 1555, the conservation of health was one of the most salient and necessary provisions of the state.[64] At first glance, the Republics of Genoa and Venice provide striking examples of political continuity as two of the three Italian Republics which survived until the invasion of Napoleon at the end of the eighteenth century. Beyond this, however, the Republics were perceived to be distinct in both theory and practice.[65] The Republic of the Venetians was widely celebrated for its remarkable longevity from its auspicious foundation on 25 March 421 (the feast day of the Annunciation of the Virgin).[66]

---

[60] Herman Roodenburg, 'Introduction: the sensory worlds of the Renaissance' in *A cultural history of the senses* (London: Bloomsbury Academic, 2016), p. 13.

[61] Paschetti, 124–8.   [62] Paschetti, 181.

[63] Rosie Cox et al., *Dirt: the filthy reality of everyday life* (London: Profile Books, 2011).

[64] ASV, Senato Terra reg 40, 41v (22 June 1555).

[65] On the distinctive features of the Genoese civic government see Christine Shaw, 'Principles and practice in the civic government of fifteenth-century Genoa', *Renaissance Quarterly* 58 (2005), 50–5.

[66] Edward Muir, *Civic ritual in Renaissance Venice* (Princeton NJ: Princeton University Press, 1981), pp. 65–103.

Giovanni Botero [*c*.1544–1617] attributed the perceived political stability of Venice in part to the city's narrow streets since the 'ease with which bridges could be closed off guaranteed peace because they fragmented the city's population and made it difficult for rebels to join together'.[67] The city's environment (urban and natural) was an important aspect of its political myth.[68] The realities of Venetian political life have been shown to include unrest, tensions and competition.[69] Nevertheless, styled as *la Serenissima*, or the 'most serene [Republic]', the city's history has been contrasted with that of early Renaissance Genoa, where events were decidedly more tumultuous. As Christine Shaw observed:

> The Republic of Genoa was renowned for its political instability, and its reputation was justified. Between 1300 and 1528, when the constitution was radically reformed under the aegis of the great Genoese naval commander, Andrea Doria, it has been calculated that there were seventy-two rebellions and changes of regime.[70]

At least in theory, after 1528 the Republic of Genoa retained its liberty from foreign domination.[71] Peter Burke has observed that, unlike in Venice, it was not a 'myth' of Genoa which was developed in political literature but rather an 'anti-myth'.[72] A comparison between the two Republics draws the lack of panegyric tradition in Genoa into sharp relief.[73] Factionalism in Genoese society and politics has been frequently observed by historians for the early communal and podestarial political systems.[74] A study of governance below the highest echelons of power can nevertheless reveal coherence of civic priorities and a consistency of practice in the sphere of environmental management which endured against the backdrop of political instability.

---

[67] Giovanni Botero cited in Filippo de Vivo, 'Walking in sixteenth-century Venice', p. 122.

[68] Robert Finlay, 'The Immortal Republic: The myth of Venice during the Italian Wars (1494–1530)', *Sixteenth Century Journal* 30:4 (1999), 931–44.

[69] Robert Finlay, *Politics in Renaissance Venice* (New Brunswick NJ: Rutgers University Press, 1980).

[70] Christine Shaw, 'Genoa' in Andrea Gamberini and Isabella Lazzarini, *The Italian Renaissance State*, p. 220

[71] The influence of Habsburg monarchy increasingly intensely felt was noted by Fynes Moryson cited in Brian Pullan, *Rich and poor in Renaissance Venice: the social institutions of a Catholic state, to 1620* (Oxford: Blackwell, 1971), p. 4.

[72] Peter Burke, 'Public and private spheres in late Renaissance Genoa', *Varieties of Cultural History* (Cambridge: Cambridge University Press, 1997), pp. 111–23. See also Carlo Bitossi, *Il governo dei magnifici: patriziato e politica a Genova fra Cinque e Seicento* (Genoa: ECIG, 1990).

[73] D. Galassi, M. P. Rota, and A. Scrivano on Agostino Giustiniani in *Popolazione e insediamento in Liguria secondo la testimonianza di Agostino Giustiniani* (Florence: L. S. Olschki, 1979) particularly pp. 9–11.

[74] Carrie E. Beneš, 'Civic identity' in *A companion to medieval Genoa*, edited by Carrie E. Beneš, pp. 193–217. See also reflections on invasions of Genoa and changes of political allegiance in Elizabeth Reid, 'Female representation, gender and violence in the ceremonial entries of the Italian Wars', *Renaissance Studies*, 36:5 (2022), 750–68.

14   CLEANING UP RENAISSANCE ITALY

Comparative scholarship on the Republics of Renaissance Italy has often focused on Venice and Florence at the expense of Genoa and Lucca.[75] Occasionally the lives and travels of individuals or families have woven the histories of Genoa and Venice together and there are suggestive examples of the enduring relationship between the two states.[76] Nevertheless the lack of comparison with Genoa in the Renaissance reflects a broader neglect of this city's history in the fifteenth and sixteenth centuries by scholars beyond the city itself.[77] Stephen Epstein observed, over two decades ago, 'Renaissance Genoa remains an obscure interval between the vibrant medieval commune and the dim early modern Republic'.[78] The following year, Peter Burke examined this 'Cinderella of the Italian Renaissance' and its increasingly-voluminous political literature (in print and manuscript) from the 1550s.[79] The decades-old call by both scholars for greater attention to be paid to the city's archival, manuscript and printed material remains relevant. Anglophone historians in particular continue to gravitate to periods of economic success in Genoa, whether the high points of medieval trade or the 'century of the Genoese' when the city became a centre for banking over the course of the 1600s.[80]

This volume suggests the utility of undertaking a comparative study on the basis of the environment, as an entity around which civic identity coalesced and a focus for governance.[81] To adopt the premodern terminology, there are enticing similarities in both the body politic and macrocosms of these two

---

[75] For the traditional comparisons between Florence and Venice see S. Bertelli, N. Rubinstein, and C. Hugh Smyth (eds), *Florence and Venice: comparisons and relations* (Florence: La nuova Italia, 1980). Brian Pullan, *Rich and poor in Renaissance Venice*, p. 4. On Lucca see, for example, M. E. Bratchel, *Medieval Lucca and the evolution of the Renaissance state* (Oxford: Oxford University Press, 2008). Abigail Brundin, Deborah Howard, and Mary Laven, *The sacred home in Renaissance Italy* (Oxford: Oxford University Press, 2018), pp. 36–7 contests traditional, historiographical 'centres' and 'peripheries' in Renaissance Italy.

[76] Brendan Dooley, *A mattress maker's daughter: the Renaissance romance of Don Giovanni de'Medici and Livia Vernazza* (Cambridge MA: Harvard University Press, 2014). For the enduring relationship see Brian Pullan, *Rich and poor in Renaissance Venice*, p. 55. Comparisons for the fifteenth and sixteenth centuries have tended to be made in business history or economics. For example, Avner Greif, 'Political organisations, social structure and institutional success: reflections from Genoa and Venice during the commercial revolution', *The Journal of Institutional and Theoretical Economics* 151:4 (1995), 734–40.

[77] Excellent studies of Genoa and Ligurian history have been developed by Ennio Poleggi, Edoardo Grendi, and Rodolfo Savelli, 'Dalle confraternite allo stato: il Sistema assistenziale Genovese nel Cinquecento', *Atti della Società Ligure di Storia Patria*, nuova serie, XXIV/1 (1984).

[78] Stephen Epstein, *Genoa and the Genoese, 958–1528* (Chapel Hill NC: University of North Carolina Press, 1996), p. 272.

[79] Peter Burke, 'Public and private spheres in late Renaissance Genoa'.

[80] Stephen Epstein, *Genoa and the Genoese* has yet to be surpassed. For the tendency of (particularly anglophone scholarship) to focus on periods of economic success see Carrie E. Beneš (ed.), *A companion to medieval Genoa*.

[81] This has been recognized of the 'state within a state', the bank of the Casa di San Giorgio. See Christine Shaw, 'Principles and practice', pp. 57–64. The argument can also be made for two parts of the government, founded at an early point in the Republic's history: the Padri del Comune and the Ufficio della Misericordia.

INTRODUCTION 15

maritime cities.[82] Trade was vital to both economies. A rebalancing of the Genoese economy began in the fifteenth century as merchants increasingly utilized smaller ships. Large storms during the seventeenth century (especially in 1613) encouraged this trend. Nevertheless, the port continued to be the lynchpin of the city.[83] During the period of this study, Venice was a cosmopolitan and vibrant trading emporium. Accounts of the city's relative or absolute economic decline during the seventeenth century are long-standing but the centrality of its commercial economy endured through the centuries under consideration here.[84]

The port districts of both cities were vital to the cities' economies and systems for supply yet remained highly vulnerable to environmental change—particularly through siltation. This threatened to cause economic disruption and corruption of the air. In Liguria, this problem was not limited to the capital city of Genoa but affected much of the 'fragile mosaic' of the territorial state which extended along the coastline for approximately 180 miles.[85] The Ligurian landscape

> has been officially described as comprising 65 per cent mountains and 35 per cent hills...Dante, wishing to convey the terror induced by looking up, in his vision, at the forbidding face of the mountain of Purgatory, compared this to the coast of Liguria.[86]

Ports were vital because overland transportation over mountain tracks was laborious and expensive, for example on the Salt Road through the mountains to Piedmont. This perhaps explains why Peter Paul Rubens maintained of the Genoese that 'they plough the seas and walk the land'.[87]

In Venice, fragmentation has already been emphasized as a feature of the city's urban fabric, which constituted numerous tiny islands [Image I.2]. Hundreds of

---

[82] John M. Najemy, 'The Republic's two bodies: body metaphors in Italian Renaissance political thought' in Alison Brown (ed.), *Language and images of Renaissance Italy* (Oxford: Oxford University Press, 1995), pp. 237–62.

[83] Francesco Podestà, *Il porto di Genova dalle origini fino alla caduta della repubblica Genovese* (Genoa: E. Spiotti, 1913) and *Il porto di Genova 1128–2000* (Genoa: Consorzio Autonomo del Porto di Genova, 1971). The works of Robert Lopez remain valuable for Genoese economic history in the early part of the premodern period. On building materials see Anna Boato, *Costruire 'alla moderna' materiali e tecniche a Genova tra XV e XVI secoli* (Genoa: All'Insegna del Giglio, 2005).

[84] The classic study is Richard Rapp, *Industry and economic decline in seventeenth-century Venice* (Cambridge MA: Harvard University Press, 1976). For a turning point in the Venetian trade economy in 1569 see Claire Judde de Larivière, 'The "public" and the "private" in sixteenth-century Venice: from medieval economy to early modern state', *Historical Social Research* 37:4 (2012), 76–94 which also contains useful references to wider literature.

[85] Biondo Flavio, *Italy illuminated*, Jeffrey A. White (ed. and trans) (Cambridge MA: Harvard University Press, 2005) p. 43. For reflections on the characterization of the 'fragile mosaic' of the state see Edoardo Grendi, *Il Cervo e la Repubblica. Il modello ligure di antico regime* (Turin: Einaudi, 1993), p. 26.

[86] Jane Garnett and Gervase Rosser, *Spectacular miracles*, p. 60.

[87] Cited in Donatella Calabi, *The market and the city: square, street and architecture in early modern Europe* (Marlene Klein, trans.) (Aldershot: Ashgate, 2004), p. 4.

Image I.2 Map of Venice from Tommaso Porcacchi, *L'isole piu famose del mondo* (1572), © Wellcome Collection. Attribution 4.0 International (CC BY 4.0).

bridges were constructed but the network of canals continued to be essential for transport and communication. Many essential supplies, including both foodstuffs and drinking water, were imported. Both commercial Republics were also the centres of Empires. Genoese territory encompassed Liguria and Mediterranean colonies including Chios (until it was ceded to the Ottoman Turks in 1566) and Tabarca—an island off the coast of Tunisia, which was settled during the sixteenth century.[88] Tabarca and Chois were the sources of vital commodities (gum mastic and coral respectively).[89] Venetian territory on the mainland was contested

---

[88] Historians of Genoa have debated the significance of the centre versus localities in premodern Liguria. See Giovanni Assereto, 'L'amministrazione del dominio di terraferma' in *La metamorfosi della Repubblica. Saggi di storia Genovese tra il XVI e il XIX secolo* (Savona: Daner, 1999); Edoardo Grendi, *Il Cervo e la repubblica*; and Osvaldo Raggio, *Faide e parentele: lo stato genovese visto dalla Fontanabuona* (Turin: Einaudi, 1990). On Chios see the works of Philip Argenti including *The occupation of Chios by the Genoese and their administration of the island 1346–1566* (Cambridge: Cambridge University Press, 1958). On Tabarca see the brief discussion of the Lomellino family (and the use of coral in distinctive garden grottos) in Stephanie Hanke, 'The splendour of bankers and merchants: Genoese harden grottoes of the sixteenth century', *Urban History* 37 (2010), 412.

[89] Giovanni Assereto and Marco Doria (eds), *Storia della Liguria* (Rome: Gius Laterza et Figli Spa, 2007). On coral in Genoa see Onorato Pàstine, 'L'arte dei corallieri nell'ordinamento delle corporazioni Genovesi (secoli XV–XVIII)', *Atti della Società Ligure di Storia Patria* 61 (1933), 277–415.

INTRODUCTION   17

throughout this period but at times stretched almost to Milan.[90] The *stato da mar* comprised territories along the Adriatic coast and in the Mediterranean.[91] Familial and corporeal metaphors of early modern statecraft were invoked in both contexts.[92]

Both ports were tied to localities elsewhere through their cosmopolitan populations.[93] Genoa was described as the 'port for the world' and Venice as a 'hotel for the people of the world', by early modern visitors.[94] Ennio Poleggi has noted the structures of assistance, hospitality and devotion which were established for communities of visitors and 'foreigners' in Genoa from the medieval period.[95] The identification of distinct spaces for groups of different nationalities was seen to complement the shaping force of the city's *alberghi*, the districts which were dominated by leading families of the city.[96] Important foreign communities in Genoa derived from the Italian peninsula, for example Tuscan merchants, and particularly the *Lucchesi* who were high-profile artisans in the city.[97] Genoa was also the natural port for merchants of Lombardy and there was a Greek community based close to the port, complete with a consulate and a *loggia*. Venice was described as 'secure port' for the Greek Nation, because of the facility for this community to protect its cultural and religious identity and also accommodated important communities from Dalmatia, Albania and the southern Slavic

[90] For the Venetian *terraferma* see the essays in Humfrey Butters and Gabriele Neher (eds), *Warfare and politics: cities and government in Renaissance Tuscany and Venice* (Amsterdam: Amsterdam University Press, 2019).

[91] For the *stato da mar* see Benjamin Arbel, 'Venice's maritime Empire in the early modern period' in Eric Dursteler (ed.), *A companion to Venetian History 1400–1797* (Leiden: Brill, 2013), pp. 125–253.

[92] For example, in 1575 the Venetian state was described as a mystical body ('...*perche la citta di Verona non potrice il danno di questo interdetto in se sola ma anco tutto il rimanente di questo dominio (che'e quasi un corpo mistico))*' in ASV, Sanità, reg. 13 169r. The *Podestà* of Savona, in a letter of 5 June 1589, wrote that the subject communities were like muscles in the body whereas the city of Genoa was the head, on which depends the vital spirits of the corporeal whole.

[93] See Miri Rubin, *Cities of strangers* and recent work on mobility as a vital dynamic in this period. The review essay by Craig Clunas, 'Modernity global and local: consumption and the rise of the West' *The American Historical Review* 104:5 (1999), 1497–1511 observed the tendency to conceptualize a 'world' of goods and consumption which was, in practice, highly localized in its examples and limited in its global coverage. Broad, comparative work remains exceptional although the seven-volume *Cambridge World History* with Merry E. Wiesner-Hanks as general editor. On the cosmopolitan ports of the Mediterranean see Alireza Naser Eslami and Marco Folin (eds), *La città multietnica nel mondo mediterraneo: porti, cantieri, minoranze* (Milan, 2019).

[94] Genoa was described as *porta nostri orbis* by Giannozzo Manetti (1436-7) and *Ostium tocius Italie* by Anselmo Adorno in 1470. Venice was described as '*Dico adunque che questa gran bella Città, la quale fu sempre cortese e fedel albergo alle genti del Mondo*' in Rocco Benedetti, *Relatione d'alcuni casi occorsi in Venetia al tempo della peste l'anno 1576 et 1577* con le provisioni, rimedii et orationi fatte à Dio Benedetti per la sua liberatione (Bologna, 1630), p. 17. For an excellent overview of different systems of citizenship in medieval Europe see Miri Rubin, *Cities of strangers*, pp. 16–18.

[95] Ennio Poleggi, 'La topografia degli stranieri nella Genova di Antico Regime' in Donatella Calabi and Paola Lanaro (eds), *La città italiana e i luoghi degli stranieri XIV–XVIII secolo* (Rome-Bari: Laterza, 1998), pp. 108–20 and Alireza Naser Eslami and Marco Folin (eds), *La città multietnica*, pp. xvii–xxvii.

[96] On the Genoese *alberghi* see, for example, Edoardo Grendi in Ennio Poleggi and Paolo Cevini, *Genova* (Rome-Bari: Laterza, 2003), p. 36.

[97] Giustina Olgiati (ed.), *Genova porta del mondo. La città medievale e i suoi habitatores* (Genoa: Brigati, 2011), p. 21.

18 CLEANING UP RENAISSANCE ITALY

countries.[98] These cosmopolitan contexts reflected differently on issues of citizenship, however; in Genoa, a varying period of up to three years of tax-paying residency qualified an individual to apply for citizenship, in contrast to the fiercely protected rights of citizenship in Venice.[99]

With respect to the place of Jewish communities the cities' histories diverge significantly. In Venice in 1516, the government chose to develop a ghetto in which the Jewish communities were forced to live. Although enacting considerable constraints, the Ghetto did afford a more secure place to live in the city than was provided in Genoa. Periodic expulsions, as well as the imposition of distinguishing signs, meant that Jewish residence in Genoa remained, at best, precarious. An obvious example of the efforts made to ensure that a Jewish community did not develop in the city came after the Spanish Alhambra Decree in 1492.[100] A significant number of Jewish migrants were accommodated in a camp at the Genoese port—affording a setting which was clearly intended to be seen as transitory. In some instances, individuals were able to take up residence in Ligurian towns following expulsion from Genoa and some well-respected physicians were able to use their reputations to remain in the city. Nevertheless the Jewish population remained small and fragmented: 'atomized' in the words of Flora Cassen.[101]

Further contrast between the two cities has been drawn on the basis of the use of wealth. Both Republics were financial centres during the early modern period but, of the two, Venice was seen to surpass Genoa in its grandeur. Giovanni Botero attributed this to the fact that, in the course of their mercantile endeavours, Venetians had enriched public interests to the neglect of private ones, whereas the Genoese had done the reverse.[102] An awareness of the vulnerable nature of the environment in Venice has been said to have necessitated giving priority to public

[98] Jonathan Harris and Heleni Porfyriou, 'The Greek diaspora: Italian port cities and London, c.1400–1700' in Donatella Calabi and Stephen Turk Christensen (eds), *Cities and cultural exchange in Europe, 1400–1700* (Cambridge: Cambridge University Press, 2007), p. 66. See Benjamin Ravid, 'Venice and its minorities', https://primolevicenter.org/printed-matter/venice-and-its-minorities/ (accessed 23 May 2021).

[99] Diane Hughes, 'Kinsmen and neighbors in medieval Genoa' in Harry A. Miskimin, David Herlihy, and Abraham L. Udovitch (eds), *The medieval city* (New Haven and London: Yale University Press, 1977), p. 96. Brian Pullan, *Rich and poor in Renaissance Venice*, pp. 101–7. The *fondaci* and structures for hospitality in Venice are discussed in chapter 1 pp. 38–9.

[100] This episode was overseen by a short-lived *Officium Hebraeorum*.

[101] Expulsions took place in 1503 (prohibiting a stay in the city of more than three days), 1505, 1516, 1550, and 1567. The latter included most towns of Liguria in addition to the city of Genoa. See Flora Cassen, 'No Jews in Genoa' in *Marking the Jews in Renaissance Italy: politics, religion and the power of symbols* (Cambridge: Cambridge University Press, 2017), pp. 154–87.

[102] Giovanni Botero cited in Thomas A. Kirk, *Genoa and the sea: policy and power in an early modern maritime republic, 1559–1684* (Baltimore MA: Johns Hopkins University Press, 2005), p. 46. See also this reputation amongst historians as referenced in Christine Shaw, 'Principles and practice', 45.

INTRODUCTION 19

rather than private endeavours.[103] It has been suggested that collective interests in Genoa were only realized through economic organizations such as the *alberghi*, the *maone* in the context of colonies and the Casa di San Giorgio.[104]

A similar contrast in public and private priorities can be found in the traditional characterization of welfare and healthcare. During the sixteenth century, across the Italian peninsula, hospital structures became larger in size and more specialized.[105] In Genoa, private interests and initiatives supported the city's principal hospitals: the *Ospedale Maggiore* (known as the *Pammatone*), the *Incurabili* (also known as the *Ospedaletto*) and the plague hospital (*lazzaretto*).[106] Each of these institutions, which carried out important public functions, operated with a significant amount of delegated responsibility.[107] In Venice, in contrast, Renaissance authors and modern historians have emphasized the extensive coordination of charity and healthcare by the state.[108] Three of the four *Ospedali grandi*—the *Incurabili* for the incurable sick, the *Mendicanti* for beggars and the *Derelitti* for the destitute—were founded by the government during this period and the fifteenth century hospital of the *Pietà* for orphans was further developed, with the intention of creating a comprehensive system of welfare and healthcare for those deserving of civic care.[109] Nevertheless, in both cities, the tensions that existed between the priorities of individuals, households, parishes and wider communities are visible in the records of health and environmental management. In neither city were social groups immune from putting individual needs above those of the collective good.

The envisioned role of the state in healthcare differed between these two cities.[110] The branches of the Republican government in Venice were active in

---

[103] Edward Muir and Robert Weissman, 'Social and symbolic places in Renaissance Venice and Florence' in John Agnew and James Duncan (eds), *The power of place: bringing together geographical and sociological imaginations* (London: Unwin Hyman, 1992), p. 92 and Peter Burke, 'Public and private spheres in Genoa', p. 13.

[104] Christine Shaw, 'Principles and practice', 45.

[105] John Henderson, *The Renaissance hospital*.

[106] Loredana Pessa, 'Pammatone e Incurabili: due grandi ospedali pubblici a Genova' in *Le antiche spezierie degli ospedali genovesi di Pammatone e degli Incurabili* (Genoa: LOG, 2005), p. 5. The Pammatone was established in 1420 by Bartolomeo Bosco and came to take responsibility for the city's sick, as well as for abandoned children. The only groups not provided for in this complex were those with the French disease, the plague and those with mental illness. Giovanni Assereto, *'Per la comune salvezza dal morbo contagioso'. I controlli di sanità nella Repubblica di Genova* (Genoa: Città del silenzio, 2011), p. 68. The *lazzaretto* was said to have been financed by Doge Fregoso, the Banco di San Giorgio, and private benefactors.

[107] Rodolfo Savelli, 'Dalle confraternite allo stato', p. 182.

[108] Brian Pullan, *Rich and poor in Renaissance Venice*. For details of community networks see Joanna Kostylo, 'Pharmacy as a centre for Protestant reform in Renaissance Venice', *Renaissance Studies* 30:2 (2016), 236–53.

[109] See Bernard Aikema and Dulcia Meijers (eds), *Nel regno dei poveri: arte e storia dei grandi ospedali veneziani in età moderna 1474–1797* (Venice: Arsenale Editrice, 1989). For a comparative study of the Pietà hospitals in Bologna and Florence see Nicholas Terpstra, *Abandoned children of the Italian Renaissance: orphan care in Florence and Bologna* (London: Johns Hopkins University Press, 2005). Jane Stevens Crawshaw, *Plague hospitals*.

[110] On the language of public health in Venice and that of the port in Genoa see pp. 6–7.

20 CLEANING UP RENAISSANCE ITALY

justifying, undertaking and monitoring work. In Genoa, in contrast, the government's role concentrated upon the first and third of these stages. Workers were utilized, but not directly employed, by the state to clean up the city. The oversight of health and the environment was also organized differently in Genoa and Venice with a single government office overseeing this work in the former city and multiple offices involved in the latter.

In Genoa, the office of the Padri del Comune or 'fathers of the Comune' (founded during the thirteenth century) had responsibility for the condition of the port, streets and aqueduct.[111] By the fifteenth century, its responsibilities had expanded to include the cleanliness, paving, viability and maintenance of streets, all waterways, the water supply, dangerous or dilapidated buildings as well as any domestic or trade structures that encroached upon public space. It regulated fishing, the sex trade and the city's lotteries, as well as approving changes to the fabric of the city. Unlike in Venice, the Genoese Health Office in this period was largely concerned with public health for maritime trade.[112] The archive of the Padri del Comune is particularly rich from the 1450s, a period described by Guido Zazzu as characterized by serious economic, political, cultural and social problems and yet the work of the Padri is broadly characterized by continuity.[113] The language of the port galvanized a sense of collective identity. It is no coincidence that it was this magistracy that commissioned monumental views of Genoa including the earliest image of the city in 1481 (which survives in a copy from 1597 by Cristoforo Grassi) [Image I.3].

In Venice, as was characteristic of the Republic's governance structures, responsibility for public health and the environment was split between three magistracies. The Provveditori di Comun had been founded in 1312 with oversight of public works, the regulation of trades, citizenship applications and lotteries.[114] It undertook the regulation of public space, dealt with dilapidated buildings and oversaw the dredging of the city's waterways until 1520, when this responsibility for the Grand Canal and the *rii* was given to the Water Office (the *Savi ed*

---

[111] The Padri has attracted attention from local historians, who have used the rich, surviving archive to great effect, notably in studies which have reconstructed much of the development of the urban fabric during the medieval and early modern periods. See, in particular, the works of Francesco Podestà [1831–1912], Ennio Poleggi, Paola Massa Piergiovanni, and Raffaela Ponte.

[112] Towns and cities in Liguria developed their own Health Offices on an ad hoc basis during the fifteenth century and a number of these were formulated on a permanent basis during the sixteenth century, including that of La Spezia. For information on the fifteenth-century development of the Health Office (initially on an ad hoc basis as was common on the Italian peninsula) and more formal organization during the sixteenth century see see Giovanni Assereto, 'Per la comune salvezza dal morbo contagioso', pp. 16–21.

[113] Zazzu references the financial crisis of the Bank of San Giorgio, the impact of the fall of Constantinople, the vulnerability of colonies in the East, internal political instability, and increased incidence of plague in G. N. Zazzu, 'Prostituzione e moralità pubblica nella Genova del '400', *Studi genuensi* 5 (1987), 45–67.

[114] See the discussion of the office in relation to other magistracies in Giovanni Caniato and Michela Dal Borgo, *Le arti edili a Venezia* (Rome: Edilstampa, 1990).

Image I.3 Genoa city and port, 1597. Painting by Cristoforo Grassi, copy of an older picture from the end of the 1400s, it shows the naval parade commemorating the Battle of Otranto, 1481. Genoa, Museo Navale di Pegli. © 2020. DeAgostini Picture Library/ Scala, Florence.

Esecutori alle Acque). The Water Office in Venice was established in 1501.[115] By 1542, officials were supported by a technical office, consisting of a superintendent and three expert advisers (or *proti*): one for the lagoon and channels between the *lidi* islands, one for rivers and one for the *lidi* themselves. There were also three deputy advisers and three assistants.[116] Finally, the Venetian Health Office, the Provveditori alla Sanità, was created on an ad hoc basis from 1456 and made permanent in 1486.[117] During the sixteenth century, this magistracy undertook a wide regulation of perceived economic and social dangers, such as butchers and the sex and second-hand trades.

Archival material from each of these magistracies is analysed alongside a range of printed and material culture sources (including architecture, objects and paintings) which help to establish the myriad of ways in which the connections between people and place were represented and revealed in Genoa and Venice. There are, of course, issues relating to the silences of the archive. Environmental management often involved the sorts of tasks which people generally only noticed when they were not completed. The voices preserved in the archive are either

---

[115] Roberto Berveglieri, *Le vie di Venezia: canali lagunari e rii a Venezia: inventori, brevetti, tecnologia e legislazione nei secoli XII–XVII* (Sommacampagna, 1999), p. 110.
[116] Roberto Berveglieri, *Le vie di Venezia*, p. 114.
[117] Excellent studies include the works of Richard Palmer and Michelle Laughran and the PhD thesis of the former remains unsurpassed for the insight it provides into the Venetian Health Office: R. Palmer, 'The control of plague in Venice and northern Italy 1348–1600' (unpublished PhD thesis, University of Kent, 1978).

22 CLEANING UP RENAISSANCE ITALY

limited to the elite or, at least, filtered through them. Neither city is well served in terms of criminal records relating to health and the environment and there are few surviving records attesting to resistance to these areas of governance.[118]

Beyond this, the nature of the archival material in the two cities is distinct and complementary. For Genoa, a significant number of proclamations survive in the archive of the Padri del Comune, which reveal the process by which issues were raised and dealt with by this government body. Proposals could be initiated by individuals, groups or parts of the government.[119] Most commonly, requests were attributed to individuals (often from elite families). The Padri would review the proposal (perhaps in conjunction with its technical experts) and a proclamation would then be read in the streets which provided an overview of the supplication and invited residents to raise any objections.[120] This same system applied in and beyond the city itself.[121]

In Venice, letters or supplications were sent directly to government offices and concerns might also be raised through anonymous denunciation by passing a slip of paper into one of the famous 'lion's mouths', which became part of the fabric of civic governance in the city. Instructions were read aloud in squares and key locations across the city. Government officials also recognized the significance of rendering their aural proclamations as visible and durable parts of the fabric of the streets.[122] Elizabeth Horodowich has explored such inscriptions in relation to the regulation of blasphemy. One from San Zaccaria in 1620 forbade the playing of games along with riotous commotion (*tumultar*), shouting, obscene words, dishonest meetings, or the creation of rubbish. The combination of social, religious and environmental prohibitions illustrates the ways in which bad behaviour, sin and dirt might be aligned.[123]

In both cities, the reports of expert advisers were utilized. In Genoa, an official known as the *cavaliero* was intended to oversee the streets and was responsible for walking through these spaces just before nightfall to ensure that they were clear

---

[118] On silences in the Venetian archive relating to protest see Maartje van Gelder and Filippo de Vivo, 'Papering over protest: contentious politics and archival suppression in early modern Venice', *Past and Present* (2022).

[119] For example, ASCG, PdC, 29-86 (18 October 1586) for a proclamation initiated by a resident whereas 29-92 (13 November 1568) was made 'in the public interest' by the Sindico dela detta Camera.

[120] George Gorse, 'A classical stage for the old nobility: the Strada Nuova and sixteenth-century Genoa' *The Art Bulletin* 79:2 (1997), 309. As Stephen Milner has noted, these proclamations were written in order to be read aloud and so reverse the usual process encountered by historians whereby the oral is recorded in surviving written records. Stephen Milner ' "Fanno bandire, notificare et expressamente comandare": town criers and the information economy of Renaissance Florence', *I Tatti Studies in the Italian Renaissance* 16:1/2 (2013), 118. Jennifer Richards, *Voices and books in the English Renaissance: a new history of reading* (Oxford: Oxford University Press, 2019).

[121] ASCG, PdC, 19-103 (15 November 1546).

[122] On 'stone laws' see Fabrizio Nevola, *Street life*, pp. 199–204.

[123] Julia Romborough has explored the ways in which social regulation was deeply linked to sonic regulation in early modern Florence and that many of the stone laws addressed the noises associated with parts of society which provoked broader moral concern. Julia Rombough, 'Noisy soundscapes and women's institutions in early modern Florence', *The Sixteenth Century Journal* 50 (2019), 467.

INTRODUCTION 23

and accessible, with all rubbish having been moved to allocated areas as instructed.[124] In Venice, the expert adviser to the Provveditori di Comun was required to walk through the city and inspect, where necessary, bridges, streets, *fondamente* (paved streets which adjoined canals), wells and other structures.[125] These government officials developed a sensitivity to the characteristics of localities by observing the city and making reports which assessed areas according to their sights, smells, sounds and materials.[126] Officials did not concentrate their investigations on the key political or economic zones of the city. Instead, their observations were widespread and were intended to facilitate preventative, as well as restorative, interventions. The concept which operated at the heart of a well-governed urban body—that of regulated movement—shaped a central component of the exercise of environmental governance: expertise and insight were developed through walking and observing in order to assess the appropriateness of conduct, morality and setting across the city.[127]

Chapter Structure

Adequate management of the environment and health necessitated the clear articulation of ideals alongside the organization and regulation of practice. Some of this constituted regular, routine work and is the focus for part one of this book. Here we see efforts to ensure an adequate flow of elements, materials and people through the streets, water supply and environmental bodies. In part two, we consider the perceived impact of Renaissance societies on their settings through waste production and experiences of natural disasters.

Chapter one considers the specific infrastructure for health and the environment in ports and engages with scholarship from the built environment which argues for the distinctiveness of ports and their societies across the longue durée. This chapter also develops the 'Renaissance' context for this study by reflecting on the forms of ideal ports developed in Renaissance architectural theory. In particular, the work of Antonio Averlino [c.1400–69], known as Filarete, on the ideal port of Plusiopolis is explored. This chapter sets Genoa and Venice in a broader Mediterranean context by considering how such ideals were developed elsewhere on the Italian peninsula and beyond. The second section of this chapter assesses

---

[124] ASCG, PdC, 20-91 (15 November 1549). A salaried official in the Padri with responsibility for cleaning of the streets was noted in the statutes from the 1460s. See Cornelio Desimoni, *Statuto del Padri del Comune della Repubblica Genovese* (Genoa, 1886), pp. 36–7. Different times were noted to apply for the six months of year with the shortest days and threat of the most severe weather (between October and March) in ASCG, PdC, 22-130 (5 September 1555) and 22-190 (8 July 1556).

[125] ASV, Comun, b.9, 44v (10 November 1518).

[126] These reports are contained in the *Atti* series in the government archive.

[127] This was particularly pronounced in Venice where the patriciate made a point of walking through public spaces. See Filippo de Vivo, 'Walking in sixteenth-century Venice'.

24 CLEANING UP RENAISSANCE ITALY

characterizations of port societies and the challenges posed to community health, as well as urban and natural environments, by their cosmopolitan and often-transient population. The chapter ends with a comparison between the port structures and society of Genoa and Venice.

Chapter two highlights the underlying motivations for public works in ports which were designed to ensure free-flowing movement through the streets. These physical structures played a vital role in binding people in neighbourhoods. Concepts of cleanliness and salubrity lay at the heart of being a good citizen and a good neighbour. Tensions between individuals or families might be articulated using the system for denunciations relating to cleanliness and health. The quality of the streets was seen to affect the quality of behaviour and, as a result, regulations focused on the materiality, cleanliness, safety and use of these spaces.

In Chapter three, on the infrastructure of water supply (including canals, drains, the Genoese aqueduct, fountains and wells), it becomes clear that the management of these elements had important moral ramifications. Access to water was believed to be a vital charitable enterprise and was one of the Christian works of mercy. If water sources were damaged, society as a whole was affected but the poor most acutely. As a result, their development, maintenance and protection were often designated as pious or charitable acts.[128] Water infrastructure also had significant social and political associations.[129] The forms of water infrastructure in Genoa and Venice were distinct but the importance of adequate access to clean water for washing, the care of animals, artisanal processes and also drinking, was common. This chapter considers how governments responded to the strain on water supplies caused by demographic growth, urban change and periods of drought. Neither city saw fundamental changes to infrastructure.[130] Instead, interventions focused on the careful allocation of existing resources.

Chapter four highlights the system which developed in both ports to generate forms of technology intended to deal with the principal environmental challenges of the day, including siltation and stagnant water. Although decision-making power remained in the hands of the few, there was a broad cast of those involved in this work. Occupational groups, such as fishermen and sailors, acted as environmental experts and provided reports on specific projects and proposals to government magistracies. Petitions and privileges were granted for new machines, often marketed as 'secrets'. These were submitted by residents and foreigners, who sometimes moved between ports and used their specialist

---

[128] ASCG, PdC, 3-10 (2 May 1469) on the pious work of the Padri del Comune in Genoa's port district.

[129] For the political issues of grain and wood supply see Paul Warde, *The invention of sustainability* and Karl Appuhn, *A forest on the sea.*

[130] Such shifts in earlier centuries saw sewage systems develop from open channels to underground drains for example. See Francesca Bocchi, 'Regulation of the urban environment by the Italian Communes from the twelfth to the fourteenth century', *Bulletin of the John Rylands Library* 72:3 (1990), 63–78.

technologies in order to find a place for themselves in new locations. Working with infrastructure and the environment could not only play an important part in sustaining and defining communities, as outlined in previous chapters, but also accessing them. The chapter also emphasizes the major environmental interventions undertaken in both cities, principally in the form of major dredging projects during the sixteenth century.

Chapter five explores cultures of waste disposal and reuse in Renaissance ports, arguing for the place of waste in discussions of cleanliness and dirt.[131] In particular this chapter highlights the systems established by both governments to regulate the repurposing of waste. Material from building projects was used to construct environmental defences (particularly against floods) or for ballast in maritime vessels. By illuminating the cultures and structures to manage waste this chapter also establishes the significance of those whose job it was to collect, remove and reuse these materials. A variety of individuals were involved in such work, including those employed directly by the government, some who accessed work through corporations or guilds and others whose work was irregular and informal. In all cases, those handling waste in Genoa and Venice were male although the processes for identifying waste materials in domestic and artisanal settings would certainly have involved women.

The final chapter explores visual and written accounts of natural disasters, including storms and floods as well as the earthquakes of 1511 in Venice and 1536 in Genoa. The place of cleanliness and dirt in explanations of natural disasters is clear, as is the importance of piety for early modern understandings of effective environmental management. Rather than sparking particular or new initiatives, natural disasters intensified discussions of human culpability and responsibility. As a result, what changed as a result of these events was the emotional and social context of environmental management more than the activities themselves. This context reaffirmed contemporary beliefs about the impact of human behaviour on the environment and often sparked concern about the spaces in which 'dangerous' groups were located.

Overall, this book adds to revisionist scholarship on premodern cities, which moves beyond traditional assessments of stinking, premodern settings, in which unsophisticated inhabitants were content to wallow in mire, and which portrayed public health as characteristic of modernity.[132] It explores the responsibility for commissioning and undertaking the work of environmental management and demonstrates the extensive efforts to ensure cleanliness, broadly conceived, in Renaissance Genoa and Venice.

---

[131] It is interesting to note that these same pairs are amongst the ideas which structure Daniel Schneider's study of biological sewage treatment during the twentieth century: *Hybrid nature: sewage treatment and the contradictions of the industrial ecosystem* (Cambridge MA: MIT Press, 2011).

[132] For an overview of this rich and ongoing debate see Guy Geltner, *The roads to health.*

1

Constructing Ideals and Practices in Renaissance Port Cities

Of the surviving representations of ideal Italian Renaissance cities, few are better known than this painting (Image 1.1) attributed to Fra Carnevale [active *c*.1445–84]. A central, ornate fountain supplies a pristine *piazza*. Four statues represent the cardinal virtues of justice, prudence, fortitude, and temperance (the latter is represented by a pitcher of water to mix with a basin of wine).[1] Commissioned for Federico da Montefeltro of Urbino's [1422–82] *studiolo* this image would likely have been set into the wooden panelling on the walls at shoulder height or higher. Viewers could have gazed outwards from that seat of political power, as if through a window, onto a scene of idealized, geometrically ordered beauty.[2] Unlike other depictions of its kind, this panel includes people. A woman collects water in a pitcher at the fountain. Another approaches with her basin. A beggar walks through the foreground.[3] Two children pass behind the central archway, under attentive female supervision. Women, the poor, and children were notoriously unruly and potentially troublesome elements of Renaissance society whose natures were seen as distinct and problematic in the humoural framework of the time.[4] Here, the cityscape is shown to be sufficient to be able to organize and control even those parts of society whose bodies and behaviours could be a cause for concern.

This painting is not just about the ways in which social problems might be diffused through the urban form. Space is also afforded to those elements of society more readily associated with order and authority: a group of elite males enters from stage right. Unlike in Leonardo da Vinci's [1452–1519] ideal city, social groups are not separated across distinct urban layers. Instead, each has the opportunity for unimpeded movement through the square. The importance of the flow of elements (such as the water in the fountain) and people in Renaissance

---

[1] 'The ideal city, attr. To Fra Carnevale in the Waters Art Museum' in M. S. Hansen and J. Spicer (eds), *Masterpieces of Italian Painting* (Baltimore MD: The Walters Art Museum in association with D. Giles Ltd, 2005).

[2] https://art.thewalters.org/detail/37626/the-ideal-city/. See Jane Stevenson, *The light of Italy: the life and times of Federico da Montefeltro* (London: Apollo, 2021).

[3] Tom Nichols, *The art of poverty: irony and ideal in sixteenth-century beggar imagery* (Manchester: Manchester University Press, 2007) particularly chapter one 'The beggar's place', pp. 17–48.

[4] On attitudes to women and efforts to limit spatial movement see Dennis Romano, 'Gender and the urban geography of Renaissance Venice', *Journal of Social History* 23:2 (1989), 339–53.

Cleaning Up Renaissance Italy: Environmental Ideals and Urban Practice in Genoa and Venice. Jane L. Stevens Crawshaw, Oxford University Press. © Jane L. Stevens Crawshaw 2023. DOI: 10.1093/oso/9780198867432.003.0002

Image 1.1 Painting of an Ideal City (c.1480–4). © The Walters Art Museum, Baltimore (CC0 license).

cities will emerge in this chapter and those that follow as one of the driving principles of Renaissance urban design.

The ideals expressed in this panel were intended to say as much about governance as they were about the built environment.[5] This connection, of course, was also evident in early modern Utopian writing.[6] When represented visually, idealized locations (whether entire cities or individual buildings) often appeared as highly stylized, geometric forms in which order and balance were principles of form and function. This chapter will examine these dynamics in the specific context of premodern ports and dilate upon the impact on concepts of health and cleanliness.[7] Leonardo da Vinci, for example, designed round rather than angular staircases for his ideal city, which had both aesthetic and practical benefits. In a clear reflection on the relationship between space and behaviour, da Vinci noted that these spaces would not only look beautiful but also no one would be tempted to urinate in the structures since they lacked the usual corners.[8] San Bernardino of Siena had preached that the placing of the holy cross in public places helped to dissuade people from urinating on communal architectural structures, such as the walls of the city. In Rome, street corners were often used for urination and the stench was well documented. Pope Paul V [1605–21] paid for drinking fountains to be constructed on a corner at which many pilgrims tended to relieve themselves before crossing the river to St Peter's. The run-off water from the fountains was to be used to sluice the streets of the area.[9] These

---

[5] See the exploration of this idea in Fabrizio Nevola, *Street life*, p. 11.
[6] R. Eaton, *Ideal cities: Utopianism and the (un)built environment* (London: Thames & Hudson, 2002).
[7] I concentrate on permanent rather than temporary constructions. On a temporary structure to accommodate poor migrants in Venice see Danielle Abdon, 'Sheltering refugees: ephemeral architecture and mass migration in early modern Venice', *Urban History* (2021), 1–21. The representation on the de'Barbari map may be one of the square communal rubbish containers discussed in chapter four.
[8] Douglas Biow, *The culture of cleanliness in Renaissance Italy*, p. 6.
[9] Katherine Rinne, *The waters of Rome*, p. 179.

28 CLEANING UP RENAISSANCE ITALY

were just some of many reflections which explored ways of shaping space in order to shape behaviour and cleanliness in the Renaissance.

Imagining Renaissance Ports

Variety, wrote Francesco di Giorgio Martini [*c*.1439–1501], lies at the heart of the natural world. Foodstuffs of diverse virtues and effects grow in the places best suited to their survival. Against this backdrop, a port is an essential structure that allows men living in one part of the world to have the same comforts (*comodità*) as those living in another.[10] Ports facilitate the movement of merchandise and foodstuffs, as well as other things necessary to the art of navigation. Ports, then, were a construction which enhanced environments and strengthened commercial relationships.[11] They were entirely compatible with the natural order of things. Indeed, they were an essential part of it.

In relation to the Asian port city, Peter Reeves, Frank Broeze, and Kenneth McPherson have noted that the existing historiography largely studies ports either with 'no reference to the cities to which they relate' or discuss ports 'as if there were no specific maritime functions that could influence the spatial and social evolution of the city'.[12] Modern ports are often located at a distance from urban centres because of the space required to meet technological demands but this was not the case in earlier centuries. Historians have not always sought to distinguish ports in premodern urban studies but Peter Rietbergen has offered a useful method for doing just that by suggesting that urban settlements should be characterized as ports if the port area is the organizing principle of the city.[13]

Ports, of course, were not necessarily maritime but many of the concerns articulated during the Renaissance about the environment and health of such sites coalesced around the impact of proximity to the sea.[14] Leon Battista Alberti [1404–72] noted that cities should be constructed either on the shore itself or a good distance inland. The effect of a sea breeze was said to make air potentially thick and mucus-like. Many authors were influenced by Classical thinkers including Plato [?429–347 BC] who had advised that a city should be located ten miles

---

[10] Francesco Giorgio di Martino, *Trattati di architettura, ingegneria e arte militare* in *La città ideale nel Rinascimento*, edited by G. C. Sciolla (Turin: UTET, 1975).

[11] For later comparisons see Brad Beaven, Karl Bell, and Robert James (eds), *Port towns and urban cultures: international histories of the waterfront c.1700–2000* (Basingstoke: Palgrave Macmillan, 2016).

[12] Peter Reeves, Frank Broeze, and Kenneth McPherson, 'Studying the Asian port city' in Frank Broeze (ed.), *Brides of the sea: port cities of Asia from the 16th–20th centuries* (Kensington N.S.W: New South Wales University Press, 1989), pp. 29–53.

[13] Peter Rietbergen, 'Porto e citta o citta-porto? Qualche riflessione generale sul problema del rapporto fra porto e contesto urbano' in Simonetta Cavaciocchi (ed.), *I porti come impresa economica*, (Florence: Le Monnier, 1988), p. 617.

[14] Josef Konvitz, *Cities and the sea: port city planning in early modern Europe* (Baltimore MD: Johns Hopkins University Press, 2019).

CONSTRUCTING IDEALS AND PRACTICES IN RENAISSANCE PORT CITIES   29

from the sea, for reasons of security as well as health. The Venetian Marco Foscari [1477–1551], cousin to Doge Andrea Gritti [1455–1538], wrote that a good city 'must not be maritime and placed right above the sea, so as to be free of contagions and pestilences that can be so easily carried there by sailors, and also the different vices that the foreigners can send out into a well-established city'.[15] Health issues were compounded not only by the environmental vulnerability of ports but also by their social composition. In 1464, the authorities in Pisa petitioned Florence for permission to develop a plague hospital on the grounds that this would be:

> One of the best remedies to repel the plague and avoid contagion, particularly in a maritime city, where it is necessary to accommodate a diversity of people, who carry more danger of contagion than others arriving beyond the coast.[16]

Ports faced a number of environmental and social challenges (principally the risk of siltation, social flux, and the importation of disease). Many of these challenges were addressed in Renaissance tracts on architecture, including works by Leon Battista Alberti [1404–72], Francesco di Giorgio Martini, and, particularly, Antonio Averlino [c.1400–69].[17] Despite suggestions that Renaissance harbours and ports were 'not embellished with the spatial vocabulary of the Renaissance', these texts also demonstrate the intended impact of Renaissance architectural ideals on the ports of this period.[18]

Francesco di Giorgio Martini identified three ideal shapes for a port and highlighted the features which were necessary in a well-functioning port district. The area in front of the harbour, he wrote, should contain a square with wells and warehouses, and a *loggia* to protect foreigners and citizens from extremes of weather and climate. A lighthouse should be located in an 'eminent' site. The Arsenal itself should be capacious. The breakwater must be kept clear, clean, and well maintained so that, during the summer, the low volume of water did not lead to corrupt air and ill health. He built into his design a structure to accommodate the ebb and flow of the tides and allow for the evacuation of filth in order to prevent siltation.[19] The facilities of his port included a marketplace, a church, a house for the superintendent of the port, and—paying particular attention to ingenious uses of water supplies—vessels for storing fish which were fed with fresh water. Some of the features of a port were divided by di Giorgio Martini into those for merchants (predominantly those which allowed for easy loading

---

[15] Douglas Biow, *The culture of cleanliness*, p. 76.
[16] Richard Palmer, 'The control of plague in Venice and Northern Italy', p. 49.
[17] For a study of architectural theorists on the streets, see Fabrizio Nevola, *Street life*, chapter one 'Planned streets and urban renewal in Renaissance Italy', pp. 22–129.
[18] Josef Konvitz, *Cities and the sea*, p. 14.
[19] Francesco di Giorgio Martini, *Trattati di architettura*, p. 487.

30   CLEANING UP RENAISSANCE ITALY

and unloading of their merchandise and storage in warehouses) and sailors (principally taverns and a brothel).[20]

Di Giorgio Martini considered fortifications to be crucial in what were intrinsically open locations. Leon Battista Alberti also wrote that ports should be protected using a breakwater, rampart, chain, or equivalent obstacles. Renaissance authors showed considerable interest in such defences and their origins. Pliny the Elder's [d.79 AD] *Naturalis Historia* included a story which was said to have inspired the development of breakwaters (*moli*) in ports. A whale, attracted by a sunken ship carrying hides, fed on the cargo and inadvertently dug itself into the seabed and became trapped under a mound of sand that built up over it, carried by the waves. The protective potential of such a structure became clear and artificial imitations came to be widely incorporated into port design. In 1589, a reflection on the health of the Ligurian town of Rapallo expressed concern that the high quality of the air was being corrupted by a stagnant marsh, the stench from which was causing considerable problems for the health of inhabitants. The inhabitants proposed the restoration of a collapsed breakwater, the absence of which had left houses exposed to the ravages of the sea.[21] An addition of a breakwater was considered to be an adaptation of the natural form of ports and based on an example from the natural world.

A detailed consideration of Renaissance port structures was provided by Antonio Averlino, known as Filarete, in his vernacular treatise on architecture which was composed between 1461 and 1464.[22] It remained unpublished until the 1880s but circulated in manuscript form. Filarete worked for Francesco Sforza and sought to honour his patron in the name chosen for his ideal city, Sforzinda.[23] Lesser known in his work is the port which he designed to accompany Sforzinda. Known as 'Plusiopolis', it was situated between a bay and the foot of a mountain. Although a number of drawings are missing from the text, considerable detail is included regarding its form and architecture.

Filarete's discussion of Plusiopolis expressed some similarities in form and style between cities and ports. He wrote:

The walls and towers were to be built just as at Sforzinda. The form of the circumference would have been surrounded by walls if the site had been suitable. The 'village' contains a *piazza* in the middle with two others beside it, like those in Sforzinda, and follows the same order and modes for the greater part.

---

[20] Francesco di Giorgio Martini, *Trattati di architettura*, p. 488.

[21] ASCG, PdC, 2-122 (15 February 1589).

[22] Pamela O. Long, *Openness, secrecy, authorship: technical arts and the culture of knowledge from Antiquity to the Renaissance* (Baltimore MD: Johns Hopkins University Press, 2001) contextualizes Filarete's authorship on pp. 129–32.

[23] This city was said to be the inspiration for the star-shaped Sabbioneta, commissioned by Vespasiano Gonzaga [1531–91]. See F. P. Dibari and E. Marani, *Sabbioneta e Vespasiano Gonzaga* (Sabbioneta, 1977).

CONSTRUCTING IDEALS AND PRACTICES IN RENAISSANCE PORT CITIES   31

Earlier in the text, Filarete had described the *piazza* of Sforzinda, highlighting a series of interconnected spaces. One, dedicated to the merchants, included the butcher, chicken, and fish shops and behind this unit were the brothels, public baths, and inn or taverns. The central square was surrounded by a channel of water. This was traversed by nine bridges which led to six entrances onto the square itself. In the centre was a cruciform church. Water was to be brought

> especially into the *piazza*. At its centre I want to make a reservoir arranged in such a way that when you want to wash the streets you have only to open certain spouts, enough water will come gushing out to wash all the streets and *piazzas* in such a way that they will be set in good order.[24]

Finally, because of the plentiful water supply, many of the roads would, in fact, operate as canals so that the number of carts passing through the city would be minimized. Carts with iron-bound wheels had long been recognized as noisy and damaging.[25] In Plusiopolis and Sforzinda, the remaining streets were to be paved with good stone in order to ensure that their condition did not deteriorate.[26]

Despite some overlap in the design of the ideal city and port in Filarete's work there were elements which were specific to the port of Plusiopolis, some of which were elaborated in the course of a detailed story relating to the setting of the foundations at the site. In the course of this work a square stone was discovered, which displayed ancient characters. Inside was a lead box and a large book of gold, as well as two, antique gold vases, which, at first sight appeared to contain dust. The book was a Greek text commissioned by King Zogalia [Galeazzo] (an ortho-graphical tool which allowed Filarete to relate the history of the Sforza dynasty). Inside the lead box was a golden head with a crown set with precious stones. Beyond this, there were coloured jewels and an ornate, covered cup. Filarete wrote that the rest of the interior was

> filled with different colours and forms of stone, some large and some small . . . as many as those in the one in the sacristy of *San Marco* in Venice. It even appeared to have a few more in it than there were in the one from Candia that was stolen in my lifetime. Nor were there fewer than the ones in Rome at *San Giovanni* that decorate the reliquary of the heads of Saints Peter and Paul.

Filarete associated the material culture of this port with that of Venice, Candia, and Rome. As illustrated by Michele Bacci, ports were connected by those who

---

[24] John R. Spencer (ed.), *Filarete's treatise on architecture* (New Haven CT: Yale University Press, 1965), Book VI.
[25] Carole Rawcliffe, *Urban bodies*, p. 139.   [26] John R. Spencer (ed.), *Filarete's*, Book VI fol. 44r.

32   CLEANING UP RENAISSANCE ITALY

visited them as points of reference in a wide-reaching religious network.[27] Bacci uncovered a manuscript list of a series of miraculous shrines which encompassed much of the Mediterranean. In earlier centuries, the development of these ports as centres for religious importance was shaped by the perspective of them as 'safe spaces' for reliquaries to be housed away from the reach of pirates.[28] Later these shrines were believed to offer enduring protection for those at sea. They were not intended to be simply utilitarian, practical sites. Considerable care was taken over the design and materials used in construction. Filarete's court at Plusiopolis, for example, was constructed of coloured marble and represented an elaborate expression of wealth, embellished to create a meaningful and magnificent place of arrival.

In the account of Plusiopolis, the 'dust' in the vases was revealed to be such that,

> spend money as you will, it will never be lacking, for the contents of one vase are related to the sun and of the other to the moon ... This makes a great multiplication in the god who cut off the head of Argus of the hundred eyes.

This was a reference to Mercury, who was ordered by Jupiter to kill Argus—a giant with a hundred eyes all over his body, some of which were said to be always open. Juno had set Argus to watch Io, Jupiter's lover and, at his death, she placed his eyes onto the feathers of her bird, the peacock. John Spencer has illustrated that Filarete employed Mercury throughout this text as the patron of trade. This imagery was deployed more broadly in depictions of Renaissance ports. In the best-known image of Venice from the Renaissance period, that of Jacopo de'Barbari from 1500, a depiction of Mercury includes the text, 'I Mercury shine favourably over this above all other emporia' ('*Mercvrivs pre ceteris hvic favste emporiis illvstro*'). Ports, therefore, were conceptualized within networks of religious and commercial provision.

Filarete further explained and illustrated the urban form of the port city. Plusiopolis had a portico with a parapet so that a person could traverse the whole area freely, emphasizing the importance of unimpeded passage. This encircled the whole area, with a stair at either end for access. A canal divided the portico in half, which transported water from the countryside. Numerous mills and crafts made use of this water supply. The important issue of defence was also addressed: a castle was to be supplied with water using cisterns and a conduit. Everything was to be built as was shown in the golden book—a literary

---

[27] Michele Bacci, 'Portolano sacro. Santuari e immagini sacre lungo le rotte di navigazione del Mediterraneo tra tardo Medioevo e prima età moderna' in Erik Thunø and Gerhard Wolf (eds), *The miraculous image in the Middle Ages and Renaissance* (Rome: 'L'Erma' di Bretschneider, 2004), pp. 223–48.

[28] Giustina Olgiati (ed.), *Genova, porta del mondo*, p. 3.

CONSTRUCTING IDEALS AND PRACTICES IN RENAISSANCE PORT CITIES   33

device which emphasized the significance of ancient ideas for Renaissance port architecture.

Filarete's text, like many of the ideal city tracts, paid particular attention to the issues of the supply, flow, and display of water. The court was constructed with a gap in the walls of one and a half arm's length (*braccia*). This space was used for stairs, chimneys, latrines, and drains, which collected both rainwater and the water used in the halls. The court also included a fountain arranged in such a way that the water would be displayed to a height equivalent to the building itself. The water was transported into the city from a place of high altitude, through a conduit which then separated to serve fountains and feed the fishpond. The excellent water supply meant that a large, fertile garden could be nurtured, replete with fruit. Finally, water could be used in ambitious, awe-inspiring constructions such as a carved, cylindrical memorial which included a mechanism through which water could be channelled. Filarete's text illustrates in richer detail than many of those written by his contemporaries that there was a clear Renaissance vision for the form of port cities, which highlighted strong fortifications, the flow of people and goods, and the display of water, as central to the health and preservation of the setting.

In addition to the reflections in ideal tracts, ports featured prominently in city views produced during the early modern period. These were 'chorographic' representations which were intended to produce a sense of the nature of a place rather than a precise depiction of the physical reality.[29] Designs became more individual during the early modern period, although it was not until the eighteenth century that cartographic representations were produced. Matteo Pagano, for example, produced an early aerial plan of Cairo in which many buildings looked 'resolutely Venetian in appearance' but it was labelled as a 'true description' and included vignettes of daily life, including customs and dress, animals (crocodiles), date pickers, historical events, and a man defecating into the Nile, translating unfamiliar sights for a European audience.[30]

The translation of unfamiliar places for European 'armchair travellers' was one of the functions fulfilled by visual representations of spaces produced by painters and printmakers. Such images could also be used to celebrate and commemorate the familiar and the local or display the exotic. They could also be emblematic of knowledge and understanding of the wider world. Paolo Cortesi [1471–1510] in *De Cardinalatu* wrote that the proper way to decorate summer rooms of palaces was with mathematical concepts and painted pictures of the world (in maps and charts). Maps were central to concepts and expressions of power: 'to map a

---

[29] For a discussion of the notion of resemblance and similitude in portraits and these views with particular reference to Rome see Jessica Maier, 'A "true likeness": the Renaissance city portrait', *Renaissance Quarterly* 65:3 (2012), 711–52.

[30] Nicholas Warner, *The true description of Cairo: a sixteenth-century Venetian view* (Oxford: Oxford University Press, 2006).

territory was seen as tantamount to possessing it'.[31] Expressive of the ambition of the Catholic-Reformation Papacy was the creation of the gallery of maps in the Vatican (largely completed by 1581–2).[32] These images were more than just plans because place was recognized to be more than just a setting. Location was believed to be instrumental for explaining and understanding differences. Specific print genres, such as the *Isolarii* (books of islands), aligned visual representations with textual descriptions and could provide considerable detail on landscapes, political systems, and social structures.[33] A broad range of such works were created within networks of patronage and demonstrate that painters and printmakers played a vital role in promoting the reputation of a place and its governance through the representation of space.

Travel writing engaged in a specific process of translation and display, which often featured port cities. Benjamin Arbel has drawn attention to the volumes of travel literature that include descriptions of provincial capitals and principal ports of the Levant.[34] He highlighted visitors' interests in elements of urban forms. In Alexandria, which had two port structures (one serving the naval squadron and the other Western commerce) the history of the city was celebrated. In addition to its famous lighthouse and spaces associated with Alexander the Great or early Christian martyrs, travellers described the city's water supply system, 'based on huge, vaulted cisterns periodically filled with water brought from the Nile during its summer flow'. They recorded a contrast between the impressive fortifications and harbour spaces and the disordered city beyond. European travel accounts blamed poor sanitary conditions on the misgovernment of Muslim rulers rather than the environmental problems, which were caused by two lakes adjacent to the city and poor-quality drinking water from the Nile.

Renaissance writings also explored the ports of the ancient world. Particularly well known are the reconstructions of classical ports by the antiquarian Piero Ligorio [*c.*1512–83], who served as the architect to Pope Paul IV [1476–1559].[35] Further interest in the ports of Antiquity was shown by Cesare Cesariano

---

[31] See the Stanza del Guardarobe in the Palazzo Vecchio, the images of 96 cities in the Louvre created by Louis XIII, the Camera delle città in Mantua and the Alcazar in Madrid. R. L. Kagan, 'Philip II and the art of the cityscape' in R. I. Rotberg and T. K. Rabb (eds), *Art and history: images and their meanings* (Cambridge: Cambridge University Press, 1986), pp. 115–37 and *Urban Images of the Hispanic World 1493–1793* (New Haven CT: Yale University Press, 2000).

[32] Lucio Gambi, Antonio Pinelli et al., *La Galleria delle carte geografiche in Vaticano* (Modena: Panini, 1994).

[33] Bronwen Wilson, *The world in Venice: print, the city and early modern identity* (Toronto: University of Toronto Press, 2005) and Bronwen Wilson and Paul Yachnin (eds), *Making publics in early modern Europe: people, things, forms of knowledge* (London: Routledge, 2010).

[34] Benjamin Arbel, 'The port towns of the Levant in sixteenth-century travel literature' in Alexander Cowan (ed.), *Mediterranean urban culture 1400–1700* (Exeter: University of Exeter Press, 2000), pp. 151–64.

[35] R. W. Gaston (ed.), *Pirro Ligorio: artist and antiquarian* (Milan: Silvana, 1988).

CONSTRUCTING IDEALS AND PRACTICES IN RENAISSANCE PORT CITIES   35

[1475–1543] through his reconstruction of Halicarnassus.[36] The best-known classical port was that of Ostia, the significance of which was at its height during the second and third centuries AD. The port gradually silted up and was largely abandoned until the remaining village was fortified by Pope Gregory during the ninth century and renamed as Gregoriopolis. The site acted, therefore, as a significant reminder of the importance of managing the environment of ports. Amalfi (one of the four medieval maritime Republics along with Venice, Genoa, and Pisa) had been devastated by a storm described by Petrarch.[37] The vulnerability of ports to environmental changes or natural disasters was widely recognized and Renaissance authorities looked to surpass the greatness of ancient (and more recent) ports in their designs and governance. Indeed, a number of ports literally built on the example of Ostia, since material was taken from the ruins for Gregoriopolis, for the building of the cathedral at Pisa in 1063, and medieval Genoa.[38] Later, similar symbolism was employed when the huge harbour chains of the port of Pisa were taken by Genoa after a victory in 1342. Both Pisa and Genoa vied for the role of preeminent medieval Italian port. Neither the symbolism of looted materials nor the cautionary tale of Ostia's decline would have been lost on the authorities or observers of Renaissance ports.

Port Societies

Leon Battista Alberti wrote, 'so that the inhabitants can live amongst one another in peace and as far as possible without discomfort and free of molestation, it is necessary to consider the place [in which they live]'. The associations between the body of the city and the bodies of inhabitants were clearly conceived in this period. Buildings, cities, and ships were each represented by the metaphor of the body.[39] Such imagery had a long history but, as Ian Maclean has argued, a new image of the body emerged during the Renaissance period, far more appreciative of ideal proportions, under the influence of Andreas Vesalius's [1514–64] work on anatomy. This meant that 'health (construed in terms of proportion, balance, and harmony both in quality and quantity) came to be seen as the "nobility of the body" and associated not only with moderate physical exercise but also the act of

---

[36] Peter Fane-Saunders, *Pliny the Elder and the emergence of Renaissance architecture* (Cambridge: Cambridge University Press, 2016).

[37] Francesco Petrarch, *Epistolae familiares*, v.5.

[38] Sonia Gallico, *Guide to the ruins of Ostia* (Venice: ATS Italia, 1985), p. 7. Some material was also removed to Orvieto.

[39] On the ship as a body see Diego García de Palacio's 1587 shipbuilding book cited in Pablo Emilio Pérez-Mallaína Bueno, *Spain's men of the sea: daily life on the Indies fleets in the sixteenth century* (Cambridge MA: Harvard University Press, 1998), p. 65.

36 CLEANING UP RENAISSANCE ITALY

beholding beauty in works of art and nature'.[40] Healthy cities required beauty and proportion in their architecture and environment. Individual parts were intended to be appropriate to the nature of the bodies they contained.

During the Renaissance, there was a close relationship between the nature of the *urbs* and that of the *polis*. In the urban body, discontent or social unrest might result from any imbalance or *disumore*. As a result, the works on ideal cities considered in the previous section were also works on ideal societies, however explicit the authors chose to make that link. Leon Battista Alberti wrote of ordered planning:

> we should divide the city into zones, so that not only are foreigners segregated into some place suitable for them and not inconvenient for the citizens, but the citizens themselves are also separated into zones suitable and convenient, according to the occupation and rank of each one. The charm of a city will be very much enhanced if the various workshops are allocated distinct and well-chosen zones... Anything foul or offensive (especially the stinking tanners) should be kept well away in the outskirts to the north, as the wind rarely blows from that direction, and when it does, it gusts so strongly as to clear smells away rather than carry them along.

If each group was allocated a clear and appropriate place in the cityscape, then society as a whole should remain stable and harmonious. These ideas were exported from Europe to colonial and imperial contexts. Ports were utilized by Spanish officials in their campaigns. One such location, Puerto Real is known to have been one of the first planned European towns in the Americas, arranged in a regular rectangular format, with segregated areas for particular groups.[41] In these contexts, moral regulation was attempted through urban design.

European port societies had a specific occupational make-up.[42] Fishermen, like sailors, had a distinct sub-culture in early modern Europe and one which was largely masculine.[43] In Venice, shipbuilders lived largely in the vicinity of their workplace (the vast Arsenal of Castello) and deep-sea fishermen clustered in San Nicolò dei Mendicoli and Angelo Raffaele.[44] Eel-fishers and other small-boat

---

[40] Ian Maclean in Klaus Bergdolt and Ingo F. Herrmann (eds), *Was ist Gesundheit? Antworten aus Jahrhunderten* (Stuttgart: Franz Steiner Verlag, 2011), p. 99.

[41] Kathleen Deagan (ed.), *Puerto real: the archaeology of a sixteenth-century Spanish town in Hispaniola* (Gainesville: University Press of Florida, 1995).

[42] Robin Quillien and Solène Rivoal, 'Boatmen, fishermen and Venetian institutions: from negotiation to confrontation' in Maartje van Gelder and Claire Judde de Larivière (eds), *Popular politics in an aristocratic Republic: political conflict and social contestation in late medieval and early modern Venice* (London: Routledge, 2020).

[43] Peter Burke, *Popular culture in early modern Europe* (London: Temple Smith, 1994), pp. 43–6.

[44] See R. C. Davis, *The war of the fists: popular culture and public violence in late Renaissance Venice* (Oxford: Oxford University Press, 1994), pp. 19–28 for a discussion of the 'factional landscape' of the city.

CONSTRUCTING IDEALS AND PRACTICES IN RENAISSANCE PORT CITIES   37

lagoon fishermen lived in Sant'Agnese and San Trovaso.[45] In Genoa many were said to live in the area around the port where, because of its lower elevation, the air was heavy and humid. It was damp because of its proximity to the sea and also the site where a number of subterranean drains emptied into the water causing fetid vapours. As a result, the air in this part of the city was more humid and less salubrious than the air in the rest of the city, which was predominantly warm and dry. The Genoese doctor Paschetti recorded that, with good reason, this area of the city was not inhabited by nobles but only by a few artisans, sailors, and foreigners.[46] Ennio Poleggi has illustrated that this was a district in which artisanal clusters also existed, such as that for shipbuilding around the Molo.

Ports were recognized as having distinctive social forms, notably the turnover of people as a result of migration and a cosmopolitan social mix. At times port populations also contained higher proportions of women because of seasons spent by men at sea.[47] Port districts were spaces in which the 'marginalised majority worked and passed'.[48] Mary Elizabeth Perry, in her study of early modern Seville, noted that after 1503 when the Crown of Castile decreed that all ships between Europe and the New World should pass through that river port the city was described as 'a Great Babylon', flushed with new people and wealth: 'beggars, prostitutes, thugs and thieves alongside merchants, bankers, shippers and soldiers'.[49]

There were recognized benefits to the congregation of a diversity of people in maritime centres. Flavio Biondo wrote 'it is obvious that nothing serves more to increase wealth than a large concourse of travellers, and that people tend to collect in places where there are opportunities for gain'.[50] Many of these individuals might be occasional visitors, whose periods of residence were short-lived. Others settled as longer-term members of foreign communities, sometimes receiving citizenship of their host city and resulting in a 'fertile exchange of ideas, attitudes and behaviours' as well as tensions and conflict.[51] There is no doubt that, during the premodern period, the principal benefit to a port of this congregation of people was seen to be economic.

---

[45] R. C. Davis, *The war of the fists*, p. 24.   [46] Paschetti, p. 124.

[47] Peter Lee, Leonard Y. Andaya, Barbara Watson Andaya, Gael Newton and Alan Chong, *Port cities: multicultural emporiums of Asia, 1500 1900* (Singapore. Asian Civilisations Museum, 2016).

[48] Rosa M. Salzberg, 'The margins in the centre: working around Rialto in sixteenth-century Venice' in Andrew Spicer and Jane L. Stevens Crawshaw (eds), *The Place of the Social Margins, 1350–1750* (London: Routledge, 2017), pp. 135–53.

[49] Mary Elizabeth Perry, *Crime and society in early modern Seville* (Hanover NH: University Press of New England, 1980), p. 1.

[50] Biondo Flavio, *Italy illuminated*, Jeffrey A. White (ed. and trans) (Cambridge MA: Harvard University Press, 2005), p. 33.

[51] Marc Boone and Heleni Porfyriou, 'Introduction' in Donatella Calabi and Stephen Turk Christensen (eds), *Cultural exchange in early modern Europe II: cities and cultural exchange in Europe, 1400–1700* (Cambridge: Cambridge University Press, 2006), p. 61.

38 CLEANING UP RENAISSANCE ITALY

Ports are often believed to have been more accommodating of foreigners in order to prioritize commercial potential.[52] The extensive historiography on Jewish communities has established that they constituted important communities in a number of ports.[53] Ghettos and sites for foreign merchants might be developed with the intention of facilitating economic contact.[54] Pope Paul III [1534–51] encouraged Sephardic, Levantine Turkish, and other merchants to trade in the port of Ancona, and prohibited the prosecution of New Christians for heresy without explicit papal order. Cosimo I granted similar privileges in 1549 as did Ercole II of Ferrara in 1550.[55] Natalie Zemon Davis has illustrated that members of these communities were aware of the utility of such international connections, as well as the suddenness with which the 'wheel of fortune might turn' in the form of persecution and expulsion.[56] For this reason, families often engaged in a strategy for marrying some children close to home and others in distant cities.[57] Such an ambiguous status could bring with it commercial advantages as well as intense social vulnerability and injustice, just as it could more generally for foreign merchants.

In port cities, resident foreign populations often rented, rather than owned, accommodation. More often than not, they rented from others of the same nationality. Otherwise, in some port cities, institutions developed on the model of the Islamic *funduq*.[58] These *fondaci*, as they were known in Italian, developed across the trading cities of the early modern world.[59] Benjamin Arbel cites a Flemish traveller, van Ghistele who described one of the two Venetian *fondaci*, in 1480:

> These *fondigos* are vast square buildings... divided inside into several floors and alleys, along which are the lodgings of foreign merchants. The lower part has vaulted chambers or casemates, where the merchandise is stocked and

---

[52] Barrington Moore Jr, 'Ethnic and religious hostilities in early modern port cities', *International Journal of Politics, Culture and Society* 14:4 (2001), 687–727.

[53] See the essays in David Cesarani and Gemma Romain (eds), *Jews and port cities 1590–1990: commerce, community and cosmopolitanism* (London: Vallentine Mitchell, 2006).

[54] Donatella Calabi, 'The Jews and the City in the Mediterranean Area' in Alexander Cowan (ed.), *Mediterranean urban culture 1400–1700*, p. 68 and R. Po-Chia Hsia and H. Lehmann (eds), *In and out of the Ghetto: Jewish-Gentile relations in late medieval and early modern Germany* (Cambridge: Cambridge University Press, 1995), pp. 125–37.

[55] Kim Siebenhüner, 'Conversion, mobility and the Roman Inquisition in Italy around 1600', *Past and Present* 200 (2008), 12.

[56] Debra Kaplan, *Beyond expulsion: Jews, Christians and Reformation Strasbourg* (Stanford CA: Stanford University Press, 2011).

[57] Natalie Zemon Davis, *Women on the margins: three seventeenth-century lives* (Cambridge MA: Harvard University Press, 2003), pp. 12–13.

[58] The Italian term developed from the same root as the Arab term *funduq*. See Deborah Howard, *Venice and the East: the impact of the Islamic world on Venetian architecture 1100–1500* (New Haven CT: Yale University Press, 2000), pp. 120–31.

[59] See Olivia R. Constable, *Housing the stranger in the Mediterranean world: lodging, trade and travel in late Antiquity and the Middle Ages* (Cambridge: Cambridge University Press, 2003).

CONSTRUCTING IDEALS AND PRACTICES IN RENAISSANCE PORT CITIES   39

which are called magazines in this country...At the centre there is a place where merchants bring their goods, exchange them, sell them, pack and unpack them...In the evening, the emir's employees come to close the *fondigos* to ensure that the merchants dwelling there would not be disturbed by the Saracenes.[60]

In Venice, *fondaci* were established to accommodate valuable commodities and foreign merchants.[61] This included the *fondaco della farina* (a warehouse for flour) which was developed to deal with the problem of famine, and the German *fondaco* for merchants, designed to keep a demarcated distance between the foreigners and the wider city whilst facilitating contact between them for trade. The German *fondaco* was described as completely isolated ('*tutto in isola*'). It had an entrance which was locked up at night, highlighting an obvious parallel with the city's Ghetto which had been established in 1516 on an island with a single entrance which was locked at night for the city's Jewish community.[62] A decision was made to establish a *fondaco* for Turkish merchants in 1573 but a site was not chosen until 1621. Such spaces were located through the city, although the German *fondaco* was situated close to the mercantile centre at Rialto. Felix Faber described the *fondaco* as a 'building from which goods flow towards other districts like water from a fountain'.[63] This is an appropriate simile, given the association between ideal ports and the display of water supply. It is also an interesting image to have applied to Venice. As we will see in chapter three, although a number of fountains were decorated in other European cities as a sign of the state's benevolence in providing for its citizens' needs, Venice's most famous early modern fountain distributed wine rather than water.[64]

A similar institution, influenced by Ottoman examples, was the *bagno* or *seraglio* for slaves. Giorgio Vasari the Younger, in his 1598 architectural tract, designed a port and determined, in particular, the site which was ideal for the *seraglio*. In contextualizing this part of the structure, he mentioned that there was one in Malta and another in Algiers as well as other locations. A well-known *bagno* was established in Livorno, a Tuscan free port which was developed by the architect Bernardo Buontalenti [c.1531–1608] under the patronage of Duke Ferdinando I de Medici [r.1587–1609].[65] The port was intended to accommodate merchants from 'any nation, Eastern Levantines and Westerners, Spanish,

---

[60] Benjamin Arbel, 'The port towns of the Levant', p. 155.

[61] See Deborah Howard, *The architectural history of Venice*, pp. 33–4.

[62] On similarities between the Ghetto and the *fondaco* see Ennio Concina, Ugo Camerino and Donatella Calabi, *La città degli Ebrei. Il Ghetto di Venezia: architettura e urbanistica* (Venice: Albrizzi, 1991), pp. 211–16.

[63] 'una casa della quale le merci profluiscono verso altre contrade come l'acque della fonte' cited in Ennio Concina, *Fondaci: architettura, arte e mercatura tra Levante, Venezia e Alemagna* (Venice: Marsilio, 1997), p. 9.

[64] Robert C. Davis, 'Venetian shipbuilders and the fountain of wine', *Past and Present* 156 (1997), 55–87.

[65] Corey Tazzara, *The free port of Livorno*.

40   CLEANING UP RENAISSANCE ITALY

Portuguese, Greeks, Germans and Italians, Jews, Turks and Moors, Armenians, Persians and others'.[66] In this context, the *bagno* combined military and commercial practices, with those of healthcare and, unlike those in North Africa, did not segregate the slaves according to their religion, gender, or class.[67] As with the *fondaci*, the buildings had 'permeable walls' and 'slaves in Livorno were employed as barbers and vendors of water, wine, tobacco and used clothing in and near the *bagno*'.[68]

Fernand Braudel and Ruggiero Romano termed Livorno the 'Algiers of Christianity' because the privileges of the port protected religious minorities and 'granted immunity to debtors and criminal delinquents whose crimes were committed outside the Tuscan Duchy'.[69] These policies prompted the Venetian resident in Tuscany, Giovanni Ambrogio Sarotti, to report to the Senate in 1652 that 'Livorno is a nest of dishonest people'. A similar image was employed by Alberto Bolognetti, papal nuncio in Venice in 1578–81 in a report on the German *fondaco* when he described that 'the Venetian government ought to realize that to allow so much freedom to Germans in the middle of the city is to nurture a viper in their own bosom'.[70] In many early modern cities, architectural and spatial controls have been associated with social restrictions but in ports, the characterization has been the opposite, that of potentially dangerous levels of social diversity and access.

Ports were also associated with other spaces located in places of 'ambiguous centrality'.[71] Urban governments often developed municipal brothels inside city walls, although sometimes they were assigned an extramural location. Regardless of the precise area chosen, there was an early and widespread attempt to establish a designed place for the sex trade in ports, in part to ensure effective financial control of this space as a potentially valuable source of income for the state. It has been widely acknowledged that authorities struggled to regulate brothels, in part because of the changing complexion of the trade. Changing economic conditions, whether at different stages in the life cycle or because of external factors, meant that women might undertake this work in a cyclical or temporary manner. In 1496 when residents of San Donato in Genoa, realized that a nearby building was being inhabited by sex workers, they reflected on the many dishonest and disgraceful activities which were against divine law and good character to the detriment of the

---

[66] Stephanie Nadalo, 'Negotiating slavery in a tolerant frontier: Livorno's Turkish *Bagno* (1547–1747), *Mediaevalia* 32 (2011), 276.

[67] Stephanie Nadalo, 'Negotiating slavery', 278.

[68] Stephanie Nadalo, 'Negotiating slavery', 296. On the notion of permeable walls in relation to hospitals see Graham Mooney and Jonathan Reinarz (eds), *Permeable walls: historical perspectives on hospital and asylum visiting* (Amsterdam: Rodolpi, 2009).

[69] Stephanie Nadalo, 'Negotiating slavery', 277.

[70] Cited in David Chambers and Brian Pullan, with Jennifer Fletcher, *Venice: a documentary history, 1450–1630* (Oxford: Blackwell, 1992), p. 331.

[71] Diane Ghirardo, 'The topography of prostitution in Renaissance Ferrara', *Journal of the Society of Architectural Historians* 60:4 (2001), 406.

CONSTRUCTING IDEALS AND PRACTICES IN RENAISSANCE PORT CITIES   41

whole of the Genoese state (*civitatis*). The general issue was intensified by the nature of the district which was one in which children were often found in the streets.[72] Part of the issue with this rental of properties, of course, was the semi-permanent nature of the presence of these women who were intended to be confined to a brothel in order to ensure that any associated immorality did not seep into the city.[73] In her article on the topography of prostitution in Renaissance Ferrara, Diane Ghirardo observes that it was not the immoral activities of the women which preoccupied civic authorities but the 'conjunction of space and sex'. In other words, having demarcated a place for the trade, the authorities' concern was to confine it. Connections, of course, endured; in seventeenth-century Amsterdam, the brothel was a site of news and socialization, a space in which letters and messages were passed on to wives and sweethearts.[74] Networks of knowledge could also be important; evidence from the inquisition in Ferrara has portrayed brothels as sites to which respectable women ventured in order to obtain love potions.[75]

The intended sense of separation between the brothel and the community was seen in the language used to describe these spaces, such as the blocks of houses in Venice in which sex workers were supposed to live which were termed *castelletti* (little castles) because they were only accessible through one bridge and could therefore be closely monitored.[76] The city's Ghetto was also referred to as a *castello* and had been placed on a self-contained island in the city.[77] In his description of the site, the diarist Marin Sanudo emphasized that it had only one entrance which could be closed up and guarded.[78]

A sense of intended security was deliberately rendered in port locations in diverse ways. In the next chapter we will see that the walls of Genoa were extended during the premodern period and, in both cities, defensive structures

---

[72] ASCG, PdC, 6-140 (22 September 1496).

[73] On the efforts made to ensure that brothels were genuinely confined social spaces see Julia Rombough, 'Noisy soundscapes'; Diane Ghirardo, 'The topography of prostitution', 402–31; Saundra Weddle, 'Mobility and prostitution in early modern Venice', *Early Modern Women* 14:1 (2019), 95–108 and Jane Stevens Crawshaw, 'Cleaning up the Renaissance city: the symbolic and physical place of the Genoese brothel in urban society' in Andrew Spicer and Jane Stevens Crawshaw (eds), *The place of the social margins*, pp. 155–81.

[74] Lotte van de Pol, *The burgher and the whore*, pp. 164–5.

[75] Diane Ghirardo, 'The topography of prostitution', 411; Kathy Stuart, *Defiled trades and social outcasts*, chapter six: 'The executioner's healing touch: health and honor in early modern German medical practice', pp 149–85.

[76] For the *castelletti* see Michelle A. Laughran, 'The body, public health and social control in sixteenth-century Venice' (unpublished PhD thesis, University of Connecticut, 1998), p. 57.

[77] Sanudo described the Ghetto as '*come un castello*' in *I Diarii di Marino Sanuto*, volume 22 col 72–73. Donatella Calabi and Paola Lanaro, *La città italiana e i luoghi degli stranieri*, p. 152. For works on the Venetian Ghetto see Gaetano Cozzi (ed.), *Gli ebrei a Venezia secoli XIV–XVIII* (Milan: Edizioni Comunità, 1987); Ennio Concina, Ugo Camerino and Donatella Calabi, *La città degli Ebrei* and Robert C. Davis and Benjamin Ravid (eds), *The Jews of early modern Venice* (Baltimore MD: Johns Hopkins University Press, 2001).

[78] Marin Sanudo cited in Ennio Concina, Ugo Camerino and Donatella Calabi, *La città degli Ebrei*, p. 27.

42 CLEANING UP RENAISSANCE ITALY

were constructed or reinforced, although the specific nature of the Venetian environment meant that the physical defences of the city comprised bodies of water rather than structures of stone. In the mid-sixteenth century the perceived Ottoman threat in the Mediterranean prompted the fortifications of many port cities to be strengthened. This work was undertaken by prominent Renaissance architects, including Donato Bramante [d.1514], Michelangelo [d.1564], and Antonio da Sangallo [1484–1546] at Civitavecchia and the aforementioned Buontalenti at Livorno and Cosmopoli.[79]

Buontalenti's designs for the Tuscan port of Livorno became particularly widely known. The siltation around Pisa meant that, by the twelfth century, the magistracies concerned with the management of water in the area had largely turned their attention to rivers and ditches.[80] Livorno emerged as a potential successor. An Arsenal was developed, on a small scale, from 1559. A proposal was made to pave the principal street and two small squares in 1562 for reasons of public health although it was not until 1574 that the streets were paved on a larger scale. By 1575, Bernardo Buontalenti had been selected by Francesco I to develop the new city and it was only at this stage that the canal which linked Livorno with Pisa was completed. Buontalenti was an experienced architect, with expertise in military and hydraulic engineering and he developed a pentagonal plan for the new port.[81] On 28 March 1577 the first stone was laid but progress was halted by the difficult economic circumstances in Tuscany during the 1580s. The scale of the new city was ambitious and was intended to accommodate approximately twelve thousand people.[82] This would make it the second city of the territory, larger than Pisa which at the time had eight thousand inhabitants. It developed famous privileges as a result of the 1591 and 1593 'Livornina' and, with the development of a free port, became a significant rival to Genoa during the seventeenth century.[83]

The principles which shaped the design of ideal ports reflected broader notions of political and social order. Contemporaries recognized the importance and specificity of ports, as well as the inherent dangers posed by the specific social and environmental contexts of such locations. An interest in port design, then, was widespread in this period but it was recognized that individual locations required specific forms to accommodate particular people and places.

---

[79] Giuseppe M. Battaglini, *Cosmopolis: Portoferraio medicea storia urbana 1548–1737* (Rome: Multigrafica editrice, 1978).

[80] Elena Fasano Guarini 'Regolamentazione delle acque e sistemazione del territorio' in G. Nudi (ed.), *Livorno e Pisa: due città e un territorio nella politica dei Medici* (Pisa: Nistri Lischi, 1980), pp. 43–75.

[81] For the breadth of his experience see Amelio Fara, *Bernardo Buontalenti* (Milan: Electa, 1995).

[82] The official statistics note that the population had risen from approximately 500 to 900 in 1592, 3,118 in 1601 and 5,046 in 1609 in Dario Matteoni, *Livorno* (Bari: Edizioni Laterza, 1985), p. 29, however, Nicholas Terpstra has identified that the city would have included approximately an equal number of slaves and prisoners who were not included in these figures.

[83] Thomas Kirk, 'Genoa and Livorno: sixteenth- and seventeenth-century commercial rivalry as a stimulus to policy development', *The Historical Association* (2001), 3–17.

Port Spaces and Society in Genoa and Venice

Dennis Romano has remarked that, 'probably no Italian city, with the possible exception of Genoa, had more space dedicated to commerce than did Venice'.[84] In Venice, the district of Rialto was the preeminent marketplace for domestic and international trade.[85] In 1414, a decision by the Senate referred to the customs house ('*doana*') in Rialto and the area served vital public functions, accommodating important government magistracies, alongside elements such as the public scales at the foot of the Rialto bridge (from 1493), and the public clock at San Giovanni Elemosinario (from 1410).[86] From as early as 1322, a world map was displayed at Rialto. This image, about which little is known, was repainted during the fifteenth century and would have been a centrepiece of commercial business of the district.[87] Rialto took on many of the principal features of a port, along with the area around the Bacino close to the Piazza San Marco. The latter site brought together the officials and spaces of customs primarily for goods arriving by sea. In 1677, the existing buildings for customs officials and warehouses were replaced by the grand Dogana di Mare which survives today.[88]

In Venice a *renovatio urbis* was undertaken by Jacopo Sansovino [1486–1570] at the behest of Doge Andrea Gritti [1455–1538], who was doge between 1523 and 1538. The work concentrated on the Piazza and Piazzetta San Marco. A description by Giorgio Vasari [1511–74] of Jacopo Sansovino's commissions reminded readers that:

> In the year 1529, there were between the two columns in the *piazza* some butchers' stalls, and also between one column and the next many wooden huts for the convenience of people's natural needs, something most foul [*bruttissima*] and shameful for the dignity of the palace and the public square, as well as for strangers, who coming to Venice by way of San Giorgio saw on their arrival all that filthiness before anything else [*nel primo introit cosi fatta sozzura*].[89]

The money-changing booths, meat and vegetable stalls, latrines, five hostelries, and a meat market were replaced over time with Renaissance designs for a *loggetta* for patricians to meet and mingle, the Zecca (mint) and the Marciana library.

---

[84] Dennis Romano, *Markets and marketplaces*, p. 58.

[85] Donatella Calabi describes the 'port functions' of Rialto from the fifteenth century in Donatella Calabi and Paolo Morachiello, *Rialto: le fabbriche e il Ponte 1514–91* (Turin: Einaudi, 1987), p. 21f.

[86] Donatella Calabi, *The market and the city*, p. 56.

[87] Donatella Calabi, *The market and the city*, p. 25. A brief discussion of the fourteenth-century version is made in Dennis Romano, *Markets and marketplaces*, p. 157.

[88] Marin Sanudo described the 'sora canal, che e il porto nostro' to describe the ripa Sancti Marci as cited in Ennio Concina, *Venezia nell'età moderna. Struttura e funzioni* (Venice: Marsilio, 1995), p. 26.

[89] Douglas Biow, *The culture of cleanliness*, p. 82.

A further association with ideal city principles can be drawn using an unusual example of surviving material culture. A glass tile survives in the collection of the British Museum which displays an impression of Andrea Gritti, along with his initials [Image 1.2].[90]

The tile was produced with a silvered background and gold relief portrait.[91] Filarete's aforementioned ideal city tract included a dialogue about a 'noble and beautiful pavement' which was to be produced by Master Angelo da

Image 1.2 Sixteenth-century Venetian glass tile showing Doge Andrea Gritti from the collection of the British Museum. © The Trustees of the British Museum.

---

[90] J. V. G. Mallet, 'Tiled floors and court designers in Mantua and Northern Italy' in Cesare Mozzarelli, Robert Oresko, and Leandro Ventura (eds), *La corte di Mantova nell'età di Andrea Mantegna: 1450–1550* (Rome: Bulzoni, 1997), pp. 253–72.

[91] John Mallet has suggested that surviving bronze medallions in the collection of the Museo Correr intimate that glass tiles of Andrea Gritti's predecessor, Antonio Grimani, may also have existed in 'Tiled floors and court designers', p. 256.

CONSTRUCTING IDEALS AND PRACTICES IN RENAISSANCE PORT CITIES   45

Murano, the head of an important family of Venetian glass makers who worked in Constantinople, Rome, Naples, Florence, and Milan.[92] Filarete proposed that reliefs in glass should be set above a seat in the loggia. Glass mosaic decorations were also to be made for the hospital suggesting a link with both beauty and cleanliness. This reflected broader interest in the use of glass in architecture. In 1473, Federico Gonzaga wrote about a possible commission for Venetian glass-makers of a pavement of glass tiles with gilt designs. In 1517, Filippo de Catanei of Murano applied to open a furnace to make glass pavement tiles in the form of the Gritti tile.[93] The lack of wear on the surviving Gritti tile suggests use as a wall rather than floor tile, which is what Filarete suggested for Sforzinda for a room in which the floor was to depict the four seasons of the year, the four elements, and a description of the earth.[94] There is no doubt that glass tiles remained rare and elite settings would more commonly have made use of maiolica tiles or marble for flooring and wall decoration. The survival does suggest the potential influence of Renaissance architectural tracts on Venetian rulers such as Gritti. Nevertheless, the distinct nature of the city's environment meant that some of the points of emphasis in ideal ports, including the extravagant display of water and develop-ment of strong fortifications, were not feasible in Venice.

In many ways, the Genoese port area was more conventional in its design. Genoa was said to have been an important strategic site from as early as the second Punic war [218–201 BC] because of its natural harbours.[95] In 1535, Agostino Giustiniani described the port of the city as, 'a maritime port, which is large and secure, sheltered from every wind direction except la Provenza'. He praised its various landing stations, the ample water supply and the shops and warehouses. It included a series of warehouses and taverns, spaces for artisans and trades (including ironworkers and fishermen), and an important church.[96] It also accommodated government officials working for the Salt Office and Padri del Comune. It had an important breakwater and, to avoid siltation and protect the area from the impact of the prevailing winds of the *scirocco*, this structure was lengthened over time. By 1535, according to Giustiniani, it was 450 metres long.[97] An iron chain blocked the port entrance from 1319.[98] The port also included various landing stations (*ponte*) used to unload particular materials. Many of these structures, originally made of wood, were rebuilt in stone during the fifteenth century.

---

[92] John R. Spencer (ed.), *Filarete's Treatise on architecture* Book IX fol 67r.

[93] See the discussion of glass objects in Luke Syson and Dora Thornton, *Objects of virtue: art in Renaissance Italy* (London: British Museum, 2001), chapter five: 'Glass and maiolica: art and technol-ogy', pp. 182–228.

[94] John Mallett, 'Tiled floors and court designers', p. 257.

[95] Biondo Flavio, *Italy illuminated*, p. 33.   [96] Francesco Podestà, *Il porto di Genova*, p. 156.

[97] Francesco Podestà, *Il porto di Genova*, p. 21.

[98] Francesco Podestà, *Il porto di Genova*, p. 24.

46 CLEANING UP RENAISSANCE ITALY

The lighthouse for the Genoese port was prominent, valued, and celebrated. The first lighthouse, as opposed to the earlier signal tower for the port, was constructed in the fourteenth century. The structure was damaged in 1512 and reconstructed by the Padri del Comune in 1543 adopting the same form that can be seen in the city today. The building, and position of lighthouse keeper, were funded through ships dues. Instructions given to the two custodians in 1558 noted that they must ensure that the lamp remained very well cleaned so that the light which was emitted could be seen from a significant distance and remain resplendent. The level of brightness needed in the lighthouse was seasonal: thirty lamps were lit through the winter (November to February), eighteen in autumn, and twelve in spring.[99] Equivalent structures in Venice were located further from the city centre but close to the entrance to the lagoon from the sea at San Nicolò and also at Sant'Elena. There the lighthouse keepers were retired pilots who worked for the Admiral of the Port (a role created in 1407).[100]

Further development of the Genoese port took place during the 'renovatio genuae' in the sixteenth century during the service of Galeazzo Alessi [1512–72].[101] George Gorse has outlined the ways in the which Vitruvian principles were put into place by Alessi as he expressed the city as a city-port, where 'architecture and urban space converged in a unified programme, analogous to that described by Vitruvius in his accounts of the city-ports of Ancient Rome'. Alessi added a triumphal arch to the wall of the breakwater (molo) at the spot where Andrea Doria had disembarked in 1528 to 'liberate' the city from the French.[102] Alessi brought about his vision between 1548 and 1557 through a series of fortresses, churches, palaces, roads, and houses.

Pietro Cataneo [d.1569] in his I Quattro primi libri di architettura wrote that, despite the advice of Plato, the situation of a city on the water did not condemn the area to poor quality air, citing Constantinople, Genoa, Naples, and Venice as prime examples of port cities with healthy environments.[103] Paschetti claimed that the generally healthy situation of Genoa was unusual for a maritime city, which would more commonly have poor quality air, as in Venice, Livorno, Civitavecchia, and Ostia. He noted, however, that Venice was inhabited by people of striking longevity, despite its location. He attributed this apparent contradiction to the purification of the city's air by the fires of the glass furnaces on the island of

---

[99] ASCG, PdC, 23-186 (1 January 1558).

[100] Frederic C. Lane, Venice, a maritime republic (Cambridge MA: Harvard University Press, 1973), pp. 17–18.

[101] George L. Gorse, 'Genova: repubblica dell'Impero' in Claudia Conforti and Richard J. Tuttle (eds), Storia dell'architettura italiana: il secondo Cinquecento (Milan: Electa, 2001), p. 244.

[102] George L. Gorse, 'Genova: repubblica dell'Impero', p. 245.

[103] Pietro Cataneo, I quattro primi libri di architettura di Pietro Cataneo. The early seventeenth-century history of Great Yarmouth by Henry Manship noted that the position of the port on the east coast of Britain meant that it basked in 'the first rising of the sun ... which doth disperse the mists and vapours from off the earth, whereby it purgeth and cleanseth the air'. Henry Manship cited in Carole Rawcliffe, Urban bodies, p. 122.

CONSTRUCTING IDEALS AND PRACTICES IN RENAISSANCE PORT CITIES   47

Murano, the regular tolling of the bells, and the many people who lived and passed through there (*corregendo et purificando quell'aria i fuochi, i suoni delle Campane et la moltitudine delle persone, che vi habitano et vi concorrono*), conveying the importance of the movement of people, not just elements, in abstractions of healthy, early modern ports. Beyond improving the quality of the air through movement, bells were believed to play an important role in providing protection from epidemics and storms. In fifteenth-century Leuven, a bell inscription read '*vivos voco, mortuos plango, fulgura frango*' ('I call to the living, I mourn the dead, I break up lightning'). The latter point about breaking up (or fracturing) lightning would have been particularly significant in an urban centre with a housing stock which was largely of wooden construction.[104] The broader protective associations of bells are reflected in the fact that they might be dedicated to donors or, frequently, to the Virgin Mary in medieval Europe. These attitudes were being criticized by the early sixteenth century but such practices nevertheless continued into the seventeenth century.[105]

The quality of the air in Venice was widely celebrated. A number of early modern authors found proof of its purity in the longevity of the lives of many of its patriciate.[106] The Venetian Senate observed that the city had a miraculous site in the middle of a body of water and this was responsible for the good and calm nature of civic life (*vivere*) in the city as well as the health of its inhabitants. Indeed, connections between social or political characteristics and the nature of a location became commonplace in accounts of both maritime Republics. Tommaso Ravenna also wrote of the low-lying nature of the location of Venice and noted the environmental problems which would have resulted but for the large number of fires and the furnaces at Murano, the abundance of people in such a restricted space (*unita in luogo strettissimo*), and the movement of the air as a result of their breathing (*l'abondanza del fiato*). Finally, the tidal movement of the water removed all rubbish and dirt (*sporchezzo seco*).[107]

The precious but precarious environmental balance in both Genoa and Venice was an important focus for government intervention. The two localities presented distinct challenges in terms of the management of space and society. In both cities, however, the importance of the flow of people and the elements as the basis for commercial success and broader prosperity was fundamental. This general point influenced the specific oversight of the streets, to which we now turn.

---

[104] Matthew S. Champion, *The fullness of time: temporalities of the fifteenth-century Low Countries* (Chicago IL: University of Chicago Press, 2017), p. 38.

[105] Matthew S. Champion, *The fullness of time*, p. 17.

[106] F. di Zorzi, *Dell'aria e sua qualità...dove specialmente si scuopre quale egli si sia in Venetia; et si leggono altre cose notabili d'intorno cosi potente e maravigliosa città* (Venice, 1596).

[107] BMC, Op Cic, 3.10 (78.10) *Consiglio del Magnifico Cavaliere et Ecc Fisico M Tomaso Filologo Ravenna: Come i Venetiani possano vivere sempre sani* (Venice, 1565).

PART ONE

THE EBBS AND FLOWS OF DAILY LIFE

2

Channelling Health

The Flow of the Streets

When the road reaches a city, and that city is renowned and powerful, the streets are better straight and very wide, to add to its dignity and majesty...Within [a fortified town] it is better if the roads are not straight, but meandering gently like a river flowing now here, now there, from one bank to the other. For apart from the fact that the longer the road seems, the greater the apparent size of the town no doubt it will be of great benefit in terms of appearance and practical convenience, while catering to the requirements of changing circumstances.[1]

For Leon Battista Alberti, the urban body required robust ligatures in the form of streets that were appropriate to the setting. These might draw inspiration from the natural environment. The notion of the road as akin to a river highlights the centrality of both structures to effective communication, trade, and healthy living in the Renaissance city.[2] It also emphasizes the principal focus of this chapter: the need to facilitate and regulate the flow of elements, material, and people through the streets as a cornerstone of the management of health and the environment. Attending to the nature of the streets could be a way of shaping behaviour and morality, as well as environmental conditions.

Many Renaissance architects reflected on the ideal form for the streets in order to anticipate and prevent urban problems in a way which drew upon ancient ideas. Vitruvius (c.80–15 BC) had advised laying out the main roads in relation to prevailing winds: 'cold winds are disagreeable, hot winds enervating, moist winds unhealthy'. Streets should be orientated so that they did not 'run full in the face of the winds' and houses directed away from the 'quarters from which the winds blow, so that as they come in they may strike against the angles of the blocks and their force thus be broken and dispersed'.[3]

---

[1] Leon Battista Alberti cited in Fabrizio Nevola, *Street life*, p. 31.

[2] For regulation which predates the periods of this study see Guy Geltner, 'Urban *viarii* and the prosecution of public health offenders in late medieval Italy' in *Policing the urban environment*, pp. 97–119 and Fabrizio Nevola, *Street life*, p. 40 on the office of the *petroni* which built on fourteenth-century work with a new focus on quality of buildings within Siena.

[3] Vitruvius describes eight principal winds: Solanus from due east, Eurus from south-east, Auster from the south, Africus to the south-west, Favonius from due west, Corus from north-west, Sententrio from the north, and Aquilo from the north-east. See Vitruvius, *The ten books on architecture*, Morris Hicky Morgan (trans) (New York NY: Dover Publications, 1960), p. 26.

Cleaning Up Renaissance Italy: Environmental Ideals and Urban Practice in Genoa and Venice. Jane L. Stevens Crawshaw, Oxford University Press. © Jane L. Stevens Crawshaw 2023. DOI: 10.1093/oso/9780198867432.003.0003

52 CLEANING UP RENAISSANCE ITALY

Once planned, it was essential that streets were managed to channel people, materials, and elements through the city without impediment. In 1465, inhabitants of Genoa were instructed to ensure that all streets remained open, accessible, 'highly agreeable and comfortable for all citizens in order to preserve their physical health'.[4] Discarded rubble or objects could block the flow of people and the air itself, reducing the salubrity of space.[5] It was also widely recognized that where rubbish or mud built up in the streets, this could generate foul smells, corruption of the air, and potentially result in outbreaks of infectious disease.[6]

Streets had the potential to stand as 'ornaments' for the city and the Renaissance period included the construction of some magnificent thoroughfares, such as the Strada Nuova in Genoa.[7] As we will see, there were also efforts to widen and improve some streets in Genoa but, in both cities, many of the routes through the city would have remained narrow and cramped. Government interventions in this period largely focused on street paving as well as the maintenance, cleanliness, and use of these spaces.

The development of urban infrastructure rested on the principle, common to Italian civic statutes from the medieval period and beyond, that a service should be paid for by those who made direct use of it.[8] Costs were allocated to the owners of the surrounding houses and land who were described as interested parties ('*interessati*'). An interesting suggestion of tensions relating to this issue survives from Rome in 1513 when protests were made at the costs of street improvements and ephemeral displays in Siena to celebrate the visit of the newly elected Pope Leo X. These took the form of posters displayed across the city which read, 'The loan will be paid, the earth will be removed, the Pope will not come.' The reference to the earth was likely to be literal as well as symbolic and suggested the threat of political uprising.[9]

During the sixteenth century, the quality and quantity of thoroughfares changed within and beyond city walls. Routes were increasingly paved in the city, as were roads which traversed territory. Any damage was said to be problematic both for residents and those travelling through these areas, in other words there was a local and collective benefit to the quality of these thoroughfares.[10] The principle of private funding for public schemes also applied in the Ligurian and Venetian mainland states. In Genoa, lists survive which detail how the costs were allocated to local residents for the paving of roads in Sampierdarena, Campi, Coronate, Fassolo, Pegli, Cornigliano, Borzoli, Fegino, Rivarolo, and Promontorio

---

[4] ASCG, PdC, 1-143 (17 April 1465).   [5] ASCG, PdC, 1-152 (27 June 1465).

[6] ASV, Sanità, 728 7r (28 August 1539).

[7] George Gorse, 'A classical stage for the old nobility: the Strada Nuova and sixteenth-century Genoa' *The Art Bulletin* 79:2 (1997), 301–27.

[8] Francesca Bocchi, 'Regulation of the urban environment', 69. See, for example, ASCG, PdC, 19-103 (15 November 1546).

[9] Fabrizio Nevola, *Street Life*, p. 60.   [10] ASCG, PdC, 29-118 (7 February 1569).

in 1548, for example.[11] In Venice, the decentralized administration of issues such as street paving meant that this work was both organized and funded at local level.

Once paved, streets and roads were cleaned regularly by sweeping and sometimes washing. The control of animals, clearing of dumps, instructions as to the correct locations in which to sell foodstuffs, and measures which address the place of marginal groups were issued in order to protect the quality of these spaces. In both cities, officials issued instructions about civic thoroughfares in general as well as targeting issues in localities.[12] Even when announcements were focused on a specific district, the governments emphasized the connections between the health of localities and the wellbeing of the city as a whole. One such letter from 1468 requested the closure of a Genoese *carruggio* (a narrow alleyway characteristic of the city's port district) because it was being used to dump rubbish. The supplicant asserted that the risk of the materials being carried into the port justified intervention in the public interest for the comfort and beauty of the city.[13] The natural geography of the city, with its incline towards the sea, meant that any material left in the streets or squares was thought to risk being transported into the port during periods of rainfall.[14] The potential impact of rubbish and rubble on the port was described in a number of ways—some more explicitly health-related than others. Terms such as '*dano*' (damage), '*lesiuni*' (injuries), and '*nocumento*' (noxious harm) were employed.[15] Related concerns were articulated in Venice about the risk that rubbish would pass from streets and squares into the canals. For both cities, the accumulation of such material in these bodies of water prompted large-scale and expensive interventions in the form of dredging, as explored in chapter four. As in so many other circumstances relating to premodern health and the environment, therefore, government officials recognized that prevention was better than cure. As a result, they issued hundreds of proclamations which were intended to prohibit the disposal of waste and building materials and regulate behaviour in these spaces.

The town criers of Renaissance governments ensured that the streets were full of audible reminders of how these spaces should function.[16] Known as the *preco* or *cintracus* in Genoa and *publico comandador* in Venice, these public figures were responsible for proclaiming decisions in a 'loud and intelligible voice' and often

---

[11] ASCG, PdC, 22-219 (11 July 1548).
[12] See, for example, specific concerns about flow and access through the area of the Darsena, including a specific entranceway in ASCG, PdC, 7-33 (28 July 1500).
[13] ASCG, PdC, 1-211 (15 January 1468).   [14] ASCG, PdC, 19-149 (2 September 1547).
[15] ASCG, PdC, 1-169 (5 May 1460) uses '*nocumento*' and 1–187 (9 December 1467) refs to '*dano o lesiuni*'.
[16] On these figures see Stephen Milner '"Fanno bandire, notificare et expressamente comandare"' and Evelyn Welch, *Shopping in the Renaissance: consumer cultures in Italy, 1400–1600* (New Haven CT: Yale University Press, 2009), pp. 186–96 for discussion of these workers' roles as auctioneers. See also Fabrizio Nevola, *Street life*.

54   CLEANING UP RENAISSANCE ITALY

'with the sound of the trumpet' (*sono tube*).[17] The archival attestations by the *preci* which confirmed that they had fulfilled their role often included details regarding the locations in which they had issued proclamations and how many times they had been repeated. Sometimes this information was of a very general nature: '*in locis opportunis*' or '*per universari civitatem*'. It could be much more specific. In 1555, the crier in Venice noted a proclamation given in the 'usual places' of Rialto and San Marco as well as on ninety bridges and squares across the city. These include each of the city's 72 parishes as well as additional sites including the Jewish Ghetto.[18]

Once announced in the public spaces of the city, the proclamations were intended to cross the thresholds of households and workshops. In Genoa, householders were specifically instructed to inform their servants of the Padri's proclamations.[19] The responsibility for regulating the behaviour of children was commonly given to fathers; in some cases, responsibility was split between both parents. These latter instances, such as warnings in 1530 that no one should steal the timber and other materials destined for the construction of a pontoon, do not appear to be gendered issues.[20] Instead, it may have been that when governments sought to remind individuals about the overall responsibility for the unit of the household (including the behaviour of women, servants, and children) these things were the remit of the father whereas behaviours associated particularly with children were held to be the responsibility of both parents.

---

[17] Emilio Podestà, *Storia di Parodi Ligure e dei suoi antichi Statuti* (Ovada: Accademia Urbense, 1998), p. 49 describes the role as 'il *Cintracus* che ha mansioni importanti, di custodia e di rappresentanza, ma che, nei secoli successivi, scadrà come ruolo, limitandosi a quello di banditore e di semplice messo'.

[18] ASV, Comun, Atti b.1, 353 notes that the proclamation was made in the usual places at Rialto and San Marco as well as: Santa Marta, San Nicolo, San Raffaele Arcangelo, Sant'Agnese, San Vidal, San Gregorio, Spirito Santo, La Carita, San Trovaso, Ognissanti, San Basegio, Santa Maria dei Carmeni, Santa Margherita, San Barnaba (on the bridge at Ca' Macello), San Pantalon, Ca'Foscari (on the bridge), Santa Maria Maggiore, Tre Ponti, San Simeone Piccolo, San Simeone Grande, San Giacomo dal Orio, San Zan Degola, in Rio Marin, in the square of the Becharie, San Cassiano, Santa Maria Mater Domini, San Stai, San Silvestro, San Polo, at the Frari (on the bridge), San Rocco, San Tomà, Sant'Aponal, Sant'Agostin, San Stin, San Boldo, Santa Lucia, San Geremia, San Giobbe, San Leonardo, San Marcuola, in the Ghetto, San Geronimo, Sant'Alvise, Santa Maria dell'Orto [Madonna dell'Orto], Santa Maria dei Servi, la Maddalena [353v] Santa Fosca, San Marcilian [San Marziale], alla Misericordia, San Felice, Santi Apostoli, I Crociferi, Santa Caterina, San Canciano, at the warehouse (magazen) in Biri, San Giovanni Grisostomo, San Bartholomeo, San Salvador, San Luca, San Paternian, Sant'Anzolo, San Samuele, Santo Stefano, San Maurizio, Santa Maria Zobenigo, San Moisè, San Fantin, San Beneto, San Domenego, Sant'Isepo, San Pietro di Castello, de qua dal ponte, in Campiello, alla Zana, San Martino, San Giovanni in Bragola, Campo di doi Pozzi, Santa Ternita, San Francesco della Vigna, Santa Giustina, San Zuan latern, San Zanipolo[Santi Giovanni e Paolo], alla Madonna di Miracoli, Santa Marina, San Lio, Santa Maria Formosa, San Lorenzo, San Severo, Santi Filippo e Giacomo, San Antonin, and San Zulian.

[19] 'E li patroni serrano obligatti per li servitor e servitrice e li padre per li figlioli notificando aciaschaduno che delle predette cose se ne fara dilligente inquisicione e rigida punicione' in ASCG, PdC, 26-68 (30 August 1563).

[20] ASCG, PdC, 13-59 (22 May 1530).

CHANNELLING HEALTH   55

The nature of materials left in the street varied but the obstructions of greatest concern to government officials were those related to the building trades. Although, in theory, supply to building sites was done on a daily basis, it is clear that both waste and construction materials were retained in the streets. Just a few days after a proclamation in 1467 which reminded residents not to deposit rubble, ash, dirt, or rubbish in the streets, workers were instructed to remove lime, rubbish, or other by-products of their trades within three days of work being undertaken.[21] Failure to do so could cause an obstruction or blockage in the streets, which threatened to pass into the bodies of water, and a build-up of dirt and filth which risked both stench and disease.

Stench was identified as a significant public health issue in both cities; 'vapours', 'fumes', and 'excretions' were all frequently mentioned as causes for concern.[22] In 1500, Venetian Health Office officials reiterated that one of the most important ways in which governments might work to keep their territories healthy was to oversee effectively the removal of matter which caused stench and illness. They were aware of an area in Santo Stefano where large quantities of rubbish were taken on a daily basis.[23] The site was such, however, that it could not be easily removed because of the narrow *rio*. As a result, the rubbish rotted away, emitting an unbearable smell. This posed a threat to the wellbeing of those living there as well as those who walked through the area. In 1517, a supplication from the brothers of Santa Maria di Castello in Genoa requested the closure of an alleyway because of the rubbish which was being deposited on a daily basis, which was said to be causing enormous harm to the infirmary of the monastery.[24] In 1530, it was said to have been brought to the attention of the Padri that excrement and rubbish (*dure et immondicie*) was being left in an alleyway close to the women's ward of Genoa's Incurabili hospital. This was said to be contemptible ('*in maximo vilipendio*') and a disgrace to the city and to those using the streets.[25] It was emphasized that these streets were not only close to religious or charitable institutions but also that the part of these institutions being affected was set aside for medical treatment where the quality of the air was of paramount importance.

In 1555 the Padri reminded residents close to the church of Santa Marta that they should desist from throwing rubbish out of their windows as they had become accustomed to doing. Previously, a ditch had run behind the church and presumably the habits had been formed in relation to that structure but the subsequent building of an alleyway over the top of the ditch had not changed

---

[21] ASCG, PdC, 1-210 (18 December 1467).
[22] Joseph Wheeler, 'Stench in sixteenth-century Venice' in Alexander Cowan and Jill Steward (eds), *The city and the senses: urban culture since 1500* (Aldershot: Ashgate, 2007), pp. 25–38. Sandra Cavallo and Tessa Storey, *Healthy living*, p. 6. See, for example, ASCG, PdC, 1-59 (11 February 1460).
[23] ASV, Sanità, 725, 63v (9 January 1500).   [24] ASCG, PdC, 10-183 (5 July 1517).
[25] ASCG, PdC, 13-73 (28 July 1530).

56 CLEANING UP RENAISSANCE ITALY

practices of rubbish disposal. All houses which had a window onto the lane were notified.[26] As Joseph Wheeler noted in his chapter on stench, evidence of environmental 'abuses' could suggest 'very real limits and inefficiencies of early modern health controls and urban government' or that the 'nature of the fight against stench was so controversial since ingrained habits, the normal processes of certain trades and the routine actions of the poor were all criminalised'.[27]

Whether reported from within or beyond a locality, health provisions reveal a specific form of urban community: those that were linked by elements of the built environment including doorways or windows onto the same spaces or shared water supplies. Neighbours had the potential to soothe or aggravate the senses through the noise, smells, and sights that permeated walls. In 1548, communities in Bisagno were reminded that they should not burn stumps or twigs (*sterpi*) in the evenings or at night because of the impact of the strong stench upon neighbours.[28] This proclamation, as later equivalents, was issued during the summer and referenced the stench (*fettore*) which was preventing people from keeping their windows open.

The multi-sensory impact of neighbours was widely acknowledged. In accordance with social and religious prejudices of the time, however, some neighbours were believed to exert a more pernicious impact than others. In Dana Katz's article on windows of the Jewish Ghetto, she reminded us that, in 1560, the *Cinque Savi alla Mercanzia* (or Board of Trade) required the Jewish community to wall up the windows, balconies, and doors which faced onto the canal surrounding the Ghetto.[29] Although Katz emphasizes the threat to the Christian community that was posed by lines of sight in and out of the Ghetto, as well as the later *Fondaco dei Turchi*, later chapters will show that the authorities were also concerned about issues of stench and rubbish disposal from these parts of the city.

Similar concerns underpinned efforts to demarcate the boundaries of sacred space around parish churches and religious institutions in the city.[30] In Venice in 1543, at the request of the parish priest of San Geremia, it was proclaimed that no one was permitted to play ball games of any kind near the church.[31] The intended alignment between piety, cleanliness, and quiet was frequently asserted.[32] Religious institutions might be associated with high levels of salubrity. Francesco Sansovino, when describing the cleanliness of the multi-coloured stone

---

[26] ASCG, PdC, 22-105 (9 May 1555).

[27] Joseph Wheeler, 'Stench in sixteenth-century Venice', p. 37.

[28] ASCG, PdC, 19-204 (29 July 1548) and ASCG, PdC, 23-135 (1 July 1558).

[29] Dana E. Katz, '"Clamber not you up to the casements": On ghetto views and viewing', *Jewish History* 24:2 (2010), 133.

[30] On the reach of sacred space beyond the walls of boundaries in Renaissance Italy see Fabrizio Nevola, *Street life*, p. 83.

[31] ASV, Comun b.11 reg 24 163v (6 March 1543).

[32] On noise see Julia Rombough, 'Noisy soundscapes and women's institutions'.

floors in Venetian elite houses, wrote that these were polished so that 'you would say that you were entering into a well-managed and clean church of nuns'.[33]

At times, the obverse was also considered to be true: filthy terrain was a stage for moral and social problems. In 1566, a Genoese notary, Francesco Frugoni, described a rocky plot of land in San Nicolo Castelletto as wasted and dangerous. He characterized the area as one of commotion, as a result of the children and youths who congregated there, and indecency, caused by their games and the presence of sex workers (*per pueros et iuvenes discolos exerceant' corpia et inhonesta tam circa ludum quam mulieres*).[34] As with other interventions in urban forms and natural environments, therefore, schemes to alter the form and material culture of the streets were intended to have social and moral effects.[35] This might involve the large-scale redesign of a particular thoroughfare or a change to the decoration of a locality.[36] In 1573, the prior of the monastery of Sant'Agostino in Genoa and the inhabitants of the area around the street of Mezzagalera decried the killings, atrocities, and enormous sins which were committed on that thoroughfare.[37] The inhabitants expressed that 'for the honour of God and extension of the city' they could see no alternative to the demolition of a number of houses there which were in a severely dilapidated state and within which a number of women of poor reputation (*male fame et pessime conditionis*) were living. The costs of the work were, as was customary, to be divided between those who would receive 'benefit or comfort' (*utile o commodita*). The quality of the street was seen to nurture sinful behaviour and threaten honest women resident in the area. The consequences of these connections prompted broad regulation of the cleanliness, safety, and accessibility of the streets.

The Quality of the Streets

Cleaning formed a substantial part of preserving the material conditions of cities. The responsibility for the regular cleaning of the streets lay partly at the door of residents in both Genoa and Venice during the Renaissance. In chapter five, we will consider the role played by government officials in collecting rubbish from districts and transporting it to designated locations. In Venice, civic employees were also tasked with cleaning the streets but this was intended to supplement rather than replace the responsibilities of residents. In 1556, the Provveditori di

---

[33] '*Ben culta et polita Chiesa di suore*' cited in Douglas Biow, *On the importance of being an individual in Renaissance Italy: men, their professions, and their beards* (Philadelphia PA: University of Pennsylvania Press, 2015), p. 165.

[34] ASCG, PdC, 2-73 (4 September 1566).   [35] ASCG, PdC, 6-140 (22 September 1496).

[36] See, for example, the insights provided in https://hiddenflorence.org/stories/giovanni/ for the parish of Sant' Ambrogio in Florence with its streetcorner Madonnas.

[37] ASCG, PdC, 32-4 (8 January 1567).

58 CLEANING UP RENAISSANCE ITALY

Comun issued a reminder that no water or rubbish was to be thrown into the street at Santi Apostoli and that all of the residents of the area were required to keep the drains (*gatoli*) and the streets in front of their doorways clean.[38] Government officials in Venice were also reminded that they were expected to set an example and keep their own buildings clean ('*mondato e netto*').[39] In Genoa, homes, doorsteps, and the street in front of properties, whether domestic or artisanal, were intended to be cleaned by residents on a weekly basis.[40] Every Saturday, these spaces should be swept (*spaciar*) and rubbish removed.[41] This was expected to be done at the start of the day before approximately 9 a.m. (*da hora de terza*) so that the muleteers (*mulatori*) or those from the Bisagno ('*besagnini*') would be able to remove the rubbish easily (*comodamente*).[42] Fines were generally set for those who failed to follow these regulations.[43]

At times, when the conditions on the streets had deteriorated markedly, the residents of homes and workshops in Genoa were instructed to ensure that streets were cleaned and swept in their entirety (*da ogni lato*). They were required to do the same for squares and to set the rubbish aside so that it could be collected and taken beyond the city. Officials reminded inhabitants of Genoa that public proclamations outlined the minimum expectation and obligations placed upon them: they should sweep the streets every Saturday and feast days as commanded, as well as every other day in which they had the opportunity and need.[44]

The central principle relating to the streets, on which the authorities acted, was to ensure that people, merchandise, and elements could move unimpeded and safely. This ideal was, of course, far more complex in practice. There were social groups whose presence or movement in the streets might be damaging or threatening. The passage of people through the city was intended to be purposeful: for commerce, work, or exercise. In 1559, the Venetian authorities bemoaned the considerable increase in the number of young rogues and swindlers who were wandering through the principal squares of the city. At night, they slept under the porticoes. They exercised no trade and were predicted to grow into thieves.[45] Once resident in the city's municipal brothel, women were forbidden in Genoa (as elsewhere), from circulating freely in the streets. Saturday was the 'day granted to

---

[38] ASV, Comun, b.13 reg 19 (unfoliated) (6 March 1556).   [39] Rompiasio, p. 251.

[40] Sandra Cavallo and Tessa Storey established a clear intersection between health concerns and the construction of the physical domestic environment in their *Healthy living in Renaissance Italy*. By 1526 all bridges, sewers, drains, and streets leading to the river in Rome were supposed to be cleaned once a week. Pamela Long, *Engineering the Eternal City: infrastructure, topography and the culture of knowledge in late sixteenth-century Rome* (Chicago IL: University of Chicago Press, 2018).

[41] ASCG, PdC, 1-178 (30 August 1466).

[42] The calculation of time in Renaissance Italy can be complex and I have used the table provided by Ernesto Screpanti, *L'angelo della liberazione nel tumulto di Ciompi: Firenze giugno–agosto 1378* (Siena: Protagon, 2008), p. 340.

[43] ASCG, PdC, 1-187 (9 December 1467) refers to '*una multa da soldi 5 a soldi 10*'.

[44] ASCG, PdC, 13-10 (3 December 1528).   [45] ASV, Sanità, 730 229r (4 March 1559).

them'. In 1540, the women were reminded not to loiter in the streets or in doorways of buildings but remain inside the buildings.

In other cases, governments worked to ensure that it was safe to walk the streets, physically as well as morally. In Venice, the Comun inspected fireplaces, for example, that at the house of Signora Camilletta in Madonna dell'Orto which was old and threatened to collapse with the risk of causing death.[46] The poor state of repair noted by the advisor to the Comun in relation to many buildings may have been, in part, due to the tendency to undertake piecemeal fixes for structural problems because of the high cost and complex engineering involved in building from scratch.[47] Ennio Concina has suggested that the proportion of houses in a poor condition or ruined, as recorded in the *Decima* records did decline through the sixteenth century and has observed that these structures were also not spread evenly through the city. It does appear that officials had some success in improving the state of repair of the urban fabric by the 1580s. Nevertheless, damaged and dilapidated buildings continued to threaten public and personal safety.[48]

In Genoa in 1546, a request was made to the Padri to be able to pull down an old and unusable stone tower, which posed a threat to nearby residents as well as those passing through the streets.[49] These concerns regarding the structure of buildings were by no means limited to the dwellings of the poor. In Venice, the local parish priest reported the poor state of a wall which formed part of a house adjoining the church of San Fantin.[50] The brief report of the official in response allows a glimpse through the window, at the fruit and vegetable store on the ground floor and the rooms occupied by the church's priest on the floor above.[51] Nor were these structures located far beyond the central squares and principal thoroughfares of the city. In 1536, the Comun officials expressed concern regarding a house near the Grand Canal which was at risk of collapsing and causing the deaths of many people. The building was owned by patrician families and included units which were being rented to six different people including a barber and a widow.[52] In all instructions of this type, the Comun ordered the patrons to execute the necessary repairs in a specific timeframe, often eight days. Otherwise, the works would be undertaken by the Comun and the costs would be charged to the owners. Concerns might relate to entire buildings or specific elements of the architecture.[53] In both cities, officials came to be concerned about the state of buildings which had been inherited, which were particularly likely to be left to deteriorate.[54]

---

[46] ASV, Comun b. 16 reg 37, 8r (25 August 1586).
[47] Giorgio Gianighian and Paola Pavanini, *Venezia come* (Venice: Gambier Keller, 2014), p. 42.
[48] Ennio Concina, *Venezia nell'età moderna*, chapter eight '*De quelli lochi ruinosi*', pp. 177–92.
[49] ASCG, PdC, 19-73 (13 May 1546).   [50] ASV, Comun b.11 reg 24 13r (3 December 1541).
[51] ASV, Comun b.11 reg 25 40r (17 October 1547).
[52] ASV, Comun b.10 reg 21 189v (29 November 1536).
[53] ASV, Comun b.14 reg 33 91r (20 October 1565).
[54] ASV, Comun b.12 reg 27 119v–120r (2 April 1552).

60 CLEANING UP RENAISSANCE ITALY

In addition to the repair of buildings, the use of space around windows and balconies was regulated. In 1560, when Nicolo del Zorzi, a carpenter at the Venetian Arsenal, wanted to keep a window box with plants in San Martin at the Ponte dal Marco, he required permission to do so. This was granted, on the condition that the window box rested upon two stone slabs (*dui modione di piera viva*) for the safety of those walking beneath.[55] The nobleman Andrea Spinola also included details of a particular form of rubbish in the streets of Genoa: the bones from cooked meat, which people threw out of their windows and which he said he had seen hit passers-by on a number of occasions, which risked breaking people's necks. Spinola suggested that those who were looking to do good works in the city could pay two or three runners (*garzoni*) to collect these bones and in so doing would by carrying out an act equivalent to a donation of thousands of lire to establish a religious institution (*hermittaggi*).[56]

Across the Italian peninsula, the presence of balconies was carefully controlled because of their impact on light and the movement of air, as well as implications for the stability of buildings.[57] It is clear that, where they were constructed, there were concerns for public safety. In 1536, the Genoese Padri recorded that a vase of flowers had fallen from the balcony of a house in San Donato. It had struck a poor artisan (*povero artifice*) and brought him to the point of death (*lo percose a termine di morte*).[58] Across the city there were said to be many such vases of flowers which were attached to walls or balconies.[59] Nearly twenty years later, the same office reiterated its concerns about the safety of the streets. This time, it was rods and oars which were the focus for concern. They noted that such objects had fallen from windows or from balconies, posing a considerable threat to passers-by, and instructed residents to remove these and all other wooden objects from these spaces.[60] Four years later, the Padri recorded that inhabitants had returned to the bad habit of keeping rods at the window or on balconies against the instructions of the officials and that, in the past, a number of these objects had fallen on the street below.[61] In 1566, concern once again centred upon the vases with flowers and herbs which were being kept on windowsills and balconies.[62] Similar items are visible in the depiction of Venice close to the Rialto bridge by Vittore Carpaccio (*The Miracle of the True Cross*). Here plants can be seen in pots and vases perched

---

[55] ASV, Comun b.13 reg 31 155v (2 April 1560).

[56] Andrea Spinola, Il Cittadino della Repubblica di Genova...diviso in 4 tomi (n.d.) [hereafter Spinola], 'Nettezza della citta'.

[57] Francesca Bocchi, 'Regulation of the urban environment', p. 71 and Fabrizio Nevola *Street life*, p. 249.

[58] The term '*artifice*' was applied in Genoese regulations to distinguish between citizens and artisans in, for example, ASCG, PdC, 13-10 (3 December 1528).

[59] ASCG, PdC, 15-62 (15 December 1536). The flower is known as a '*ganofolo*'.

[60] ASCG, PdC, 23-113 (18 April 1558).   [61] ASCG, PdC, 25-98 (2 January 1562).

[62] ASCG, PdC, 27-142 (10 June 1566).

CHANNELLING HEALTH 61

precariously on the small balconies and windowsills on buildings on both sides of the canal.

Whilst some thoroughfares were indispensable elements of the networks of communication that flowed in the city, other streets or alleys were found to be rarely used. In his recent analysis of Italian Renaissance streets, Fabrizio Nevola highlighted the essential mobility and movement contained therein. In Genoa during the Renaissance, concerns were raised about streets which were barely utilized, in part because they were often sites for the accumulation of rubbish.[63] These streets were not only of concern because of potential dirt and a lack of movement, however. Disused streets were also perceived to be at risk of a confluence of types of filth.[64] In 1500, Hieronimus Logia requested the closure of an alleyway close to his house in the corner of the Piazza San Giorgio which had become virtually impassable because of the rubbish which was dumped illicitly at night-time. Even worse, the alleyway had become a place in which armed men congregated, often drunk, to engage in vile conduct with dishonest serving girls.[65] It was suggested that the alleyway should be closed at its entrance and exit in order to restrict access. In 1558, the representative of the Monasterio de Pama described a street close to the convent which was partially closed. It was said to be used for nothing else than the dumping of enormous quantities of rubbish and being a haven for immoral acts (*recetaculo de molte cose inhoneste*).[66] The rector of the church of St Mark in Genoa described a space 'like a street' between the city walls and those of the church. The fact that it resembled a street but served no transitory purpose meant that a significant amount of rubbish had built up in the area but that it had also become a site for 'unspeakable sins' (*peccatti nefandi*) which were neither good nor lawful in any site, let alone near to a church which was a house of God. The rector requested that two gates should be used to close off the space.[67] Unlike in cities elsewhere, it does not appear that the government in Genoa targeted such spaces for 'stone laws' but, instead, looked to limit access in order to reshape behaviour.[68] Ironically, some streets were subsequently reopened because nearby residents found that closure led to a build-up of rubbish.[69]

Concerns about filth and damaging movement coalesced in regulations targeting animals in cities.[70] Proclamations often addressed animals alongside concerns

---

[63] ASCG, PdC, 29-111 (11 January 1569).   [64] ASCG, PdC, 2-34 (7 July 1446).
[65] ASCG, PdC, 7-17 (7 December 1500).   [66] ASCG, PdC, 5-9 (6 April 1481).
[67] ASCG, PdC, 221-218 (8 March 1604).
[68] Fabrizio Nevola notes that many stone laws were more likely to be in side streets or narrow alleyways, or sensitive locations, in Fabrizio Nevola, *Street life*, p. 200.
[69] ASCG, PdC, 7-6 (6 January 1500) and 21-215 (1 August 1553).
[70] ASV, Comun, b.9 36v (16 September 1518) the inhabitants of the campo dei do pozzi were instructed not to keep chickens nor throw rubbish into the square and b.14 reg 32 8r (4 May 1560) includes regulations for campo San Pantalon. Karl Appuhn, 'Ecologies of beef: eighteenth-century epizootics and the environmental history of early modern Europe', *Environmental History* 15:2 (2010), 276. Dennis Romano, *Markets and marketplaces*, p. 73 and Ennio Concina, *Venezia nell'età moderna*, p. 58.

62 CLEANING UP RENAISSANCE ITALY

about waste. In Venice in 1561, for example, the residents of the courtyard at the Ponti di Mori were instructed not to deposit rubbish or keep hens or animals of any kind.[71] In 1548, the Comun noted the enormous costs which were being incurred every day as a result of the damage to squares, *fondamente*, and streets by the large number of pigs which passed freely through the city. Owners were instructed to keep the animals in the boundaries of their own property in 1548 and again in 1587.[72] In Genoa in 1554, the Padri expressed its dismay that people were allowing pigs to roam freely through the streets of the city without any supervision. Residents were reminded that this was not permitted in the city or suburbs.[73] In the seventeenth century, Venetian Health Officials expressed the urgency of intervention needed at the cemetery of San Nicolo del Lido. Here, the openness of the site meant that animals, particularly pigs, were able to run roughshod through the cemetery, trampling over corpses.[74]

It was not simply that animals were considered to pose a threat when allowed to roam through the streets. In Genoa, the Padri frequently reiterated that mules and other animals, whether loaded with materials or not, should not be tied up in the square in front of the cathedral of San Lorenzo. Owners were instructed to use designated sites, particularly the Piazza del Vastato.[75] Nearly ten years later, the regulations were clearly not being adhered to. The Padri reminded owners that they were not entitled to tether pack animals in the Piazza de Marini.[76] Ten years after that, owners were told not to rest their mules underneath the Dogana del pane because of the damage which was being caused to the structure.[77]

Fabrizio Nevola has highlighted the dangers which were associated with ox-carts in a number of Italian cities and the ex-votos that attest to accidents involving these animals and their equipment.[78] As a result, the routes taken by animals through the city might be stipulated by officials. The Piazza Banchi in Genoa was obviously a popular—but officially prohibited—route since in 1524, 1540, and 1558, owners of pack animals were instructed not to cross the square (whether loaded with cargo or not).[79] This square was situated close to the principal western gateway (the Porta di San Pietro). It included the seat of the city's famous financial institution the Casa di San Giorgio from 1408, had been the city's ancient Roman forum and was redesigned with a new Loggia dei Mercanti and a rebuilding of the church of San Pietro during the Renaissance. From 1540, animals carrying wood, charcoal, or any other material were prohibited there.[80]

---

[71] ASV, b.14 reg 33 104r (17 November 1561).
[72] ASV, Comun b.11 reg 25 16v (14 August 1548) and b.16 reg 37 107v (3 September 1587).
[73] Leges Genuensis, *Historiae patriae monumenta*, vol. 18 [95] and [115]. ASCG, PdC, 22-65 (2 October 1554).
[74] ASV Sanità 62v (24 December 1646).   [75] ASCG, PdC, 11-183 (27 January 1524).
[76] ASCG, PdC, 14-57 (15 July 1533).   [77] ASCG, PdC, 20-5 (11 January 1549).
[78] Fabrizio Nevola *Street life*, pp. 76–7.
[79] ASCG, PdC, 11-185 (27 January 1524) and 23-175 (1 January 1558).
[80] ASCG, PdC, 16-8 (7 January 1540).

CHANNELLING HEALTH   63

Central to transportation in Genoa, the specific routes taken by these animals and their owners was a threat to the safety and aesthetics of the streets and therefore regulated in key districts.

Whilst cattle were commonly used in Genoa for transportation, this was done on boats in Venice. The presence of larger animals in Venice was more commonly associated with rituals and festivals. Robert Davis has argued that bull-baiting in Venice occupied the streets as well as squares of the city and that rituals and shaming races would have been used as expressions of parish factionalism. This was largely seasonal, taking place in autumn, much like bridge battles.[81] In Venice, those who transported animals around the city were supposed to do so 'quietly, above all holding on to the ropes'.[82]

Damage to the infrastructure and health of the city might also be posed by those trades that handled animal products. As in many areas of Europe, designated areas were developed for butchers in order to limit the impact of this trade on residents.[83] It was not uncommon for butchers to be located near bodies of water into which entrails and other offensive waste products would be thrown; in sixteenth-century Mantua, for example, the fish market and butchers' premises were placed over and adjacent to a canal.[84] In Genoa a slaughterhouse was constructed beyond the Porta degli Archi at the end of the fifteenth century to bring great benefit and ornament to the future of the city (*commodo atq orna-mento urbi futurum est*), despite the inevitable smells and rubbish which would emanate from the site itself.[85] Animal markets were held in the square just outside the Porta degli Archi, in front of the new slaughterhouse.[86]

Efforts to locate this work elsewhere were met with resistance. In 1572, a letter was sent to the Genoese Padri which asserted that the appetites and greed of people had grown so substantially that the government needed to intervene to protect public interests.[87] A new butchers had been proposed beyond the desig-nated area (*volerlo fabricare fuori del cerchio delli macelli*). Such a development had not been made in living memory, would prejudice the interests of many, and cause universal damage in deforming the city (*deformer la citta*). The long-standing custom (*consuetudine lunghissima*) was that the butchers should remain separate (*restar ripartiti*) in the city. In 1595, the Padri received a supplication regarding a new butchers on the road between Malapaga (close to the port) and

---

[81] Robert C. Davis, 'The trouble with bulls: the *cacce dei tori* in early modern Venice', *Histoire Sociale/Social History* 29:58 (1997), 275–90.

[82] Robert C. Davis, 'The trouble with bulls', p. 289.

[83] In Venice from at least the mid seventeenth century communal slaughterhouses existed in Cannaregio beyond San Giobbe, see Ennio Concina, *Venezia nell'età moderna*, p. 68 and Giovanni Caniato and Renato della Venezia, *Il macello di San Giobbe: un'industria, un territorio* (Venice: Marsilio, 2006).

[84] Fabrizio Nevola, *Street life*, p. 170.

[85] ASCG, PdC, 6-143 (5 April 1497) and 8-67 (22 May 1506).

[86] ASCG, PdC, 9-40 (4 December 1508) and 9-44 (6 February 1509).

[87] ASCG, PdC, 31-53 (31 May 1572).

64   CLEANING UP RENAISSANCE ITALY

the city walls.[88] It noted that for more than 440 years the customs regarding the location of butchers had been maintained without exception (*inviolabilmente osservato*) and that there would be nothing of benefit to be obtained by introducing changes which would cause damage to an infinite number of citizens.

Butchers were also closely regulated in order to oversee the quality of foodstuffs and uphold standards of cleanliness. In 1552, butchers were reminded that they must not slaughter sick animals. A few days previously, a number of contaminated animals had been identified in Genoa and the Padri reflected on the potentially dangerous impact of this for the health of the community.[89] In 1573, the butchers at Sant'Andrea were reminded that they were not permitted to kill animals in the street but must do this inside the slaughterhouse using the benches and channels provided for the drainage of blood.[90] In the statutes of both Genoa and Savona, it was emphasized that blood should be collected in a suitable container and transported to an appointed location to keep the slaughterhouses clean (*netti e mondi*).[91]

Tanning animals pelts was also very carefully controlled. This work was concentrated on the island of the Giudecca in Venice.[92] In 1552, the Padri noted that Genoa was equipped with three tanners: one beneath the gate of Sant'Andrea and the other two in Castelletto. In 1557, the Padri reminded all citizens that these three sites were provided for public benefit and that no other site should be used for this work.[93] The strong opposition of residents elsewhere in Liguria to proposed tanners' sites expressed common concerns about such work.[94] In 1568, in Gavi, Antonio Raimondo had established a tannery in what was described by one critic of his project as the most beautiful part of the town. This was clearly believed by the residents to be an inappropriate site for such a trade. The stench produced was said to be damaging for residents and visitors using the street, the neighbourhood, and the whole of the state. It was against the statutes of the locality and the Padri were asked to intervene to settle the matter once and for all and 'impose perpetual silence' to stop this development being proposed again. Raimondo's response suggested that opposition derived from social tensions and a lack of willingness for residents to have this trade in the town at all. If such work was carried out in Genoa, he wrote—the capital of all Liguria and a city which was surpassed by no other in beauty—then surely it could be located in Gavi which was a limb (*membro*) of Genoa. He disputed that the development would be contrary to the statutes but to no avail.[95]

---

[88] ASCG, PdC, 2-141 (1 January 1595).   [89] ASCG, PdC, 21-157 (28 November 1552).
[90] ASCG, PdC, 32-52 (9 June 1573).
[91] *Statuti politici della citta di Savona: con le sue rifforme et addittioni rimesse a suo luogo, tradotti in lingua volgare* (Genoa, 1610), p. 92. Leges Genuensis, *Historiae patriae monumenta*, vol. 18 [40].
[92] See N. Spada, 'Leggi veneziane sulle industrie chimiche a tutela della salute pubblica dal secolo XIII al XVIII', *Archivio veneto*, 5th series, 7 (1930), 126–56.
[93] ASCG, PdC, 23-85 (20 October 1557).   [94] ASCG, PdC, 21-220 (25 August 1553).
[95] ASCG, PdC, 29-106 (9 December 1568).

CHANNELLING HEALTH   65

Health regulations were used in ways which might reflect broader social and economic tensions. In particular, the association between stench and the materials and processes of certain trades was sufficiently well known as to be seen as ripe for manipulation.[96] The stench produced by the workshops of grease-makers (*untori*) and rope-makers (*cordanieri*) in Santa Fede beyond the Porta dei Vacca prompted complaints to the Padri and a request for these trades to leave the area. In response to a separate accusation of the emission of dangerous smells, artisans responded that their trade had been practised in that location for well over a century and there was no recollection whatsoever amongst the inhabitants (*non e memoria d'huomo*) of such pernicious smells. The trade only sold leather, as in the shops of shoemakers in other places in the city. Instead the cause of the resentment against the artisans was said to be the dislike (*mal'odio*) and jealousy (*invidia*) often present between neighbours.[97]

The condition of the streets was seen to be essential to the wellbeing of the city, for facilitating the flow of materials and people between districts, moral behaviour, and agreeable relationships between neighbours. In the following sections, two forms of interventions will be explored for Genoa and Venice: initiatives to monitor the material and condition of the surface of the streets and to regulate trades in these public spaces. The final short section will consider the seasons of the streets in order to emphasize the changing conditions at different times of the year.

The Surface of the Streets

Street paving was undertaken from the medieval period to facilitate flow and movement and 'add to the ornament of the city and the common benefit'.[98] Paving operated like skin on the urban body—blocking offensive material whilst protecting and retaining valuable elements. In Venice, paved streets were portrayed as indispensable to the beauty (*ornamento*) and working (*bisogno*) of the city.[99] The Venetian authorities undertook early initiatives, for example, during the thirteenth and fourteenth centuries at San Marco and Rialto.[100] By the end of the sixteenth century some squares in Venice were paved in their entirety including some which were central to civic rituals such as San Zaccaria, the Frari, Santi Giovanni e Paolo, and Sant'Angelo.[101] Many, though, would have continued to live up to their name as *campi* and been grassed areas through the sixteenth

---

[96] ASCG, PdC, 26-121 (8 June 1564) [4].   [97] ASCG, PdC 26-121 (8 June 1564).
[98] Dennis Romano, *Markets and marketplaces*, p. 144.
[99] ASV, Comun, Atti b.1 98v–99v (22 May 1384).
[100] Donatella Calabi and Paolo Morachiello, *Rialto*, p. 11.
[101] Richard Goy, *Building Renaissance Venice: patrons, architects, and builders, c.1430–1500* (New Haven, CT: Yale University Press, 2006), p. 43.

66 CLEANING UP RENAISSANCE ITALY

century, such as at San Geremia and the Madonna dell'Orto. In some squares, just the area around a wellhead was paved.

In Genoa, the progression of paving within squares is less clear but developed at a slower pace than in Venice in relation to both squares and streets. Paving was undertaken from the second half of the fifteenth century.[102] At the start of the sixteenth century the decision was taken to pave the streets in Genoa in all 'necessary locations'. By 1559, the expectation of the Padri was that the city would be largely paved although it was noted that in number of localities it still remained lacking. The process of paving the streets was undertaken gradually, not least because of the quantity of materials required in order to undertake these works and the challenges of procuring these. In 1523, an official was instructed to travel to the coast to the west of the city and visit every location which produced bricks, as far as Savona. Substantial supplies needed to be secured because of the enormous demand for materials to pave the streets and squares of the city as well as restoring the city's aqueduct in many places.[103] This work was imperative since unpaved streets were believed to pose a much greater threat to the health of the city's port because dirt and mud could be easily displaced by inclement weather and carried into the port. For the same reason, rubbish disposal on unpaved streets was strictly prohibited.[104] In 1528, the Padri reminded residents of the direct connection between the cleanliness of the streets and the service, benefit, and honour of the city.[105]

The chronology of paving works in both cities broadly fits with that of urban centres elsewhere on the peninsula. In Rome from 1452, it was instructed that the streets should be paved in stone (using *selciata*, the hard, volcanic stone which had been used in Antiquity) although few were until the sixteenth century.[106] Careful attention was paid to materials. Pamela Long has noted that basalt did not absorb moisture and some feared that this would 'create excess humidity and bring about bad air or miasma'. In 1565 a papal bull instructed that streets should be paved with baked bricks.[107] Others were paved with pebbles.[108] Debates about paving were akin to those on layers of clothing in the early modern period and the extent to which these might trap moisture.[109]

Once paved, streets were intended to be maintained in a state of cleanliness and this sometimes involved the washing of the stone. In 1537, for example, the Zattere in Venice (particularly that of charcoal) was to be washed and cleaned of all rubbish (*lavate e nettate d'ogni immondizia*).[110] The impact of these standards and methods of cleanliness could produce their own health and safety

---

[102] ASCG, PdC, 5-30 (21 October 1481). [103] ASCG, PdC, 11-133 (22 April 1523).
[104] ASCG, PdC, 24-55 (12 October 1559). [105] ASCG, PdC, 13-10 (3 December 1528).
[106] Katherine Rinne, *The waters of Rome*, pp. 195–6.
[107] Pamela Long, *Engineering the Eternal City*, p. 174.
[108] Katherine Rinne, *The waters of Rome*, p. 203. [109] Susan North, *Sweet and clean?* p. 46.
[110] Rompiasio, p. 167.

CHANNELLING HEALTH   67

problems. In Genoa in particular, the smooth surface of paved streets, given the city's steep incline, were a potential source of accidents. Many proclamations were issued throughout the premodern period which forbade residents from cleaning particular streets because of the impact on the safe passage of animals. The street which led from the Porta degli Archi to the drinking trough and monastery of San Francesco d'Albaro was a point of concern because of the risk that individuals travelling by horse would fall.[111] Residents were said to be acting in a way which thought only of their own advantage in continuing to sweep and collect rubbish from this road. With such a clean surface, lacking the friction that would come from the dirt and rubbish, the road was said to be treacherous and the site for many accidents.[112] The Padri continued to insist that no one should sweep this route.[113] Despite the many accounts that we have of premodern cities and the lack of cleanliness in the streets, records such as these remind us that the day-to-day cleaning of streets was often habitual and sometimes the interventions of officials focused on limiting rather than enforcing standards of cleanliness. The smooth surface of paved streets was said to be one reason that people did not travel by horseback in Venice. Thomas Coryat described the streets of the city in 1605 as 'being both very narrow and slippery, in regard they are all paved with smooth bricke, and joyning to the water, the horse would quickly fall into the river and so drowne both himself and his rider'.[114]

One issue surrounding the cleaning of the streets focused on the moisture that might be left behind on the surface if stone was washed. Panegyrics on cities, such as that of Leonardo Bruni on Florence which depicts the city as singular in its cleanliness, described 'the cleanliness *and dryness* that you find only in the rooms of private palaces in other cities, you find in the squares and streets of Florence' [my emphasis].[115] As a result, the paving of the streets was often a moment in which the drainage would be improved.[116] In Genoa, as elsewhere on the peninsula, extensive subterranean sewage systems were constructed during the premodern period.[117] These helped to ensure dryness of the streets: an essential quality for clean Renaissance roads.

In 1508, concerns about moisture and mud prompted the paving of the road used by the pious and pilgrims to get to the 'Nuntiata' church.[118] These initiatives might be coordinated by the government but religious institutions were also seen to have responsibilities for their surrounding areas. In 1533, the friars at San

---

[111] ASCG, PdC, 12-22 (19 July 1526) and 23-138 (11 July 1558).
[112] ASCG, PdC, 12-22 (19 July 1526), 11-112 (17 May 1552), 13-116 (1 July 1531), 22-33 (11 June 1554), 22-116 (2 July 1555), and 23-44 (1 July 1557).
[113] ASCG, PdC, 21-117 (2 July 1552), 22-33 (11 June 1554), and 22-157 (1 January 1556).
[114] Thomas Coryat cited in Robert C. Davis, 'The trouble with bulls', p. 278.
[115] Leonardo Bruni cited in Douglas Biow, *The culture of cleanliness*, p. 82.
[116] ASCG, PdC, 20-152 (7 July 1550).
[117] Francesca Bocchi, 'Regulation of the urban environment', p. 73.
[118] ASCG, PdC, 9-27 (11 July 1508).

68 CLEANING UP RENAISSANCE ITALY

Domenico were instructed to pave the main street which ran from their institution to San Antonio; the friars at San Antonio would also be expected to contribute to the cost.[119] In Genoa, the government entrusted the Padri with the coordination of paving, maintenance, and cleaning of the roads in the suburbs of the city as well as the wider territory.[120] The significance of these thoroughfares in the state had been set out in communal statutes at the beginning of the fifteenth century.[121] In 1538 the need to repair the road between the broken bridge over the Bisagno and the Villa Torriglia in Fontanegli was prompted by the fact that it was almost impossible to traverse, whether on foot or horseback, without considerable effort and danger.[122] The Padri coordinated with local officials who would solicit reports from local experts and the costs of paving or resurfacing were split between the communities seen to derive immediate benefit.[123] The Padri were also called upon when issues could not be resolved adequately at the local level. In 1556, for example, a letter from two of the 'Padri' of Monterosso requested assistance in dealing with the water which was being dispersed on one of the community's principal streets by a mill. The road was said to be used by many travellers on a daily basis and the water flooding the street was noxious.[124]

In addition to the roads in the territory, the authorities in Genoa regulated the points of connection between these thoroughfares and the city, notably through the principal gateways.[125] The fourteenth-century walls of Genoa were reinforced and strengthened during the sixteenth century with particular attention paid to the port area, where additional gates were built, including the Porta del Molo designed by Galeazzo Alessi. An inscription from 1553 commemorated the strengthening of the defences there by extending the breakwater, constructing the gateway, and creating a border with the walls along the part of the city which was washed by the sea (*quacumque alluitur mari*). Gates were also built to align with the principal landing stations of the port. It was not until the following century that Genoa's walls were substantially extended in the form of the '*mura nuove*' built from 1626. Many of the gateways included inscriptions which attested to the role of the Republic in funding and directing the construction of the defences, as well as statues and dedications to saints or the Madonna. The Porta Soprana was built in the face of the political and military threat of Federico Barbarossa during the twelfth century and includes a Latin inscription which

---

[119] ASV, Comun b. 9 178r (1 September 1533).
[120] ASCG, PdC, 11-36 (30 March 1519) refers to the repair of roads in Sampierdarena, Cornigliano, and Sestri Ponente.
[121] Leges Genuensis, *Historiae patriae monumenta*, vol. 18 col. 591.
[122] ASCG, PdC, 15-152 (5 October 1538) and 22-158 (3 January 1556).
[123] ASCG, PdC, 28-97 (8 August 1567) and 2-136 (1 January 1595).
[124] ASCG, PdC, 22-159 (5 January 1556).
[125] On the symbolism of Genoa's gateways see Carrie E. Beneš, 'Civic identity' in Carrie E. Beneš (ed.), *A companion to medieval Genoa* (Leiden: Brill, 2018), p. 196.

CHANNELLING HEALTH 69

welcomed those who sought peace and repelled those who approached in the name of war.

The symbolic nature of city walls was also seen elsewhere. In Milan, the new walls built between 1548 and 1560 were said to be shaped like a human heart in order to symbolize the perfect circulation of goods and human beings in the city.[126] In Venice, of course, the preservation of the city's 'gates' was synonymous with the protection of the canals. The Venetian Cristoforo Sabbadino [c.1487–1560] wrote:

> The walls were constructed from water, the gates and the roads of water: to preserve those same walls, towers, roads and gates there was no need for stones, chalk, wood or hardware but instead only faith, prudence and justice—things which are never lacking in this Divine city.[127]

The regulation of those vital canals is considered in the next chapter.

In Genoa, gateways were essential for the security and health of the city. In 1464, the Padri instructed that planks of wood should be added to the Porta da San Nicola (presumably in Castelletto) so that the gateway could be closed when necessary to avoid the importation of plague.[128] Gateways were also important spaces for communication. When, in 1510, artisans had been washing their cloth, linen, and hides in the ditch at San Tommaso, the proclamation in response was to be read aloud and also affixed to the gateway at San Tommaso.[129] The accessibility of gateways was strictly regulated. In 1560, all citizens were reminded that they were not permitted to leave materials in the Porta di San Andrea (also known as the Porta Soprana) which would narrow the space of the gateway and cause congestion problems for travellers.[130] These gateways were busy places and in 1565 the Padri observed the great concourse of people who passed through the gateway of San Andrea each day. This was the principal site of entry into the city for those coming from an easterly direction and had become a popular site for the sale of biscuits and other similar foodstuffs. The impact was said to be a throng of people (*grande calca*). The problem, of course, was that these sellers stopped to sell their wares in a space which was designed to facilitate and regulate movement. No such selling was permitted to be undertaken without a licence.[131] The issue of impediment caused by sellers at gateways of the city was representative of concerns more generally about the need to protect the accessibility of streets

---

[126] Stefano D'Amico, *Spanish Milan: a city within the Empire, 1535–1706* (New York: Palgrave Macmillan, 2012), p. 10.

[127] 'le ha fabricate le mura di acqua: le ha fatto le porte e le strade di acqua: che amantener le mura, le torri, le strade e le porte: no' le bisogna pietri, calcina, legnami ne ferramente: ma solamente fede, prudentia e giustitia, delle quai. mai è mancata ne è per mancar questa Divina citta', ASV, SEA, 231, 1, 68v.

[128] ASCG, PdC, 1-119 (25 June 1464).   [129] ASCG, PdC, 9-130 (31 May 1510).

[130] ASCG, PdC, 24-92 (23 March 1560).   [131] ASCG, PdC, 27-19 (9 April 1565).

70 CLEANING UP RENAISSANCE ITALY

and squares in both cities throughout this period through the regulation of both the production and sale of artisanal and food products.

Selling on the Streets

Throughout the fifteenth and sixteenth centuries, government regulation addressed the processes and location of artisanal work to protect the health of the streets. This included the clear stipulation of acceptable districts for street selling, as well as restrictions on the physical form of permanent shops and their impact upon public space. Many premodern goods lacked a permanent site for distribution. In 1595, the Genoese government captured just some of items which might be sold in the streets by those who were attempting to scrape a living. Impoverished men and women offered a wide array of goods including thread, multiple silk products (including flowers, slippers, tassels or bows), *cavegerete* for head dressings, nets, bed curtains (*fenogieto*), five types of buttons, ribbons, women's collars, and embroidery.[132] The quality and location of such sellers, particularly those relating to the provision of foodstuffs, were a long-standing concern for government officials and were addressed extensively in communal statutes as well as those of guilds.[133] The general principles seen elsewhere on the peninsula were applied, challenged, and developed in the streets of Renaissance Genoa and Venice.[134]

In 1565, an apothecary in Venice noted that, for six years, he had served his community in times of sickness and health and kept his premises clean and tidy (*mondo et netto*), referencing this as good artisanal behaviour.[135] There was extensive awareness of the need for hygiene and cleanliness as part of an array of artisanal trades but perhaps none more important than for those handling consumable products. In Venice, the Health Office instructed shopkeepers not to sell rotten goods (*robe cative et marze et non sufficiente*) which deceived consumers and caused considerable risk of plague. Amongst other things, this was said to include cheese that was marked, disformed, stinking, or bad in any other way ('*formazi marzi, guasti, puzolenti*'). In addition, the cheesemakers of San Marco and Rialto were not permitted, under any circumstances, to keep cheese of that sort on the balconies or rooftops (*balchon*) of their shops in recognition of concerns that such corrupt materials could affect the health of the city by infecting the air (as well as through ingestion). Only good and sufficient cheese, whether

---

[132] ASCG, PdC, 2-152 (1 January 1595). *Firozella* was a form of silk. The silk products included *pimpinelle di seta e di firozella, scofie di seta, bossetti di seta e firozella, fiocheti et lacheti di seta e firozella, garofori di raso di seta, gasete di seta e di firozella d'ogni sorte per samarre da donna*. The list also includes *trene* and *picaglie da camisie* which have not yet been identified.
[133] Leges Genuensis, *Historiae patriae monumenta*, vol. 18.   [134] Fabrizio Nevola, *Street life*.
[135] ASV, Comun b.14 reg 33 104v (19 November 1565).

soft or firm, might be stored in such spaces.[136] The cleanliness and use of retail space, therefore, was an important part of ensuring the health of the city.

In Genoa, the Padri held responsibility for the regulation of trades and officials were concerned with the operation of street selling in the city. This included those *besagnini* who came to sell their wares on bridges and in the squares of the city as well as merchandise which came into the city by sea.[137] Sellers of some foodstuffs were required to register with the Padri.[138] The ongoing difficulties of ensuring that only registered sellers were involved in particular trades was expressed in Genoa in 1551 when the Padri recounted the number of complaints which they were receiving from the representative of the fruit sellers and from citizens of the city regarding those unlicensed individuals who walked around the city selling fruit.[139]

Street selling of foodstuffs involved both men and women. In 1518, the Padri noted the names of the vegetable sellers in the city who had been involved in the trade for the past two years. More than three hundred people were grouped according to the location in which they were permitted to sell. There were seventeen sites identified, with varying-sized groups, ranging from three in San Donato to thirty-eight around San Lorenzo. In many cases, the list recorded details of the place of origin of the seller. One third of the sellers were women, who were present in almost all sites across the city.[140] The women were never in the majority, although they were present in equal numbers to men in Piazza Fossatello. Five of these women were specifically recorded as being married and were listed with their husband's name.[141] More broadly the work of these women street sellers was often less formally organized than for their male equivalents. One of the most important resources for sale in Venice was drinking water and, as David Gentilcore has noted, many of these *bigolanti* were women who lacked a formal guild structure equivalent to the male *acquaroli*.[142]

Concerns relating to the presence of these sellers in the streets were partly practical. These men and women carried with them an array of large baskets (*corbe panieri et canestri o sia cavagni*) to sell fruit, vegetables, and other items. This impeded those on horseback and on foot. The space of the streets in Genoa was further constricted because shops and taverns were receiving money or benefits from street sellers, in return for being allowed to set up outside their properties.[143] A similar problem occurred in the vicinity of Piazza Ponticello and

---

[136] *Venezia e la peste, 1348–1797* (Venice: Marsilio, 1980), p. 121.
[137] ASCG, PdC, 2-55 (8 April 1518) and 13-36 (20 October 1529).
[138] ASCG, PdC, 11-168 (1 October 1523).   [139] ASCG, PdC, 21-45 (11 July 1551).
[140] Melissa Calaresu and Danielle van den Heuvel (eds), *Food hawkers: selling in the streets from Antiquity to the present* (London: Routledge, 2018).
[141] ASCG, PdC, 11-12 (6 May 1518).
[142] David Gentilcore, 'The cistern-system of early modern Venice: technology, politics and culture in a hydraulic society', *Water History* (2021), 20.
[143] ASCG, PdC, 31-68 (13 July 1572).

72 CLEANING UP RENAISSANCE ITALY

the Padri were moved to remind residents in the vicinity of that square that they were not permitted to facilitate the presence of street sellers outside their homes by allowing them to occupy the spaces on steps or in front of doors in return for payment.[144]

Elsewhere, concerns about these street sellers focused on associations with immorality and indecency.[145] The associations of commerce partly explain the efforts undertaken in Genoa to restrict such activities in the square around San Lorenzo, the city's cathedral.[146] In 1528, the Padri reiterated their intention to reduce the continual commerce and markets which were taking place around the cathedral at which vegetables, fruit, eggs, poultry, baskets, and other items were all being sold. Time was regulated as well as space. Commerce in the piazza was only permitted until the bells struck the hour of nine. By the time the bells rang, not only should commerce have ceased but all rubbish should have been cleared away.[147] These efforts culminated, in the early sixteenth century, in the construction of the Piazza Nuova close to the Church of Sant'Ambrogio and Palazzo Ducale. This was intended to be a commercial centre for the city with shops and warehouses.[148] In 1548, the Padri continued to bemoan the number of people who were selling in the streets, making it very difficult to pass, including along the thoroughfare which connected Piazza Nuova to San Lorenzo.[149] In 1551, the Padri reflected on the disorder occurring daily in Piazza Nuova.[150] Even once commerce was located here, the Padri were concerned with failures to situate the selling in the specific places and time slots allotted to diverse trades.[151]

For practical reasons some street sellers congregated in different types of spaces. In Venice in 1551, fruit sellers were noted as situating themselves on the bridges and in the streets, whereas vegetable sellers were more likely to be found in squares in close proximity to public wells. This was of considerable concern since the disposal of waste by these trades risked damage to the city's water supply. A similar problem was recognized in Genoa. In 1494, sellers of vegetables were instructed not to throw the pods of beans and peas or the discarded outer leaves of lettuce (*scarcio de bazano leitughe, poissi, ceriolo*) onto streets or into public fountains. They were supposed to ensure that they carried the waste, regardless of the quantity, in their own baskets and containers out of the city to the designated sites in Bisagno. This was intended to prevent these waste materials from rotting in the streets, emitting a foul stench, and potentially being carried into the port.

---

[144] ASCG, PdC, 15-51 (11 September 1536).
[145] Evelyn Welch, *Shopping in the Renaissance*, pp. 34–40, which also includes illustrations of individuals carrying the large baskets.
[146] ASCG, PdC, 1-110 (1 June 1464), 5-51 (10 April 1483), and 11-192 (9 April 1524).
[147] ASCG, PdC, 5-51 (10 April 1483).
[148] ASCG, PdC, 5-106 (23 June 1483) and 287-195 (28 February 1528).
[149] ASCG, PdC, 19-180 (14 April 1548).   [150] ASCG, PdC, 21-39 (29 July 1551).
[151] ASCG, PdC, 14-182 (15 July 1535) and 26-35 (6 May 1563).

CHANNELLING HEALTH   73

Sellers and artisans were also frequently reminded not to discard rubbish in the streets.[152] This might include scraps of cloth (*rutagli de panni*) from tailors or drapers.[153] In Genoa in 1508, those who sold fresh beans were instructed to ensure that these had already been podded before being brought into the urban centre to avoid the accumulation of large quantities of waste. The remnants (*scorzie*) were to be left outside the city.[154] In 1534, all *besagnini* and sellers of manure (*letame*), leaves (*foglie*), and plants (*erbe*) were reminded that they must keep bodies of water, streets, and squares clean and swept (*netti e spassati*) of any rubbish and ensure that it was carried to the allocated place in Bisagno.[155] That offcuts and peel of fruit and vegetables were discarded in urban streets was observed by the Mantuan ambassador to Venice who was astonished to see the poor of the city gather up bits of melon peel and relish the eating 'as though they were marzipan'.[156] Throughout this period, individuals do not appear to have been employed to clean commercial areas in Genoa and Venice as they were elsewhere.[157] Instead, the authorities emphasized the responsibility of individual sellers to ensure that these spaces were maintained in an appropriate state.

In addition to those who sold their wares in the street, officials in both ports were concerned with the extent to which shops and workspaces of artisan production encroached upon public space.[158] This activity tended to be reported by local residents, such as in 1540 when the priest of San Giacomo dell'Orio reported that Pietro the stonemason was taking over parts of the square with his work.[159] Across Venice, carpenters and stonemasons were said to be using the squares of the city like warehouses and damaging the streets.[160] This was seen to demonstrate a lack of reverence and respect on behalf of artisans as they hindered access and damaged the infrastructure of streets and squares.[161] In 1549, merchants were given permission to keep pieces of timber (*legnami squadrati*) on the *fondamenta* from San Trovaso to San Basegio as long as the surface was maintained in an appropriate state.[162] Construction work, however, often required artisans to work in the streets surrounding the building site and the impact on the access and state of the streets would have been significant.[163]

In Genoa, the Padri reflected on the way in which, for many years, the artisans of the Riva and other sites had placed merchandise, benches, tables, and other objects outside their shops and in the public streets, restricting the space and movement. The Padri reminded artisans that they were not permitted to encroach

---

[152] Dennis Romano, *Markets and marketplaces*, p. 144.
[153] ASCG, PdC, 11-204 (23 December 1524).   [154] ASCG, PdC, 9-16 (16 May 1508).
[155] ASCG, PdC, 14-136 (4 December 1534).   [156] Cini Mantova b.1489.
[157] Dennis Romano, *Markets and marketplaces*, pp. 134–5.
[158] For example, ASV, Comun b.10 reg 21 18r (20 November 1534).
[159] ASV, Comun b.10 reg 23 46r (28 July 1540).   [160] ASV, Comun reg 1 (10 September 1551).
[161] ASV, Comun b.10 reg 21 35v (16 February 1534).   [162] Rompiasio p. 185 and p. 231.
[163] Such a scene is depicted in Luca Cambiaso's painting 'The construction of the Trebisonda warehouse' in the Palazzo Lercari-Parodi, Genoa.

74 CLEANING UP RENAISSANCE ITALY

upon the streets beyond a distance of between one and two hands' length depending on the width of the street.[164] Barrel-makers were not permitted to work or to leave their goods in the streets.[165] In 1516, shop owners were instructed not to block the public streets with the exhibition of their wares.[166] These efforts to display products could take on a more permanent form and in 1569, the Genoese authorities reminded those who had tables fixed to the walls of their shops that they should remove them and ensure that their properties did not extend into the street beyond the permitted distance.[167] In 1546, the Padri noted that almost no one in the city was respecting the rule of limiting the extension of their shop or workshop.[168] The expansion of commercial and artisanal properties was narrowing the streets to the extent that they were inadequate (*tanto angusto*) and limiting the ability of people to pass through them.[169] Artisans were instructed not to place their merchandise on poles which extended into the street.[170] This may have been out of concern that—as in Pistoia in relation to awnings on supports—these could hit individuals in the face.[171]

In Genoa, shopkeepers at the Piazza dei Banchi were forbidden from encroaching on public space beyond their shops in order to prevent inconveniencing people and obstructing the prospect of the place (*offendere... il prospetto della vista*).[172] As Dennis Romano has noted, this was an important element of early proclamations relating to public space, which were designed both to prevent individuals from gaining an unfair advantage over their competitors and impeding traffic. Where these structures were 'ugly and unattractive' this was seen to be even worse and something which would leave a poor impression on visitors.[173] Ennio Concina has illustrated that the building campaigns of the sixteenth century caused some small streets in Venice to be left so that 'you never see the sun'.[174] This would have caused the environment of these areas to be perceived as less salubrious and also shaped issues of access. Dennis Romano has cited a complaint made by the bakers with shops at Rialto in Venice in 1366 that the 'darkness' (*obscuritatem*) of their location hindered sales.[175] Beauty, visibility, and access were all issues addressed by these regulations of public space. These same considerations informed practices of governance in distinct liturgical or temporal seasons.

The Seasons of the Streets

The cleanliness and accessibility of the streets were a perennial concern for urban governments but there was nevertheless a distinct sense of seasonality to

---

[164] ASCG, PdC, 30-07 (3 March 1570).
[165] ASCG, PdC, 6-59 (22 March 1492).
[166] ASCG, PdC, 10-152 (27 June 1516).
[167] ASCG, PdC, 29-229 (14 December 1569).
[168] ASCG, PdC, 19-67 (16 March 1546).
[169] ASCG, PdC, 22-124 (12 August 1555).
[170] ASCG, PdC, 29-43 (10 July 1568).
[171] Dennis Romano, *Markets and marketplaces*, p. 96.
[172] ASCG, PdC, 29-43 (10 July 1568).
[173] Dennis Romano, *Markets and marketplaces*, p. 96.
[174] Ennio Concina, *Venezia nell'età moderna*, p. 15.
[175] Dennis Romano, *Markets and marketplaces*, p. 93.

regulations.[176] On the streets of Mantua in 1459–60, for example, Pope Pius II remarked on the presence of the dust in the summer and mud in the winter.[177] In Genoa in November 1563, the Padri observed that they had arrived at the moment in the year when the rain usually arrived, making the presence of any rubbish and rubble in the streets of heightened concern.[178] Not only was this the season when material was more likely to be transported into the port, the risk of damage to vessels overwintering in the port was greater. Winter was—as the Padri noted in 1549—the most dangerous season for ships in the port since storms were more likely and there was a lower level of water in the port itself.[179]

Winter weather could cause considerable urban disruption. In Florence in 1493, the snow was so heavy that shops were forced to close.[180] In 1572, the Genoese authorities ordered the removal of snow from the front of doorways and workshops by residents. The purpose was to facilitate comfortable passage around the city and avoid a strain on the public drains when the snow melted.[181] In Venice in 1531 the diarist Sanudo noted that it had snowed (which it had not done for many years) causing severely muddy conditions on the streets.[182] In January 1560, all of the porters (*bastazi over fachini* and *capo di bastazi*) who worked in the city were instructed to clear snow from the bridges and principal streets. Presumably the porters were utilized because the work involved would have been unmanageable for the small team of street cleaners.[183] The *bastazi* were instructed to clear snow directly into the canals—again, in order to avoid excess moisture on the streets when the snow melted.[184]

Buildings, of course, sustained structural damage in severe weather. Ice and snow damaged roofs, causing significant leaks during times of heavy rainfall.[185] The same was also true of the roads and streets. In 1551, Domenico Ponte described the impact of winter weather in Gavi, including the principal roads, which proved to be incommodious in winter. The pools of water which accumulated also had an insalubrious effect on the air.[186] Equally the process of corruption was associated with heat and so this risk was particularly acute during the summer, meaning that there was a seasonality to these concerns: omnipresent but intensified during the hotter months as well as winter when levels of rainfall and other types of precipitation increased.[187]

There was also a further seasonality to the development of infrastructure and cleaning the city which was directed by the civic and liturgical calendars. In 1502, street paving was given greater impetus by the upcoming visit to Genoa of the King of France. A letter sent to Galeazzo Pannexo in Savona described the large

---

[176] See also Evelyn Welch, *Shopping in the Renaissance*, pp. 107–9.
[177] Cited in Fabrizio Nevola, *Street life*, p. 33.   [178] ASCG, PdC, 26-88 (13 November 1563).
[179] ASCG, PdC, 20-91 (15 November 1549).   [180] Fabrizio Nevola, *Street life*, p. 190.
[181] ASCG, PdC, 31-25 (14 February 1572).
[182] Rinaldo Fulin (ed.), *I diarii di Marin Sanudo*, vol. 55 col. 461.   [183] See chapter 5, pp. 151–2.
[184] ASV, Comun, b.14 reg 32, 68v (22 January 1560).
[185] ASV, Sanità, 738 119v (9 February 1618).   [186] ASCG, PdC, 21-49 (21 July 1551).
[187] ASV, Sanità, 740 10v (30 April 1643).

76   CLEANING UP RENAISSANCE ITALY

quantity of bricks needed to pave the streets and carry out other works.[188] In September of the same year, instructions were issued to remove the gravel and sand which had been scattered in the streets in order to repair holes and covered unpaved areas. Again, the motivation for such action was referenced directly as being the entrance of the King of France.[189] In 1599, the street leading to the lighthouse (from San Lazaro to la Cossia) was to be repaved because of the upcoming visit of the Queen of Spain.[190]

In Genoa in 1549, a proclamation opened by reflecting upon the great benefit which resulted to the port from the cleaning of the streets every Saturday as well as every feast day or holy day. In 1541, as the Padri were preparing for the procession of Corpus Domini, it was noted that many sites in the city were blocked by stones, rubble, and other rubbish. Inhabitants of the city were instructed to ensure that they cleaned in front of their houses, with materials being removed from all sites in the city and particularly along the route of the procession. This was an important distinction because the regulations about cleanliness were not simply issued in this context in order to ensure that processions could be undertaken along an accessible route.[191] In extending the provision beyond the procession's path, the Padri made clear that the concern was more than practical. By 1648, all inhabitants were instructed to clean in front of their properties and also encouraged to display tapestries and devotional images (*tappezzerie e quadri di devozione*).[192]

In addition to cleaning the surface of the streets in preparation for feast days, the use of the streets was also regulated at these times. It was not permitted to bring beasts of burden into the city on Sundays or feast days.[193] Any tables outside workshops were supposed to be removed along the processional routes.[194] Artisans were required to keep workshops closed and the Padri took particular care to issue reminders about the significance of these closures on Corpus Domini and the feast days of St John the Baptist and St George (the city's patron saint).[195]

The regulation of the streets also had to respond to the production of seasonal foodstuffs. In Venice in March 1565, a seller of the delicious fried carnival treats *fritole* was required to dismantle the *bottega* that he had constructed.[196] In the same month in Genoa in 1604, a chicken seller, Susannina Barbagelata had a saucepan confiscated by the town crier Giannettino Siciliano in which she had made *frissioli* (*frittele*) in the Piazza Nuova.[197] She had the item returned to her and the only mention of this incident found thus far in the archive referred to the

---

[188] ASCG, PdC, 7-115 (5 July 1502).   [189] ASCG, PdC, 7-122 (3 September 1502).
[190] ASCG, PdC, 221-142 (1 January 1599).   [191] ASCG, PdC, 16-128 (14 June 1541).
[192] ASCG, PdC, 224-387 (3 June 1648).   [193] ASCG, PdC, 3-46 (31 August 1470).
[194] ASCG, PdC, 6-160 (10 March 1498) and 7-66 (1 April 1501).
[195] ASCG, PdC, 20-66 (29 August 1553), 22-55 (28 August 1554), and 29-20 (23 April 1568).
[196] ASV, Comun b.14 reg 33 1v (9 March 1565).   [197] ASCG, PdC, 62-27 (5 March 1604).

need for the authorities to reflect further on the case whilst expressing sympathy with Susannina's right to work in the square.

The unusual ambiguity of this entry is perhaps explained by a further case recorded in the archive five years later. Here, the Sindaci di San Siro in Struppa and Bargagli reported the same Giannettino Siciliano to the Padri. He was still working in Piazza Nuova. The officials wrote that he had, for many years, and indeed almost continuously, hassled and insulted the women from Bisagno who went into the square in order to sell their produce. He extorted additional fees from them and was said to speak in shocking terms not only to married women but also to young girls and boys. They describe women being grabbed by the hair, by the collar, and by other items of clothing, causing them (and the wider community) considerable distress and shame. If the women and girls had the courage to challenge him verbally, he responded with insults and bad words and worse (*e peggio co' fatti cosa che per il passato no' si e mai piu vista'*). The entry made reference to further maltreatment and abuse which, the Sindaci noted, could be reported in minute detail by the women affected when the Padri investigated.[198]

No further material has been uncovered in the Genoese archive relating to Giannettino Siciliano and his violent and abusive behaviour. His example does remind us that, for all of the ideals of design and management on behalf of governments, the streets were, for many, a place of vulnerability and danger. Concerns about the safety of public spaces included regulations of physical infrastructure as well as behaviour and movement. In the broadest sense, these were spaces which were seen to connect the moral and physical wellbeing of communities, or the inverse of the same, and the perceived impact of mismanagement was severe. In this, the streets were joined by the infrastructure of water supply, which lies at the heart of the next chapter.

---

[198] ASCG, PdC, 67-35 (3 June 1609).

3

Preserving Purity

The Symbolic and Practical Regulation of Water

Collected illustrations of virtuous women during the fifteenth and sixteenth centuries commonly included a depiction of the Vestal Virgin Tuccia. Tuccia was one of the women who maintained the fire in the temple of the goddess Vesta, in Rome. She responded to an accusation of immorality by carrying water from the Tiber River to the temple in a sieve to demonstrate her chastity.[1] Stories such as this, and their representations, remind us of the symbolic as well as practical importance of water during the Renaissance. What was true of the element might also be true of the structures which channelled or stored it. The maintenance of water infrastructure and the purity of its supply were vital for healthy living in the Renaissance city and might also be interpreted by residents and visitors alike as a reflection of the condition of a state.[2]

The practical and symbolic significance of water had additional resonance within Catholic societies. Associations between sanctity, purity, cleanliness, and the provision of water were intricate and long-standing. A sixteenth-century Venetian holy water basin, now in the Victoria and Albert Museum (London), bears the inscription 'Aqua Salvtis Aeternae' (Water of Eternal Health).[3] The infrastructure of water supply might also be deployed in religious metaphor. St Bernard of Clairvaux [1090–1153] had praised the Virgin Mary as an aqueduct, an essential connecting force between the source of life-giving water (God) and the fountain (Christ). This association with female spirituality was particularly appropriate given that much of the handling of water in premodern Europe was gendered, from the collection of water to its domestic use and the washing of

---

[1] For example, see https://collections.vam.ac.uk/item/O125590/tuccia-chastity-tempera-painting-neroni-bartolomeo/

[2] Katherine Rinne, *The waters of Rome*; Paolo Squatriti, *Water and society in medieval Italy* (Cambridge: Cambridge University Press, 1998), and Roberta Magnusson, *Water technology in the Middle Ages: cities, monasteries, and waterworks after the Roman Empire* (Baltimore MA: Johns Hopkins University Press, 2001). See also the literature discussion in Petra J. E. M. van Dam, Piet van Cruyningen, and Milja van Tielhof, 'A global comparison of pre-modern institutions for water management', *Environment and History* 23 (2017), 335–40.

[3] http://collections.vam.ac.uk/item/O122366/holy-water-basin-holy-water-basin-unknown/. Researchers have uncovered a similar basin in the Bode Museum, Berlin, the base of which is inscribed 'Aqua expiationis quotidianae' (Water of daily purification) [accessed 6 October 2014]. See also Carole Rawcliffe, *Urban bodies* chapter four 'Water', pp. 176–229 on the religious and theological aspects of water supply.

Cleaning Up Renaissance Italy: Environmental Ideals and Urban Practice in Genoa and Venice. Jane L. Stevens Crawshaw, Oxford University Press. © Jane L. Stevens Crawshaw 2023. DOI: 10.1093/oso/9780198867432.003.0004

laundry. As with so many aspects of women's lives in the Renaissance, discussions of the proximity to, or handling of, water were often highly moralized.

Water was known to be affected substantially by the areas through which it passed. Its capacity to absorb minerals and qualities from its surroundings meant that it was affected by the seasons, prevailing winds, and proximity to sources of natural heat, such as volcanoes. It was firmly a product of its place, therefore, despite recognition of networks of flow which spanned continents. Water could corrupt (through stagnation or heat) and, once this occurred, it could not be reversed. The challenge, therefore, was to prevent the corruption of the supply in the first place.[4] This chapter considers the ways in which these factors of morality, piety, and purity infused efforts to control and preserve the infrastructure of water supply in Genoa and Venice during the Renaissance.

Genoa's water infrastructure comprised multiple structures: the aqueduct was of principal importance and this fed the city's network of wells, cisterns, drinking troughs, and fountains. The latter included both publicly funded drinking fountains as well as those paid for by private citizens for civic benefit.[5] Public drinking fountains were conceived of as *res publica* but disputes about their use reveal tensions between individual interests and the collective good.[6] The expense of developing and maintaining the networks of water supply was considerable and a lack of funds was an enduring problem. As with the maintenance of the streets, the costs of water infrastructure in Genoa and Venice were split between those who were seen to derive benefit from the investment.[7]

The supply of water in fountains was frequently described as a charitable act for the poor, who were said to lack access to other sources. In his aforementioned reflection on the role of Christ as akin to a fountain, St Bernard explained its various practical functions: to provide what was required in order to wash or clean stains, quench thirst, irrigate the land, and provide water for cooking food.[8] In Venice, where fountains were notably absent from the water infrastructure, these same essential functions were fulfilled by the city's wells.[9] Like cisterns,

---

[4] Andrea Bacci, *Del Tevere*, pp. 53–4 on the tendency of water to corrupt.

[5] Katherine Rinne, *The waters of Rome*, p. 156. Rinne identified five categories of public fountains: *beveratori* which were used for animals and workers; *fontane pubbliche* which were publicly funded drinking fountains; *fontane semi-pubbliche* (drinking fountains paid for by private citizens for public benefit); *lavatoi* (laundry basins), and *purgatoi* (purging basins for wool). See also David Gentilcore 'From "vilest beverage" to "universal medicine": drinking water in printed regimens and health guides 1450–1750', *Social History of Medicine* 33:3 (2020), 683–703.

[6] Edward Muir, 'Was there Republicanism', p. 142.

[7] ASCG, PdC, 23-137 (11 July 1558) for example and 26-103 (26 February 1564).

[8] Roberta Magnusson, *Water technology in the Middle Ages*.

[9] Robert C. Davis, see 'Venetian shipbuilders and the fountain of wine', *Past and Present* 156 (1997), 55–86.

80 CLEANING UP RENAISSANCE ITALY

these could be filled with rain water and their supply might also be supplemented with freshwater transported from mainland rivers.[10]

Just as the ample provision of pure water could enhance the reputation of port settings, the opposite was also true. The flow of fetid water, or the stench of stagnant pools, could sully their status, threatening to cause outbreaks of epidemic disease or lead to problems of siltation (which are considered in more detail in chapter four).[11] They might also be discussed with moral overtones. A petition composed during the mid-sixteenth century by the friars of San Francesco di Castelletto in Genoa, in response to the proposed relocation of the city's municipal brothel, suggested that the impact of that institution in the neighbourhood would be that the holy and blessed churches would degenerate into latrines and sinks of foul vices (*et cosi di chiese spirituali et sante saranno cloache et sentine d'ogni piu vicio nefando*).[12] Furthermore, additional social and physical effects would include the pollution of the water supply of the district, which would become muddy and unclean (*turbide et immonde*). Alongside systems of supply, therefore, this chapter will also consider the structures designed to remove dirt or impurity, including drains and ditches. Subterranean drains had been developed in Genoa as the preferred method for keeping the streets clean and limiting foul odours.[13] Indeed, these drainage channels were often constructed or repaired in conjunction with the paving of the streets.[14] The drains flowed into ditches or the city's port just as the gutters of Venice flowed into the canals. Effective use of these structures was intended to ensure the beauty and comfort of the city as well as the health and purity of the air.[15] Free-flowing, plentiful supplies of clean water in ports were known to be important for both health and piety. Investment in water infrastructure can also be seen beyond ports during the Renaissance, in Nicola Pagliera's work on Rome and Fabrizio Nevola's studies of Siena and structures developed in Pavia, Bologna (1476), and Cesena (1500–4).[16] Nevertheless, the close association between the environment and civic identity in ports made the connections between clean water, health, and piety in port settings acute.

The ideal city tracts explored in chapter one illustrated the manifold ways in which the appropriate channelling and distribution of water might enhance the wealth, reputation, and appearance of a port city. Water was also recognized to pose a powerful threat to the integrity of the streets and buildings if left

---

[10] David Gentilcore describes Venetian wells as 'well-filtered cisterns' and explores the technology employed in the city in 'The cistern-system of early modern Venice'.

[11] ASV, Comun, Atti b.1 100v (11 February 1385).

[12] Reprinted in Ennio Poleggi, *Strada nuova: una lottizzazione del '500 a Genova* (Genoa: Sagep, 1968), p. 407 and discussed in greater detail in Jane L. Stevens Crawshaw, 'Cleaning up the Renaissance city'.

[13] *Statuti politici della citta di Savona*, p. 88.   [14] ASCG, PdC, 20-152 (7 July 1550).

[15] ASV, Comun, Atti b.1 417r (19 March 1582).

[16] Nicola Pagliera, 'Destri e cucine...' in Aurora Scotti Tosini (ed.), *Aspetti dell'abitare in Italia tra XV e XVI secolo: distribuzione, funzioni, impianti* (Milan: Unicopli, 2001), pp. 63–77.

unchannelled.[17] In chapter six, we will look in more detail at the devastation wrought by natural disasters, including storms and floods. The impact of water on building structures could be more incremental, however. Early urban regulations in Milan had established the minimum distance of 43.5cm between the wall of a house and the boundary of the adjacent property which Francesca Bocchi has noted was to control the impact of rainwater and allow water to drip from the eaves and windows without damaging the fabric of the building.[18] In Venice, the Comun also intervened regarding the diversion of rainwater from houses. In 1551, a building in Cannaregio was said to be affected by rainfall, much to the disadvantage of the inhabitants and the Comun ordered the diversion of the water into the public canal.[19] In Genoa in 1569, a household requested permission to add a marble tube to an archway of the aqueduct to rechannel the moisture which was dripping onto their property.[20] The water might be diverted into wells or canals in Venice and drains or cisterns in Genoa demonstrating both the value of the resource and concerns about effective channels of flow.

Overflows: The Infrastructure of Water Supply

Wells had become common features of squares, private courtyards, and public institutions in both Genoa and Venice from the fifteenth century. They provided water for drinking and to supply the key services of the house, such as cooking. The provision of water in wells could also equip cities in the event of fires.[21] These structures required adequate supply of clean water and also regular maintenance and cleaning. Wells were a vital public resource and access was one way of shaping community.[22]

In total, there were estimated to be approximately 160 wells in Renaissance Venice, between private and public structures (and there are said to be just over 230 today), of differing sizes (some termed *pozzetto* and others a full-sized *pozzo*).[23] The names given to these wells also sometimes identify those of particularly fine quality water, including the *pozzetto d'oro* at San Canciano and *pozzo*

---

[17] *Statuti politici della citta di Savona*, p. 92.
[18] Francesca Bocchi, 'Regulation of the urban environment', p. 64.
[19] ASV, Comun b.12 reg 27 103v (3 March 1551).   [20] ASCG, PdC, 29-140 (27 April 1569).
[21] Siena's fountains were essential to strategies for firefighting. Multiple earthenware vessels would be filled at once and then thrown into the fire. Roberta J. Magnusson, *Water technology*, p. 30. Donatella Calabi and Paolo Morachiello, *Rialto*, p. 44. The diarist Sanudo also notes that the buckets and ladders which the Council of Ten had ordered to be placed around the city could not be found.
[22] On the public nature of the attack in cases of poisoned wells see Tzafrir Barzilay, *Poisoned wells: accusations, persecution, and minorities in medieval Europe, 1321–1422* (Philadelphia PA: University of Pennsylvania Press, 2022).
[23] See Robert C. Davis 'Venetian shipbuilders', p. 63. The contemporary estimate comes from Alberto Rizzi, *Vere di pozzo di Venezia* (Venice: Filippi, 2007).

82 CLEANING UP RENAISSANCE ITALY

d'oro at Santi Apostoli.[24] These structures developed an elaborate filtration system through layers of sand and stone.[25] They received rain water, as well as being supplied with fresh water from the mainland (brought by boat principally via the Rio dell'Acqua Dolce in Santi Apostoli).[26] The provision of fresh water was seen as a charitable initiative and yet it was clear that the supply did not meet demand in many of the poorer areas of the city.

The form of wellheads in Venice varied significantly, from intricate bronze versions in the city's Palazzo Ducale to others decorated with religious iconography or geometric designs.[27] In the sixteenth century, the wellheads from the Campo dei do Pozzi (the square of two wells), depicted the eponymous wells on one panel. Another showed San Martino flanked by angels because the square was situated in the parish of San Martino and SS Trinità. Public wells often displayed a saint relevant to the parish along with a representation of the Venetian Republic in the form of the winged lion of St Mark, although these latter decorative elements were largely removed after the fall of the Republic in 1797.[28] Public wells might also be marked with inscriptions, such as an example from Campo San Leonardo from 1518 which attested to funding from the Provveditori di Comun and the phrase, 'a public resource as well as an ornament for the city' (*commoditati publicae nec non urbis ornamento*). For reasons which will become clear, many of these wells were equipped with covers. For those in private courtyards, Francesco Sansovino noted that these tended to be only partially covered because fresh water was believed to stay better preserved when exposed to the air rather than in the darkness: the sunlight had a purging effect.[29]

Despite this provision, water suitable for consumption could be difficult to source in Venice. The water sellers became a guild in March 1471 which brought with them both rights and responsibilities, including the provision of 100 boatloads of water every year for the charitable and religious institutions of the city.[30] In 1494, the *acquaroli* were said to be selling water which was not clean but 'saltwater and bad (*cattive*)' from the Bottenigo and other localities. As a result, the government stipulated that only water from the Brenta was to be sold for consumption.[31] In 1540 the decision was taken to construct a canal from the Brenta which enabled water to be transported with greater ease to the city. This was completed in 1611 and was known as the Seriola.[32] In Genoa, drinking water was drawn predominantly from the city's fountains and wells and the provision of

[24] Giuseppe Tassini, *Curiosità veneziane* (Venice: M. Fontana, 1882), p. 584.

[25] See Richard Goy, *Venetian vernacular architecture: traditional housing in the Venetian lagoon* (Cambridge: Cambridge University Press, 1989), p. 86.

[26] Giuseppe Tassini, *Curiosità veneziane*, p. 10. [27] Alberto Rizzi, *Vere da pozzo*.

[28] Alberto Rizzi, *Vere da pozzo*, p. 32. [29] Alberto Rizzi, *Vere da pozzo*, p. 45.

[30] Massimo Costantini, *L'acqua di Venezia: l'approvvigionamento idrico della Serenissima* (Venice: Arsenale Editrice, 1984), p. 38 and David Gentilcore, 'The cistern-system of early modern Venice'.

[31] *Venezia e la peste*, 1348–1797 (Venice: Marsilio, 1980), p. 119.

[32] Massimo Constantini, *L'acqua di Venezia*, p. 21.

water necessitated the regulation of the aqueduct and its supply. In both cities, the process by which individuals obtained their water was strongly affected by their social status. It was recognized that artisans, citizens, and nobles were likely to have access to private wells and cisterns whereas the poor would be largely reliant on the provision of water from public structures.[33]

In ports, the need to supply ships with adequate water supply risked draining the resources of the city. In the thirteenth century, an anonymous poet described a '*fontanna bella e monda/chi a le nave l'aqgua abbonda*' in Genoa: the beautiful, clean fountain which gave water to ships in abundance. In 1567, the Genoese Padri observed of a well in the contrada del Roso that it had traditionally provided a good and abundant water supply for the inhabitants, as well as many mariners.[34] As the scale of need increased, however, and the quality of the water in some of these structures was not maintained, the system struggled to meet demand. In Venice, problems were reported of the crews of large ships using wells in the city to supply their vessels. They were instructed that they were only entitled to take three barrels of water from the city and should source the rest of their supply from the Lido where wells had been constructed for this purpose.[35]

Beyond the structures which helped to supply ships, wells were distributed throughout the two cities. In Venice in 1563, Marchio Rizo, *maestro delle stampe* at the Zecca (Mint), submitted a petition for an invention which would prevent water from stagnating and corrupting around the well heads of the communal wells.[36] Rizo included a list of 108 wells in squares around the city (which excluded the many others in courtyards and other similar spaces). He underscored the value of his invention to care for those who, because of their poverty, suffered enormously from the lack of access to good quality water.[37] These 108 wells were located in seventy of the city's main squares. Nearly a third of the squares contained more than one well, with San Nicolo, San Marco, San Canciano, and San Geremia listed as having four. There are notable differences in the number of residents in each of the Venetian *sestieri* and the number of wells, likewise, ranged from ten in San Polo to twenty-four in Castello. Public wells were distributed between the *sestieri* in a way which is remarkably similar to the distribution of the population when the percentage totals of wells are compared with residents from the 1536 census, for example.[38] Santa Croce at that time is estimated to have

---

[33] On cisterns see Gianjacopo Fontana, 'Sulla singolarità delle cisterne di Venezia', *Omnibus* (1854), 257–61. The Padri in Genoa also reminded the sellers of flour not to soak grain to bulk out the produce because of the potential damage to the health of the poor in ASCG, PdC, 22-39 (3 July 1554).

[34] 'usurpato il d'nio e possesso di detta aqua' in ASCG, PdC, 28-39 (12 March 1567). See also 2-143 (1 January 1595).

[35] ASV, Comun, b.11 reg 25 14v (8 August 1547).

[36] Petitions for inventions of this sort are considered in more detail in the next chapter.

[37] This information is taken from a list of public wells provided in ASV, Comun, b.5 reg 7 15r (22 May 1563). Details regarding the paving surrounding a wellhead have been taken from the de' Barbari map of Venice.

[38] Cambridge University Library, Ms ADD 9461.

84   CLEANING UP RENAISSANCE ITALY

contained 11 per cent of the city's residents and 12 per cent of the public wells and the statistics for the other districts are similarly aligned.

The high number of public wells in Castello is notable. Broadly speaking, Venetian elites were resident across districts and the city lacked a monumental noble street equivalent to the Strada Nuova in Genoa. Nevertheless, the district of Castello was home to a significant proportion of the city's residents and accommodated some of the city's poorest residents. In 1547, the Comun noted that three wells had been constructed at considerable expense at Sant'Isepo, Sant'Antonin, and the Campo della Tana for the comfort of the inhabitants who had been forced to spend virtually as much on water as they did on bread. The work on the wells was not done in isolation: streets were paved as part of the same initiative.[39] The parish of San Nicolò was said to be full of innumerable poor and that it was, therefore, particularly important that many public wells were available and the streets were paved.[40]

The form of Venetian wells differed in individual squares as well as across the city. In Jacopo de'Barbari's plan of Venice from 1500 some of this variety is visible. Some wells were surrounded by bare earth, some paved in the area immediately surrounding the well and others located in a square which was entirely paved. Just under half of the wells shown by de'Barbari lacked any paved surround. A slightly fewer number were paved around the wellhead. Only three of the paved squares of the city were shown to include wells. As a result, and as Rizo's petition suggests, there was a problem with the build-up of stagnant and dirty water around the city's wellheads since paving surrounding these wells was designed to channel rainwater into the system and to help to prevent the incursion of dirt and filth from the ground.

Significant efforts were made to preserve and improve the quality of well water in Venice although these efforts could not prevent wells from being affected by natural disasters, such as episodes of flooding.[41] Rizo's petition to the Comun offered an invention which would deal with the rainwater which sat around the edges and putrefied, damaging the physical structure and corrupting the water, which, he claimed, was disgusting to see and also created poor quality air.[42] In 1567, Giacomo Antonio Cortuso also targeted an invention at the preservation of well water in the summer and the prevention of what he had observed as water which was warm, muddy, impure, and unhealthy (*torbide, pocco pure et mal sane*).[43] In 1569, a Flemish man Nicolo Nicolai Cavalliero offered a

---

[39] Paola Pavanini, 'Venezia verso la pianificazione? Bonifiche urbane nel XVI secolo a Venezia' in Jean-Claude Maire Vigueur (ed.), *D'une ville à l'autre, Structures matérielles et organisatione de l'espace dans les villes européennes (XIIIe–XVIe siècle)* (Rome: École française de Rome, 1989), 496–500.

[40] ASV, Comun b.11 reg 25 168r (13 April 1547).

[41] Samuel K. Cohn Jr., *Cultures of plague*, p. 128.

[42] ASV, Comun b.5 reg 7 15r (22 May 1563).

[43] ASV, Comun b.5 reg 8 [unfoliated] (27 February 1567).

mechanism by which wells could be maintained with 'flowing, fresh, clear and perpetual' water of the same quality as the best wells on the mainland.[44]

In both cities, the authorities received requests for access to water supplies from religious and charitable institutions (situated both within and beyond the cities).[45] The Venetian Provveditori di Comun was asked to facilitate the construction of new wells, often at the expense of the state, as well as the rebuilding or repair of existing structures.[46] In 1519, the nuns of Sant'Isepo were said to be lacking a well in the convent, meaning that the community was forced to buy in water, at considerable expense.[47] In 1533, the nuns at Santa Lucia described themselves as being in true need of a well, lacking even enough water to drink.[48] In 1567, a similar supplication was sent on behalf of the whole community on Burano, where the poor numbered four thousand. They were said to be forced to purchase and drink water from the Sile, described as dangerous and the cause of illness. The community's officials requested the construction of two wells at the expense of the state.[49]

In other instances, religious institutions requested to be able to increase their water supply in order to meet better the needs of their wider community.[50] In 1559, the representatives of San Mauro on Burano noted that their well was damaged (*guasto*) and emphasized the good use to which the water was put, for the benefit of the whole of the poor parish.[51] In Genoa some repurposing of water supplies was more specific such as the case in 1519 relating to the water from a cistern at San Domenico being made available to soldiers.[52] In 1555, Stephano Torquerio de Arquata requested permission to be able to construct a subterranean pipe in order to carry water from the religious institution of the Carmine to supply a well near his house. These networks of water supply, then, crossed public and private land, as well as bridging the supply of institutions and individuals.[53]

Wells could pose risks for the community if the physical structure of the wellhead was not maintained. In 1548 in Genoa, a well in the district of the Prè, was in desperate need of repair. It was said to be so dangerous that children might fall into it and drown. Three residents of the district were appointed in order to oversee the work on the well and to ensure that those who derived the benefit of the work paid for their share of the costs.[54] In Savona any well or cistern had to be surrounded by a wall which was two and half palms from the ground so that no one would be endangered by the structure.[55] In earlier centuries, although more commonly in rural than urban areas, it was recognized that wells might act as

---

[44] Roberto Berveglieri, *Inventori stranieri*, p. 61.   [45] ASCG, PdC, 3-44 (1 July 1470).
[46] ASV, Comun b.10 reg 21 173r (9 September 1536).
[47] ASV, Comun b.1 234v (17 October 1519).   [48] ASV, Comun b.9 151r (30 June 1533).
[49] ASV, Comun b.5 reg 8 [unfoliated] (25 February 1567).
[50] ASV, Comun b.1 359v (8 August 1558).
[51] ASV, Comun b.13 reg 31 unpaginated (11 March 1559).
[52] ASCG, PdC, 11-43 (8 August 1519).   [53] ASCG, PdC, 22-90 (23 January 1555).
[54] ASCG. PdC, 19-207 (14 August 1548).   [55] *Statuti politici della citta di Savona*, p. 89.

86 CLEANING UP RENAISSANCE ITALY

'lethal booby traps for the unwary' and the cause of accidents and drownings.[56] Alexandra Bamji has shown that, in later centuries in Venice, people did fall into wells whilst drawing water as well as using them for suicide.[57]

The material culture of wells is sometimes recorded in archival sources as well as being represented in paintings such as the biblical story of the Samaritan woman at the well. In such images we can often see the chains with metal hooks from which people would hang their own wooden or metal vessels for gathering water. The structure of a well might also be altered to protect the quality of the water supply. In 1552, a grate was attached to a well in Carignano to prevent rubbish being thrown into it at night. Those nearby were permitted to have a key.[58] In other instances, key figures in the neighbourhood would be appointed as key holders and would be responsible for unlocking the well for those in the vicinity.[59] A well near the monastery of the Madonna dei Servi was being used for the disposal of rubbish because of the dimensions and design of the wellhead (which was described as very large and misshapen). The religious community offered to clean the well at their own expense, which (they noted) promised to be of huge benefit not only to themselves but also the neighbourhood and in the public good. The prior was also given permission to reduce the size of the public wellhead to a diameter of five palms.[60]

Wells were known to require regular cleaning.[61] In Savona, the statutes of the city instructed officials to oversee the cleaning of wells at least once every year and more often if necessary. The cleaning process was described as '*nettare, purgare et evacuare*'.[62] In Genoa, the steps necessary in order to cleanse a well were not always stipulated but in 1551, in relation to work on a well in Piazza del Vastato, the structure was to be swept and well cleaned (*spasare et ben netare*).[63] The same steps had been outlined in 1514 for a public well, which was also to be 'put in order' (*aconciare*) with repairs presumably being made to the physical structure in the process.[64] In 1571, a well in vico Macellari, in the district of the Pré, was said to be in need of clearing out and arranging (*evacuare et expedire*) because it was full of rubble and fetid water. The cleaning was desired by those in the neighbourhood so that they could make use of clean water for their general benefit. At the end of the proclamation relating to the cleaning of the well, the Padri reminded all

---

[56] Roberta J. Magnusson, *Water technology*, p. 136.

[57] Alexandra Bamji, 'Blowing smoke up your arse: drowning, resuscitation and public health in eighteenth-century Venice', *Bulletin for the History of Medicine* 94:1 (2020), 35.

[58] ASCG, PdC, 21-121 (3 August 1552).

[59] See, for example, ASCG, PdC, 28-39 (12 March 1567) when two shopkeepers were appointed in this way.

[60] ASCG, PdC, 29-223 (28 November 1569).

[61] On the cleaning of a well see ASCG, PdC, 10-95 (8 August 1514). See also the well-documented case in 2-114 (7 November 1571) from Pegli relating to private access to a water supply.

[62] *Statuti politici della citta di Savona*, p. 89.   [63] ASCG, PdC, 21-42 (9 July 1551).

[64] ASCG, PdC, 10-95 (8 August 1514).

PRESERVING PURITY 87

citizens that they were not to throw rubble, stones, or other rubbish into the well nor to wash directly in the well or by drawing the water from it.[65]

In Venice, the cleaning of communal wells was organized by the state and the workers (the *bastazi*) were organized by district. This group was also involved in public health work in a different context by carrying out some of the disinfection of merchandise in the city's plague hospitals.[66] In 1559, Signor Battista, in charge of the *bastazi* of San Polo was provided with a large vessel (*tomba*) in order to be able to drain the wells of the *sestiere*.[67] In 1585, it was noted that the equipment necessary to clean the wells was held by the parish priests. The tubs (*mastelle*), buckets (*sechi*), shovels (*badilli*), and other items were to be returned to the church after the cleaning had taken place.[68] This important work was recognized to expose cleaners to the unhealthy air. Tommaso Garzoni emphasized that well-cleaners needed to look after themselves well (*guardarsi bene*) because of the cold temperatures in which they worked below ground level and for the potential exposure to sulphur and alum (*solfore et allume*).[69] Depending on the condition of the well structure, they might also have been exposed to the sort of putrefaction which the physician Nicolo Massa noted in relation to the clearing of ditches which had been unused for a long time and were therefore full of putrid water.[70]

These interventions in the infrastructure of water supply were often requested by groups unified by their common use of an element of the built environment.[71] In 1509, a public well in Sarzano was said to have been badly maintained (*male curato*) and as a result the community derived little benefit or utility from the structure. Four individuals from the neighbourhood were chosen by residents to oversee the process of cleaning and restoring the well.[72] In Genoa in 1571 the costs of the cleaning of a well were split between sixty-two households giving a sense of the 'catchment' of this structure.[73] In exceptional circumstances, recommendations might be made for a city-wide clean of the wells such as in Venice following the advice of the physician Raimondo who recommended that the central chamber (*canna*) should be emptied and the drains which collected the rainwater (the *pilelle*) meticulously cleaned. In general, beyond the intended annual cleaning, the cleanliness and maintenance of communal wells was monitored and interventions were initiated at a local level.

---

[65] ASCG, PdC, 30-116 (4 May 1571).   [66] Jane L. Stevens Crawshaw, *Plague hospitals*, p. 225.
[67] ASV, Comun b.13 reg 31 117v (15 November 1559).
[68] ASV, Comun b.16 reg 36 unpaginated (16 May 1585).
[69] Tommaso Garzoni, *Piazza universale*, p. 845. For an interesting exploration of the health threats of working below ground in the specific context of mining see Guy Geltner and Claire Weeda, 'Underground and over the sea: more community prophylactics in Europe, 1100–1600', *Journal of the History of Medicine and Allied Sciences* 76:2 (2021), 123–46.
[70] *Ragionamento dello Eccellentissimo m Nicolo Massa sopra le infermita che vengono dall'aere pestilentiale del presente anno MDLV* (Venice, 1556), 24r.
[71] ASCG, PdC, 14-62 (7 August 1533).   [72] ASCG, PdC, 9-67 (23 July 1509).
[73] ASCG, PdC, 30-119 (10 May 1571).

88 CLEANING UP RENAISSANCE ITALY

In both Genoa and Venice, cisterns also formed an important part of the communal water supply. These structures facilitated rainwater collection but could also be filled from freshwater sources or, in Genoa, directly from the aqueduct.[74] Massimo Costantini has estimated that, in Venice during the sixteenth century, there were four thousand working cisterns which could have provided an estimated 5.5–6 litres of water per person per day.[75] One issue relating to the construction of cisterns was the lack of available urban space. In 1507, Ambrogio de Rovercho requested a licence to be able to construct a cistern underground in a small public alley in the Genoese district of the Molo near his home. The alley was said to be rarely frequented.[76]

The location of the cisterns was carefully regulated to prevent contamination of the water supply. In 1552, the cistern in the Piazza del Molo was restored by the Padri. An inscription attesting to the work emphasized that the cistern was for use by those living in the locality and for the crews of ships anchored in the port.[77] This structure had previously been abandoned because of its proximity to sources of contamination. The Padri del Comune had found the source, constructed a new channel, cleaned the reservoir, and issued the regulations to protect the water supply in the future. Accordingly, nothing was permitted to encroach upon the cistern. Sewers (*cloache*), sinks (*lavelli*), or drains (*condotti*) had to be situated at least twelve palms distant.[78] In 1557, citizens were reminded that they were not permitted to wash cloth or any other materials next to the cistern or to use the water for this purpose.[79]

On occasion, individuals and institutions were able to use the water from the civic aqueduct to fill their cisterns. In 1509, Pantalone Rebusso was given permission to fill the cistern which supplied his house in this way but it was emphasized that this water should not be used to serve his dye-house (*tentoria*).[80] In July 1563, the Padri del Comune granted a licence to the governors of the Incurabili hospital to use water from the public water supply to fill one of their cisterns.[81] The following summer the hospital was granted permission to use water from the aqueduct for the needs of the institution regardless of any city-wide restrictions in order to meet the needs of their patients.[82] In 1572 the Padri received a supplication on behalf of the hospital of the Pammatone where water was required

---

[74] Podestà records the 1510 discovery of an abundant freshwater source at *Ponte dei Cattani* which was channelled into a cistern for the population and a further inscription in *Il porto di Genova* pp. 165–6. Giustiniani describes the '*diane*' in Genoa which collected rainwater and fed cisterns as referenced in Paolo Stringa, *La strada dell'acque: l'acquedotto storico di Genova, tecnica ed architettura* (Genoa: Libreria Equilibri, 1980), p. 11.

[75] Massimo Costantini, *L'acqua di Venezia*, pp. 42–3.   [76] ASCG, PdC, 8-89 (14 June 1507).

[77] Francesco Podestà, *Il porto di Genova*, pp. 160–1.

[78] ASCG, PdC, 21-154 (21 November 1552).   [79] ASCG, PdC, 23-55 (14 July 1557).

[80] ASCG, PdC, 9-71 (27 August 1509).

[81] ASCG, PdC, 26-61 (26 July 1563). This was an ongoing problem and in September 1559 the cistern of the hospital was said to be depleted in 24–50 (5 September 1559).

[82] ASCG, PdC, 26-138 (18 August 1564).

particularly for cooking and drinking. Significant sums of money had previously been spent, and inconvenience incurred, in the transportation of water across large distances by barrel.[83] The ability to store sufficient water was vital, particularly for charitable institutions and the supply of these sites was prioritized in the management of the civic water infrastructure.

As with wells in both cities, the condition and form of cisterns were important for issues of both health and safety. In 1554, the Padri recorded that over the past few days two hens had fallen into the city's 'della Gratia' cistern. They were rescued 'with difficulty' to prevent them from ruining the water of the cistern.[84] In 1552, Genoese officials noted that children were throwing various types of rubbish into the cistern which had been constructed near the church of Sant'Agostino. Part of the problem was said to be large numbers of children who assembled in the square, particularly on feast days when it was a site for dancing. The Padri's response was to clamp down on the dancing and also to state in no uncertain terms that it was prohibited to throw anything into the cistern.[85]

As a result of its role in supplying cisterns and fountains, the Genoese aqueduct was vital for maintaining the balance and flow of water through the city.[86] Although such a structure was suggested in Venice from the fifteenth century, an aqueduct was not constructed there for another four hundred years.[87] The Genoese Padri attempted to protect the civic aqueduct and its water supply in a variety of ways. They prohibited the planting of trees and building of structures close to the main channel (which was not covered in its entirety until the nineteenth century).[88] In 1532, residents were forbidden from planting vines and trees, particularly figs and jasmine (gelsi) near the public aqueduct without observing the necessary distance of between ten and fifteen palms.[89] These plants were presumably singled out for their popularity as well as the scale of the disruption caused by leaves, fruits, and flowers which might fall into the water course. In 1564, these long-standing regulations were reiterated and included details about planting: that any tree near to the aqueduct had to be at least ten palms' distance. Figs, jasmine, and vines should be fifteen palms away. It was

---

[83] For Genoa's Ospedaletto see ASCG, PdC, 15-137 (24 May 1538).
[84] ASCG, PdC, 22-13 (18 April 1554).   [85] ASCG, PdC, 21-136 (14 September 1552).
[86] In 1491, the government noted the period of drought and proposed the establishment of a new magistracy with sole responsibility for the aqueduct. It would have been responsible for emptying the cisterns of the city and ensuring a good supply of water for the city but issues of fraud meant that the responsibilities were revoked and the Padri continued to be assigned this task. Francesco Podestà, L'acquedotto di Genova 1071–1879, p. 29. Claudio Guastoni, L'acquedotto civico di Genoa: un percorso al futuro (Milan: Franco Angeli, 2004) and Anna Decri, 'The historical aqueduct of Genoa: materials, techniques and history—a way to know' in Robert Carvais, André Guillerme, Valérie Nègre, and Joël Sakarovitch (eds), Nuts and bolts of construction history (Paris: Picard, 2012), vol. 1. For comparative material on Florence see Emanuela Ferretti, Acquedotti e fontane del Rinascimento in Toscana: acqua, architettura e città al tempo di Cosimo I dei Medici (Florence: L. S. Olschki, 2016).
[87] Massimo Costantini, L'acqua di Venezia, p. 39.   [88] ASCG, PdC, 1-175 (9 August 1466).
[89] ASCG, PdC, 13-249 (20 August 1532).

90 CLEANING UP RENAISSANCE ITALY

noted that the roots of such plants could damage the structure of the aqueduct and prevent the water from flowing freely. Those with land next to the aqueduct were instructed to have any trees or vines which were in contravention of the regulations cut back within eight days.[90]

It was not simply organic material which was a source of concern regarding blockages in the aqueduct. Domestic windows, gates, and openings which faced onto the aqueduct were closed to protect the quality and flow of the water.[91] At the end of the fifteenth century, Genoese residents were reminded that they were not permitted to remove the cover of the aqueduct channel, nor to wash any fabrics whether linen or wool in the water or to use the channel for the disposal of rubbish of any kind. Problems of this sort were said to be occurring on a daily basis.[92] In 1530, these restrictions were reiterated and residents were commanded that they should not even approach the structure of the aqueduct whilst carrying cloth, stone, or rubbish.[93] In 1561, the Padri had overseen work to cover the aqueduct in the city in order to conserve the water running through the channel so that it would be carried to the public fountains and issued instructions that no one was permitted to remove that covering in any part of the structure.[94] Nevertheless damage to the aqueduct was a frustratingly frequent problem for the authorities.[95]

Genoese officials managed the water infrastructure as a network. Cisterns in the city provided the Padri with an opportunity to regulate the flow of water through the aqueduct (and, by extension, the fountains) by encouraging residents to fill their cisterns in times when water was abundant in the system. In April 1540, a proclamation was issued to invite citizens to do this to avoid excess rainfall flowing into the port (and the sea).[96] Equally, officials were concerned about excess use of the civic water supply. It was often stated that citizens should not take water illegally, block the flow of public channels, or fill barrels (*botti*). The levels of use should, instead, correspond with that needed for drinking and for domestic purposes.[97] Individuals were not entitled to draw off water for irrigation unless they were given licence to do so because of the quantities of water involved in such work.[98] In 1460, for example, the Padri instructed that no one was permitted to draw water from the aqueduct and store it for their own land, possessions, or garden.[99] The Padri emphasized that these things had not been habitual or traditional uses (*non se sono solito fare per la tempi passata*) and had

[90] ASCG, PdC, 26-116 (13 May 1564).
[91] ASCG, PdC, 13-161 (5 June 1532) and 13-223 (14 December 1532).
[92] ASCG, PdC, 6-142 (4 April 1497).   [93] ASCG, PdC, 13-55 (9 March 1530).
[94] ASCG, PdC, 25-7 (2 February 1561).
[95] ASCG, PdC, 1-198 (29 July 1467), 21-110 (10 June 1552), 29-182 (6 August 1569), 29-183 (11 August 1569), and 29-198 (1 September 1569).
[96] ASCG, PdC, 16-20 (7 April 1540).
[97] ASCG, PdC, 3-39 (13 June 1470), 3-62 (19 June 1471), 3-77 (18 February 1472), and 3-121 (29 July 1474).
[98] ASCG, PdC, 5-20 (25 June 1481).
[99] ASCG, PdC, 1-169 (5 May 1460) and see also 11-179 (4 January 1524).

the consequence of overburdening the system. They instructed residents that they were only to draw water for drinking and for domestic use in a way which was honest and convenient.[100] In the Bisagno, individuals were permitted to draw directly from the river in order to irrigate their gardens.[101]

Access to the water of the aqueduct was regulated via structures known as *bronzini*—pipes with an internal diameter of one twentieth of a Genoese '*palmo*' (12.4mm).[102] These *bronzini* were part of the structure of public fountains as well as made available for private access.[103] Paolo Stringa has published a volume brimming with technical detail on this structure and has calculated that each of these *bronzini* could have supplied approximately thirty people, meaning that about one-fortieth of the population could have received water through these in 1531.[104] *Bronzini* could be given as acts of charity to hospitals and religious institutions or as gifts or acts of political diplomacy.[105]

More generally, permissions to use the water from the public aqueduct had to be requested and renewed and could be withdrawn.[106] In 1459, the Padri began a process which was repeated over the following years, which was to request all of those who possessed a *bronzino* from the aqueduct for personal use to present their permit to the office within fifteen days.[107] By establishing a system of licensing for the water supply, the Padri del Comune could summon holders of licences into the offices of the magistracy when changes needed to be communicated. The names of those who complied were recorded and their licences renewed; those who did not lost their access.

One detailed list of those with access to the Genoese water supply survives from 1519.[108] The date of the visit to the office is recorded, along with the name of the individual bringing the permit; in some cases, documents were brought on behalf of others but it was not specified why. In some cases, information is provided regarding the purpose of the access, for example to service a home in the city or beyond the walls, a religious institution or a place of work, including taverns ('*taberna*') and dye-houses ('*tintoria*'). At first glance, the list appears to contain standardized entries. A closer look, however, reveals that there were significant differences in the type of access to the aqueduct, the material of the *bronzini* and

---

[100] ASCG, PdC, 8-103 (16 October 1507).   [101] ASCG, PdC, 26-47 (12 June 1563).

[102] Claudio Guastoni, *L'acquedotto civico*, p. 133.

[103] ASCG, PdC 13-54 (8 March 1530), 14-45 (19 May 1533), and 14-174 (18 June 1535).

[104] Paolo Stringa, *La strada dell'acque*, p. 23 notes this calculation regarding supply. In theory, the *bronzini* would have supplied approximately 1,300 people at this time and were given for domestic as well as industrial use. ASCG, PdC, 2-78 (14 January 1569).

[105] ASCG, PdC, 1-168 (5 May 1466) and 26-129 (17 July 1564) which is a gift to the Spanish ambassador. On water gifts in Rome see Katherine Rinne, *The waters of Rome*, p. 77 and 183. Here the volume of water was described in terms of the diameter of the pipe delivering the water (*uncia* or *oncia* which equated to 2cm). See also Pamela O. Long, 'Hydraulic engineering', p. 1109 n. 31.

[106] ASCG, PdC, 19-198-1 (2 July 1548).

[107] ASCG, PdC, 1-23 (19 March 1459). See also 1-148 (31 May 1465) and 1-170 (12 June 1466).

[108] ASCG, PdC, 11-26 (26 January 1519).

92 CLEANING UP RENAISSANCE ITALY

the degree to which private individuals literally marked their access using symbols. Of the 118 access points, forty-seven were made of silver and thirty-five of gold. Over a third of the entries (41) relate to a single silver *taciam*. Twenty of these were marked with symbols and one specified the cost, suggesting a particularly high value.

The Padri's oversight of the *bronzini* in the city was one of the principal ways in which the magistracy regulated the water supply of the city. Officials regularly instructed that the *bronzini* should be closed because of conditions deemed to be persistent drought (*persistente siccità*) to ensure that public fountains continued to be provided with water.[109] This would apply in the city and wider territory and the *bronzini* were intended to be sealed (*chioder e serrar*) with lead.[110] By the 1560s, the seasonality of these closures was so clear that they were discussed as part of the management of the civic water supply during the summer (generally May to September). Proclamations expressed, for example, that 'the time had come for access to the aqueduct to be closed'.[111] Closures might also be introduced beyond the summer too.[112] At the end of January 1552, the Padri recorded that water was so scarce that the public fountains were dry. This was said to be particularly devastating for the poor, who lacked cisterns in their houses.[113] There is no doubt that the impact of periods of drought was felt unevenly within the population. In Genoa, the display of water in ornate grottos became part of the magnificent display of elites. Stephanie Hanke has observed that, restrictions on the supply from the aqueduct meant that 'the staging of water games, especially during the summer...became a luxury reserved only for the richest members of the upper class'.[114]

The structure of the aqueduct encompassed areas within and beyond the city. As a result, restricted access posed a challenge to the Padri in terms of effective monitoring and enforcement particularly beyond the city walls.[115] In July 1572, a representative of the Padri travelled to Montaldo in order to ensure that the regulations regarding the aqueduct had been adhered to.[116] He discovered multiple examples of *bronzini* which had not been closed and were still being used to fill cisterns or irrigate land. In one instance, the *bronzino* showed signs of having been very recently sealed with fresh mortar (*calcina frescha*) rather than lead.

---

[109] ASCG, PdC, 1-179 (18 September 1466); 19-24 (9 June 1545); 19-198-1 (2 July 1548); 20-135 (31 May 1550); 21-101 (19 May 1552); 22-20 (09 May 1554); 22-180 (07 May 1556); 23-139 (27 July 1558); 25-112 (21 July 1562); 27-34 (15 June 1565); 27-227 (1 January 1566); 30-115 (4 May 1571).

[110] ASCG, PdC, 21-193 (5 June 1553).

[111] ASCG, PdC 27-34 (15 June 1565) '*sieno venutto il tempo che si doveno serrare li pertusi dell'aqueduto*', 29-35 (21 June 1568), and 29-169 (23 June 1569).

[112] ASCG, PdC 2-54 (8 February 1518) and 24-151 (30 December 1560).

[113] ASCG, PdC, 21-83 (30 January 1552).

[114] Stephanie Hanke, 'The splendour of bankers', 414.

[115] ASCG, PdC, 21-101 (19 May 1552) and 29-187 (17 August 1569) is the report of the Padri's *cavallero* about a *pertuxo*.

[116] ASCG, PdC, 31-81 (23 July 1572).

PRESERVING PURITY 93

In another property a large fishpond appeared suspiciously well-supplied with water. The official was not always able to gain access to properties but the report attests to the ease with which regulations were circumvented. Individuals might place the priorities and needs of the household above those of the community when deciding whether to heed the instructions which were issued from the capital.

The attempted regulation of the water supply, then, required oversight of the use of water within and beyond the city to preserve the supply to the eleven public fountains located in squares across Genoa.[117] These were often marked as public structures, as in 1569 when parts of the fountain at Portanove had been replaced in bronze and the arms of the commune were carved in marble with an inscription so that it might be demarcated in perpetuity as a public fountain.[118] The preservation of the quality of the water in these fountains required extensive intervention by the Padri. In December 1499, the water in the fountain of San Toma was said to be muddy and fetid. This was thought to be caused by nearby drains or latrines (*fosse da necessari*). The Padri instructed residents who had drains, latrines, or any other channel in their houses and residences that they must ensure that these did not damage, impede, or corrupt this water.[119] The fountain at the Molo was the focus for public works in 1428 and 1552.[120] This vital fountain, which supplied local residents as well as ships, had required urgent action to clean it in order to return the water to a usable, consumable state. Problems had been caused by nearby sewage channels from latrines, sinks, and sewers. The work was said to be for the benefit of all, but particularly important for meeting the needs of the poor during the summer. In order to avoid paying out significant sums for similar work in the future, the Padri rendered a plaque to be posted about the fountain which reminded everyone that rubbish should not be thrown into the system.[121] Despite this, many young people were said to continue to do this, for the basic pleasure they took in doing something they should not.[122]

Despite efforts to distinguish the elements of the civic infrastructure, these structures were frequently damaged both by animals in the city and theft. Animals were not allowed to be tethered to fountains but it is clear that this regulation was often contravened. In the Porta di Sant'Andrea, mules and other beasts were being tied to the *cannoni* of the fountain, which was prohibited, as was leaving these

[117] These are the fountains at Porta di Vacca, Santo Marcellino, Spinoli (Ponte di Spinola), Dogana chiapa di l'olio, Ponte delli coltellieri, Molo, Sarzano, Porta da Sant'Andrea, Porta Aurea, and Palacio as listed in ASCG, PdC, 13-54 (8 March 1530). The fountains are of different scales, with the fountain at the *Molo* having eight *canoni di Genoa* and a number of the others with just two. The fountains are also listed in, for example, ASCG, PdC, 12-77 (6 December 1527) and 20-162 (1 January 1551).
[118] ASCG, PdC, 29-194 (27 August 1569).   [119] ASCG, PdC, 6-216 (20 December 1499).
[120] ASCG, PdC, 221-293 (s.d.). These are seventeenth-century transcriptions of the earlier inscriptions.
[121] ASCG, PdC, 221-293 (25 October 1552).   [122] ASCG, PdC, 21-155 (23 November 1552).

94 CLEANING UP RENAISSANCE ITALY

animals unattended in the street (whether tethered or not).[123] The theft of the apparatus from public fountains was an ongoing challenge for the Padri. In 1527, officials responded to thefts of the *bronzini* from public fountains. The proclamation noted that the majority of the *cannoni* had been removed and stolen, frustrating efforts to ensure public comfort and benefit, particularly for the poor who lacked access to water in their own homes. Information on the thefts was requested from artisans who might have been offered the *bronzini* for sale.[124] These records represent an obvious clash between public and private interests, whereby those who stole the fixtures of the fountain believed that they could do more to further their financial interests and wellbeing than the effective operation of the civic water supply by the Padri. In response, a guard and custodian of the public fountains and *canoni* was appointed, as elsewhere in Europe, to ensure that these structures remained well equipped and maintained. The first was a tin-smith (*stagnaro*) called Pantolino de la Plazia. He was presumably thought to possess the necessary practical skills to ensure careful maintenance of the structures.[125] Indeed, the tin-smiths were one of the professions tasked with denouncing individuals who attempted to sell stolen fittings from the public fountains.[126] Issues of theft continued, however. In 1572, residents living close to the fountain at the Pré (where two *cannoni* had recently been broken as a result of attempted theft) were reminded that they should take all possible care of the fountain fittings ('*per quanto sara in loro poter haver buona cura*') and any future repairs would be charged to the community.[127]

Regulations in Genoa accord with those of towns and cities elsewhere on the peninsula to preserve the quality of the water supply.[128] In Perugia, stone vases were provided for people to wash their jugs and receptacles before collecting water from the main fountain.[129] We know that *broche* (pitchers) were provided in Genoa since, in 1565, it was noted that these had been stolen from the *cannoni* of the public fountains.[130] Animals were not permitted to drink from fountain basins because of issues of cleanliness. Instead, they should use the drinking troughs provided. In Genoa, in 1520, it was emphasized that these troughs were set aside for mules, horses, and any other animals. The vessels were located in two key areas of the city (Porta dei Vacca and on the Ponte Chiavari).[131] Any animals in the western part of the city were intended to use the former and those in the east should travel to the latter.[132]

---

[123] ASCG, PdC, 7-74 (8 July 1501).   [124] ASCG, PdC, 12-77 (6 December 1527).

[125] ASCG, PdC, 12-77 (6 December 1527) and, for guards elsewhere see Roberta J. Magnusson, *Water technology*, p. 134.

[126] Tin-smiths are mentioned alongside *merscaro*, blacksmith (*ferraro*), *chiapucio*, inn keepers (*tavernario*), and 'any other artisans' in ASCG, PdC, 12-77 (6 December 1527).

[127] ASCG, PdC, 31-97 (29 August 1572).   [128] Katherine Rinne, *The waters of Rome*, p. 156.

[129] Francesca Bocchi, 'Regulation of the urban environment', p. 74.

[130] ASCG, PdC, 27-36 (27 June 1565).

[131] Reiterated in ASCG, PdC, 13-100 (8 March 1531) and 13-149 (12 January 1532).

[132] ASCG, PdC, 11-63 (16 March 1520).

Access to public fountains was seen as an important right. In 1499, a resident in Albaro had constructed a wall around a public fountain on the public street and was ordered to remove it, in response to complaints from other residents.[133] The intersection of public resources with private land might result in complex and tense contestations.[134] In 1526, the Padri heard petitions relating to a long-standing issue from Santa Maria de Monte Carmelo relating to water that flowed through the garden of the Carmine and the property of David Giordano. This was to be made accessible to the locality via a receptacle in the wall of Giardano's garden. He was required to keep this full of clear and clean water but was accused of deliberately failing to do so.[135] In 1573, the residents of Vallechiara referred back to this ruling regarding the water from the spring situated in the ditch (*fossato*) at Santa Marta and noted the delays that had occurred and requested a new instruction regarding the provision of water for the community.[136]

In larger bodies of water, a variety of materials and objects could cause dangerous and unhealthy obstructions. Across premodern Europe, the construction of bridges was recognized to be an issue which needed to be handled with care. Such structures were essential to facilitate movement and transit into or around a city and played a particularly vital role in Venice. Bridges could also, however, impede the flow of the water, catch rubbish and cause siltation, depending on their form. In Andrea Bacci's account of the 1557 flood of the Tiber, he described the narrowness and low level of the arches of the bridges as one factor which had impeded the flow of the water.[137] The use of bridges by inhabitants might also cause issues. In Genoa in 1566, the Padri sought to have *golette* (schooners) removed from the Ponte dei Cattanei and a few years later reported with frustration that Ponte Spinola was said to be being used to tether boats which were creating an impediment.[138] In Venice building works might also restrict the flow of water in the canals on a temporary or more permanent basis because of scaffolding which was installed. Furthermore, the Comun described 'a terrible and damnable corruption' which had developed whereby new buildings were constructed which exceeded their former footprint and caused a constriction of space either in the canals or the public streets.[139]

In Venice only one bridge spanned the Grand Canal, at Rialto, until 1854. In a publication of 1588 the bridge itself complained that 'nearly the whole world | I have had on my back | while they went on their way | And more than ever I am

---

[133] ASCG, PdC, 6-208 (3 October 1499).
[134] ASCG, PdC, 1-80 (1 September 1460) and 1-166 (7 March 1466).
[135] ASCG, PdC, 12-30 (26 October 1526).   [136] ASCG, PdC, 32-13 (13 February 1573).
[137] Pamela Long, *Engineering the Eternal City*, p. 27.
[138] ASCG, PdC, 27-131 (30 April 1566) and 31-84 (1 August 1572).
[139] ASV, Comun b.2, 222v (1 October 1585).

96 CLEANING UP RENAISSANCE ITALY

trampled on | but I am groaning from every side'.[140] It existed as a pontoon bridge until the end of the fourteenth century. It was then replaced by a permanent wooden structure which collapsed under the weight of the crowds of spectators watching a naval procession honouring the marquis of Ferrara in 1444.[141] The bridge was rebuilt, in wood, with a drawbridge in the centre and lined with shops, as on the Ponte Vecchio in Florence. It was not constructed in stone until 1591, under the supervision of the appropriately named Antonio da Ponte. The Water Office received models from at least 1546 and supplications emphasized the form, strength of the bridge designs, as well as the extent to which the foundations or supports would impede the flow of the water.[142]

In Venice in this period the Provveditori di Comun oversaw the conversion of other bridges from wood to stone and also the replacement of some in wood. Tommaso Porcacchi estimated that there were four hundred public and private bridges in the city.[143] Francesco Sansovino suggested that the change of material for bridges was partly stimulated by a desire to replace flat wooden bridges with arched stone structures to allow the easier passage of gondola boats which included a cabin (felce).[144] Stone bridges were widely recognized to be more robust. In 1566, for example, Jacomo di Ludovico funded a stone bridge in San Marcuola in place of wooden bridge at the cost of 255 ducats. He became a creditor of the Comun for half of the cost because of the perceived comfort, benefit, and ornament to the city. The Comun noted a clear financial benefit for the state because when the bridge was made of wood there was a need for repeated maintenance which would have been the responsibility of the government.[145] In Genoa, a similar process took place of replacing wooden with stone bridges in some key locations, such as the Ponte della Mercanzia, during the fifteenth century.[146] This was said to be important given the vulnerability of the bridge to the impact of storms and heavy rain, as well as its proximity to the Customs House, presumably indicating heavy traffic. As considered in the previous chapter, bridges in Venice might represent symbolic dividing lines between districts and became an important site for rituals of popular culture particularly after the conversion of wooden to more robust stone bridges.[147]

Changes to the location or material of bridges might be done in the name of preserving the safety of those passing through the city. In 1540, Andrea Rizo and

---

[140] Cited in Rosa Salzberg, 'The margins in the centre: working around Rialto in sixteenth-century Venice' in Andrew Spicer and Jane Stevens Crawshaw (eds), *The place of the social margins, 1350–1750* (London: Routledge, 2017), p. 137.

[141] Robert C. Davis, *The war of the fists*, p. 15.   [142] ASV, SEA, 119, 6r and 170f (1546).

[143] Tommaso Porcacchi, *L'isole piu famose del mondo* (Venice, 1576) p. 66. Gianighian and Pavanini have estimated that today approximately a quarter of the 450 bridges in the city serve a private function in Giorgio Gianighian and Paola Pavanini, *Venezia come*, p. 22.

[144] Robert C. Davis, *War of the fists*, p. 15.

[145] ASV, Comun b.14 reg 33 280v (28 February 1566).

[146] ASCG, PdC, 5-112 (18 December 1485).   [147] Robert C. Davis, *War of the fists*, p. 16.

his brothers sent a petition regarding a house in San Martino. On the wall facing their property were two very old brackets, which, it was said, could have served no purpose other than to support a bridge which would have stretched from the house to the *fondamenta*. The brothers claimed that this bridge was likely to have burned during a fire at Rialto and they sought to reinstate it for their own benefit and also for the safety (*salute*) of those who, at night, came from the Grand Canal along the streets. This route was said to be full of obstacles, causing a number of people to drown.[148]

Bridges might also cause bottlenecks in terms of the movement of people around a city particularly if the available space was used to dump materials. In Genoa builders were reminded not to leave stones and marble on bridges.[149] At other times, it might be the potential congregation of people which prompted concern. In July 1560, the Comun caught wind of a party which was being planned by a Venetian courtesan, called Donna Tiberia. Donna Tiberia was one of the *cortigiane oneste* (honest courtesans), famous amongst both tourists and inhabitants of early modern Venice.[150] On Sunday 7 July, Donna Tiberia received a visit from the captain of the Comun, notable since the lower-paid messenger (*fante*) was often responsible for communication. Donna Tiberia lived near the wooden bridge at San Girolamo in Cannaregio—on the northern outskirts of the city.[151] The captain explained that the authorities feared that the anticipated throng of partygoers would cause the neighbourhood's wooden bridge to collapse.[152] Donna Tiberia's is the only instance uncovered to date of the authorities being concerned that a private party would have such an impact on part of the city's urban fabric. She was warned that if she went ahead with the party and the bridge collapsed, all of the repairs would be made at her expense.[153] It is not clear whether the party went ahead and the bridge managed to withstand the pressure or the event was cancelled—the snippety response (*sel si rompera il cozero*) of Donna Tiberia suggests that she did not plan to stump up the money even if the bridge was affected.

The infrastructure of water supply naturally took distinct forms in Genoa and Venice but the priorities and challenges for the authorities in providing water of sufficient quality and quantity necessitated the regulation of both space and

---

[148] ASV, Comun b.10 reg 23 7r (1 April 1540).

[149] ASCG, PdC, 3-59 (21 May 1471) and 3-84 (30 April 1472). For the instructions to builders see 8-71 (1 July 1506).

[150] Margaret Rosenthal, *The honest courtesan: Veronica Franco, citizen and writer in sixteenth-century Venice* (Chicago IL: University of Chicago Press, 1992), p. 2.

[151] An excellent resource on the residence of Venetian courtesans in 1565 has been produced by Hannah Johnston and can be found on the history blog: https://historyjournal.org.uk/2022/01/05/a-sexual-tour-of-venice-mapping-a-sixteenth-century-catalogue-of-courtesans/. Donna Tiberia does not feature but other courtesans are mentioned in San Girolamo.

[152] *et questo perche essendo il ponte dl legno debile per il concorso dl populo alla ditta festa e per ruinar.*

[153] ASV, Comun, b.14 reg 32 23r (8 July 1560).

98 CLEANING UP RENAISSANCE ITALY

behaviour. Significant sums of money were spent supporting a network of supply which underpinned domestic and economic life in the city. Many of those essential tasks were located in homes and workplaces but some required additional space and resources, particularly washing and laundry which feature frequently in regulations.

Worries about Washing

In Venice in 1551, officials in Venice reflected on the work of their predecessors in office who had enhanced the beauty and comfort of the city by paving squares, streets, and *fondamente*, as well as constructing bridges and wells. The latter gave '*il comodo del acqua*' to residents and most especially the poor. This good work was said to be being extended on a daily basis in the city, at significant cost to the office.[154] One practice which was essential for health but threatened both the quantity and quality of the water supply was washing.[155] Prohibitions on the use of water from the public network for washing cloth were a common feature of proclamations, particularly in the summer because of the high quantity of water involved.[156]

References to washing in archival sources principally concern the washing of cloth rather than skin. The doctor Paschetti noted that the adoption of linen underwear (*le camiscie*) and its positive impact on the cleanliness of the body had reduced the need for bathing.[157] In Genoa, a number of elite palaces had bathing rooms built from the second half of the sixteenth century, including in the Palazzo Angelo Giovanni Spinola by Giovanni Ponzello from 1558 to 1564.[158] Public bath houses had existed in the city earlier and Ennio Poleggio has noted that one with a courtyard for ball games was proposed in 1559 near to the Porta Portello.[159] As a number of studies have shown, the focus for personal cleanliness lay on washing clothes rather than the skin and the issue of laundry in the Renaissance city was one which was closely regulated because of its potential to corrupt the network of water supplies. The belief that clothes played a role in removing dirt from the body meant that washing was a process which was seen to produce considerable quantities of filth which needed to be kept out of civic water supplies.

These concerns about washing included but went beyond fabric. In 1563, the Padri issued a proclamation in response to the problem of *le trippe* (tripe) being

---

[154] ASV, Comun, reg 1 343r (10 September 1551).

[155] Michele Robinson, 'Dirty laundry: caring for clothing in early modern Italy', *Costume* 55:1 (2021), 3–23.

[156] ASCG, PdC, 31-97 (29 August 1572).

[157] Stephanie Hanke, 'Bathing *all'antica*: bathrooms in Genoese villas and palaces in the sixteenth century', *Renaissance Studies* 20:5 (2006), 679–80 and Susan North, *Sweet and clean?*

[158] Stephanie Hanke, 'Bathing *all'antica*'.

[159] Cited in Stephanie Hanke, 'Bathing *all'antica*', 676.

washed at various places in the city's port. This was described as 'extremely damaging' because tripe was said to be 'full of filth' (*sempre piene de immondicie*). It was emphasized that between the Molo and the lighthouse of Capo di Faro tripe should not be washed in this way.[160] Regulations on washing wool, in particular, stemmed from concern that the water would be corrupted by products used in fulling raw wool before it was spun, such as alum and urine.[161] Concerns also extended to the locations used to soak (*amogio*) animal pelts.[162]

In 1572 the Padri received a supplication on behalf of the hospital of the Pammatone which stated that greater quantities of water were required by the institution, not only to meet its day-to-day needs but also to allow patients to wash linen for pious citizens of the city.[163] This was said to benefit the hospital, by occupying the resident children and young women in this work. It was also said be of broader communal advantage because if the linen was passed to the washer-women to wash in the Bisagno, it would be marked in the process. Washing was seen to be an appropriate form of work in both charitable and religious institutions. During the sixteenth century, laundries were built in convents and monasteries both to serve the resident communities and provide opportunities to supplement their income. Sometimes the symbolism of this was articulated explicitly. Katherine Rinne has cited an instance of a laundry basin built in 1576 for the monastery of Santa Maria in Campo Marzio with the inscription 'Since you clean white linen here | you have also cleaned your conscience' ['*Si come panni bianchi qui voi fate | Le consciencie monde aver curate*'].[164]

Most of the laundry work in the Renaissance city was carried out by women, often working in pairs or groups. These women were recognized to be vulnerable in the course of carrying out this essential work.[165] On occasion, abuse directed by men towards these women reached the attention of the Genoese Padri del Comune. Two women, Bianca and Nicoletta, were said to be being harassed by a certain Gregorio whilst washing cloth and spreading it out to dry next to the river.[166] Three years later, another unpleasant character, Giovanni Battista Sciaccalugo was ordered to avoid harassing and hindering the women who dried cloth on the shoreline (*greto*) of the river at Sturla.[167] Whilst washing might be dried at the same site it was washed, it was also placed by women on roofs and balconies for the latter purpose.[168]

---

[160] ASCG, PdC, 26-77 (27 September 1563).   [161] Katherine Rinne, *The waters of Rome*, p. 171.
[162] ASCG, PdC, 23-52 (12 July 1557).   [163] ASCG, PdC, 2-116 (13 January 1572).
[164] Katherine Rinne *The waters of Rome*, p. 177.
[165] On washerwomen, see Douglas Biow, 'Soap and washerwomen' in *The culture of cleanliness*, pp. 95–143 and Carole Rawcliffe, 'A marginal occupation? The medieval laundress and her work', *Gender & History* 21:1 (2009), 147–69.
[166] ASCG, PdC, 30-112 (27 April 1571).   [167] ASCG, PdC, 33-32 (26 April 1574).
[168] Alessandro Allori, *Women at work around a balcony* from Florence, Palazzo Pitti (1587–90) shown in Michele Robinson, 'Dirty laundry', p. 11. ASCG, PdC, 9-85 (12 November 1509).

100 CLEANING UP RENAISSANCE ITALY

Despite the opportunities to utilize the services of individuals and institutions for laundry it is clear that a significant number of residents continued to do their own.[169] Women's domestic recipe books included a large number of stain removal treatments.[170] Although this was essential domestic work, it became a focus for government regulation. From 1460, it had been made clear to the inhabitants of Genoa that it was prohibited to do washing in the channels of the aqueduct, whether within the walls of the city or beyond.[171] There were similar restrictions on fountains, wells, and cisterns.[172] In Sarzano in 1570, residents were reminded that they were not permitted to do washing on a step (*scalino*) belonging to Battista Magiolo because of the 'prejudice' this was causing to him and his home. Nevertheless these practices endured. In 1600, the cistern at Sarzano was said to be being used by men and women alike to provide water to soak lime and wash cloth and other work contrary to its purpose, which was to supply the poor and for basic sustenance.[173] Concerns about an adequate supply of water applied within and beyond the city.[174] In 1507, the Padri described a fountain situated on a public road near the Villa di Casamavari. A 'poor habit' (*pessima usanza*) was said to have developed in the neighbourhood and wider district in which the water from the fountain was used for the washing not only of small but also sizeable pieces of cloth and to irrigate gardens. The consequence was that water supply was often depleted. Residents and those in surrounding areas were reminded that the water should be used only for drinking and domestic purposes in a way which was 'honest and convenient'.[175]

Concerns about the pollution of the water supply, by utilizing structures for the wrong purpose, were articulated acutely.[176] Trades which worked with furs and fabrics were perceived to pose particular risk. In 1413, Venice's Maggior Consiglio had declared that dyers should not carry out their trade 'within the city' but instead on the outskirts. The products used in cloth dying, such as '*guado*' and '*sanguine*' were raised as particularly concerning regarding the production of corruption within the air.[177] Many of these trades also utilized large quantities of water. In Venice in 1536 a number of trades were prohibited from using water

---

[169] Patricia Fortini Brown, 'The Venetian *casa*' in Marta Ajmar-Wollheim and Flora Dennis (eds), *At home in Renaissance Italy* notes on p. 53 that patrician palaces might have laundry rooms on the ground floor and records that an inventory of one belonging to Piero Gritti included nine tubs, large and small, with their washboards. She also finds evidence of open courtyards being used for this purpose. In other instances wealthy Venetian families carried out large-scale laundry at their country estate rather than in the city, presumably because there was more space for drying than was available on an *altane*.

[170] Sandra Cavallo, 'Health, hygiene and beauty' in Marta Ajmar-Wollheim and Flora Dennis (eds), *At home in Renaissance Italy*, p. 176.

[171] ASCG, PdC, 3-21 (1 September 1469).

[172] ASCG, PdC, 3-30 (9 January 1470) and 9-131 (6 June 1510).

[173] ASCG, PdC, 221-122 (30 June 1600).

[174] ASCG, PdC, 1-169 (5 May 1460) '*de fora como dentro de la cita*'.

[175] ASCG, PdC, 8-103 (16 October 1507).   [176] Susan North, *Sweet and clean?* p. 273.

[177] *Venezia e la peste*, p. 118 and 364.

PRESERVING PURITY   101

from public wells: dyers, barbers, tripe sellers (*tripperi*), tanners (*pellizzeri*), laundry-workers (*lavanderi*), soap makers (*saonieri*), and sausage makers (*luganegheri*), providing a clear sense of those trades associated with filthy by-products and materials.[178] In Genoa in 1469, leather workers were forbidden from soaking hides and skins in the tub near to the aqueduct at Porta dei Vacca until the vessel had been repaired and returned to its pristine state.[179] Cordwainers (leather shoemakers) and tanners were required to provide a vessel in their workshops which would collect dirty water so that it could be properly disposed of.[180] Accusations were made against those working in these trades in relation to the corruption of public water supplies. In 1490, for example, a silk dyer was accused of having polluted (*inquinato*) a well in the district of Curlo.[181] Such trades were intended to utilize separate structures from those on which the water supply for the city relied.

The structures for removing filth from these two ports reflected an understanding of the tides and meant that any polluted materials needed to enter the waterways at key locations. These might be symbolic, such as areas beyond the Venetian *lidi* and therefore beyond the boundaries of the city.[182] In dealing with the by-products of artisanal and domestic processes, however, it was also believed to be vital that waste and pollution entered these bodies of water at a location from which they would be removed by the tides.[183] One way in which this channelling of waste took place was through the structures of drains.

Down the Drain

Urban drainage was intended to operate as a system distinct to that of water supply.[184] In Venice, domestic drains (*gatoli*) were holes which allowed materials to pass from pipes into the canals of the city from domestic dwellings as well as the apertures which allowed water to enter the purification system of wells. The officials of the Venetian Republic observed that the siltation of the canals, corruption of the air, and outbreaks of illness were partly being caused by the fact that

---

[178] Giuseppe Tassini, *Curiosità veneziane*, p. 241. The *saoneri* (soapmakers) were particularly clustered in San Polo and formed a company in 1565 in Giuseppe Tassini, *Curiosità veneziane*, p. 650.

[179] ASCG, PdC, 3-21 (1 September 1469).   [180] ASCG, PdC, 10-9 (15 July 1512).

[181] ASCG, PdC, 6-18 (15 July 1490).

[182] John Jeffries Martin, *Venice's hidden enemies: Italian heretics in a Renaissance city* (Berkeley CA: University of California Press, 1993), p. 69.

[183] In Rome, corpses, including those of murder victims, were dumped in the Tiber in Katherine Rinne, *The waters of Rome*, p. 24 and the ashes of the Dominican friar Girolamo Savonarola and his companions were thrown into the Arno to ensure that no relics would survive in Fabrizio Nevola, *Street life*, p. 265.

[184] Subterranean drains in the city were variously referred to as *condutto*, *canale*, *conilio*, *quintana*, *cloacha*, *chiavica*, and *bendo*.

102   CLEANING UP RENAISSANCE ITALY

the *gatoli* were continuously full of sludge and other rubbish.[185] This was despite money being allocated by the Comun to the cleaners of the districts.

The networks of drains in both cities were known to include both public and private elements, both of which required maintenance and cleaning. In 1535, Piero Spicier in Rio Marin was instructed to clean up the *gatolo* in front of his door.[186] The consequences of a failure to care for any element of the network this could be very damaging for buildings nearby. In Genoa, for example those who lived in homes which used the drain (*chiavica*) at the Molo were commanded to pay for its cleaning to avoid damage to the salt warehouses nearby.[187] The drains of neighbours also intersected: in 1550, Mattio Botto was instructed to deal with one of his *gattoli*, the opening of which passed into that of his neighbours Zuan Alberto and Zuane Basso.[188]

In 1505 a drain close to the Genoese salt warehouses, which served a number of properties, was said to threaten to pollute the surrounding area if it was not cleaned; the cost of this operation was to be met by those who lived in houses with pipes which flowed into it.[189] In 1567, in Rivo Turbido the streets were said to be being flooded with filth from a sewer which needed to be emptied and repaired (*evacuare et espedire*).[190] It was clear that these situations were horrendous both for those living in the vicinity and those passing through the streets.[191] The following year, a broken drain, which served many houses, was said to be causing filth to spew across the main square in Colla Soprana.[192] Earlier that year a full drain near the breakwater had caused the rubbish from many properties to flow into the streets.[193] By the end of the 1560s, the sewer network in Genoa was under considerable strain.

Behaviour in the city did not help. In the same decade, rubbish was said to be being continuously thrown out of the windows onto empty plots of land. In times of rainfall, this rubbish could be carried into public drains. In one instance this was observed to be happening at the intersection between the drain and the smaller channels of the latrines of the district. The rubbish was causing this flow to be impeded and the cost of clearing the drain would be significant. The owners of the land requested a proclamation stating that nothing should be thrown from the windows onto the empty plot or the roofs of surrounding buildings.[194] Habits did not always keep pace with changes of infrastructure. In 1557, residents were reminded not to throw rubbish, stones, rubble, or any other material in the place

---

[185] ASV, Comun reg 1 100v (11 February 1485).

[186] ASV, Comun b.10 reg 21 89r (16 September 1535).

[187] ASCG, PdC 8-46 (08 July 1505). Known as '*conilio*' into which a number of conduits and drains ran.

[188] ASV, Comun b.12 reg 27 69r (27 October 1550).   [189] ASCG, PdC, 8-46 (8 July 1505).

[190] ASCG, PdC, 28-130 (3 December 1567). Similar situation in Carrogio de Piuma in the district of the Prè in 28–140 (22 December 1567).

[191] ASCG, PdC, 26-164 (12 December 1564).   [192] ASCG, PdC, 29-69 (10 September 1568).

[193] ASCG, PdC, 29-14 (25 March 1568).   [194] ASCG, PdC, 26-108 (18 March 1564).

PRESERVING PURITY 103

where a drain had recently been constructed close to the Pammatone hospital.[195] Sensibly, in 1501, the residents of the district of the Campeto wanted to open and reconstruct a drain in the traditional location as used '*per lo tempo passato*'.[196]

There were not simply concerns about blockages of material in the drainage system. In Genoa, the network of subterranean drains included sizeable channels. It was not simply filth and waste that might flow through these underground structures. In 1501, the Padri emphasized that no one was allowed to keep piglets or pigs in sewers of the city or in any other underground channel without a licence.[197] In 1531, the Genoese government expressed concern that thieves were using the openings in order to perpetrate crimes and instructed the Padri to fit grates to the drains in order to prevent access.[198] Today, the drains below the park at Acquasola contain the remains of thousands of victims of the plague of 1656. These bodies were deposited a number of years after the plague because of reclamation work in one of the communal burial sites of the city.

Tragic stories also survive of attempts to use drains and canals in Venice for infanticide. Elena Buttaro was convicted of throwing her baby into a latrine in 1508.[199] In 1585, the maid Marieta Todesca in San Barnaba was arrested after a servant heard the cries of a baby coming from a sewer.[200] In 1694, Margherita Serena from Burano was accused of throwing a newborn baby, unbaptized, into a canal.[201] Five years later, Margarita Ventura was said to have disposed of the body of her daughter in a well close to her small village.[202] Maria Franceschini was accused of infanticide after the body of a newborn baby was found in a sewer pipe in San Marcilian.[203] This fascinating case suggested that Maria retained the loyalty of her community who kept her location from the authorities, meaning that she was able to continue to live in the city even though she was subject to official banishment. The loyalty of her neighbours may have been as a result of the circumstances of her pregnancy which, one testimony suggested had resulted from 'an outsider who had forced her once at the entrance of her house when she went to fetch water at the well'. Julie Hardwick has demonstrated that during the eighteenth century in France rivers and latrines were sometimes used in the aftermath of experiences such as termination, miscarriage, stillbirth and neonatal death. The use of waterways suggests an effort at more clandestine removal than leaving the bodies of preterm or newborn babies in small boxes in or around

---

[195] ASCG, PdC, 23-54 (14 July 1557).   [196] ASCG, PdC, 7-61 (22 July 1501).
[197] ASCG, PdC, 7-68 (17 May 1501).   [198] ASCG, PdC, 13-126 (14 October 1531).
[199] Joanne Ferraro, *Nefarious crimes, contested justice: illicit sex and infanticide in the Republic of Venice 1557–1789* (Baltimore MD: Johns Hopkins University Press, 2008), p. 117.
[200] Joanne Ferraro, *Nefarious crimes*, pp. 136-43. See also Julie Hardwick, 'Dead babies in boxes: dealing with the consequences of interrupted reproduction', https://nursingclio.org/2020/09/10/dead-babies-in-boxes-dealing-with-the-consequences-of-interrupted-reproduction/ (accessed 21 June 2022).
[201] Joanne Ferraro, *Nefarious crimes*, p. 116.
[202] Joanne Ferraro, *Nefarious crimes*, p. 147.
[203] See 'A whodunnit: Venice, 1736' in Joanne Ferraro, *Nefarious crimes*, pp. 118–36.

104   CLEANING UP RENAISSANCE ITALY

churches in order to secure burial in consecrated ground. Indeed Joanne Ferraro writes that 'large numbers of deceased infants never arrived at foundling homes, but instead were discarded in dung heaps, ditches, sewers, and rivers'.[204] These elements of the infrastructure were places to which women were expected to go in the course of their daily routines. They may have felt less conspicuous in these locations than elsewhere. In those cases which came to the attention of the authorities, though, the knowledge and use of these facilities by their community ended up leading to the discovery of the child. Of course, we cannot know how many cases passed unnoticed.

The regulation of the civic water supply was undertaken for a multiplicity of reasons but recognized the large quantities of water required to meet the specific practical needs of port societies. The regulation of the flow of water dealt both with issues of too little and too much water, as well as introducing measures to ensure its cleanliness. The channels of water in the Renaissance city were intended to run in distinct systems but social and environmental factors often caused a literal muddying of the waters. The resulting pollution of the civic water supply was of practical and moral concern on its own terms. The failure to follow the proclamations and intentions of government was also seen to be responsible, at least in part, for the siltation of bodies of water. The responses to this issue are the subject for the next chapter.

[204] Joanne Ferraro, *Nefarious crimes*, p. 11.

4

Stemming the Tide

Innovation and Purgation

In 1535 the Venetian Senate reflected on the miraculous situation of the city in water. The government confirmed its commitment to caring for the lagoon environment so as to preserve the bountiful and serene existence of the inhabitants (*bon et quieto vivere de subditi*) as well as protect their health.[1] To maintain the comfort (*commodo*) of the city, it was said to be necessary to intervene in the state of the city's canals. Bodies of water were giving off a foul stench, which was dangerous to health. A high level of siltation was blocking the natural flow of elements and people around the city.[2] A concern for the state of the environment in both Venice and Genoa prompted the development of proactive measures of environmental management (largely in the use of new environmental technologies) as well as reactive ones (through public works such as dredging). In both Genoa and Venice, governments took seriously the challenge and responsibility of shaping and preserving the natural environment because of the practical and symbolic implications of environmental issues.

Public works had been undertaken in previous centuries but were pursued with greater intensity during the fifteenth and sixteenth centuries because of the increased impact of the population upon the environment. During the sixteenth century, the Republics of Genoa and Venice combined traditional approaches with new technologies in relation to dredging, hydraulics, land reclamation, and flood defences, to improve the quality as well as quantity of available urban space. Innovation in environmental management was driven by the introduction of a system of petitions for patents and licences—as has already been studied in other contexts by scholars such as Luca Molà.[3] In this, the management of the environment can be aligned with other health initiatives, such as the licensing of medical secrets in the context of plague epidemics, where we see a similar system for encouraging and regulating innovation.[4] A focus upon these systems reveals

---

[1] ASV, Comun, Atti b.1 291v. See also '*beneficio per segurta del stado nro et essendo maxime conservation del ben agiere de questa cita*' in Atti, b.2 124r (18 January 1546).

[2] ASV, Comun, Atti b.1 381v (7 July 1572).

[3] Luca Molà, *The silk industry of Renaissance Venice* (Baltimore MD: Johns Hopkins University Press, 2000).

[4] Jane Stevens Crawshaw, 'Families, medical secrets and public health in early modern Venice', *Renaissance Studies* 28:4 (2014), 597–618. There is evidence too of concerns around the secrecy of

---

Cleaning Up Renaissance Italy: Environmental Ideals and Urban Practice in Genoa and Venice. Jane L. Stevens Crawshaw, Oxford University Press. © Jane L. Stevens Crawshaw 2023. DOI: 10.1093/oso/9780198867432.003.0005

106 CLEANING UP RENAISSANCE ITALY

the broad social make-up of those involved in the work of managing the environment in these ports. As Pamela Long's study of hydraulics in sixteenth-century Rome has demonstrated, there was considerable interaction between 'practical, technical and learned cultures' in environmental knowledge and practice.[5]

It was important that new structures and practices addressed practical considerations as well as aesthetic ones. Premodern authors described their inventions using the terms 'edificio et ingegno' (construction and product of ingenuity or talent) and reflected on the idea that the Christian God made both the environment and the human mind and endowed the latter with the capacity to develop technology for the former.[6] One supplicant wrote, when offering their invention to the Genoese government, that the arts are those things which do not simply maintain cities but ennoble them (illustrano) and bring great benefit (portano commodita). Supplicants were both native to the cities in question and foreigners. Proposals might be submitted by individuals or as companies.[7] Indeed, the patent system facilitated the entry of 'outsiders' into the social and economic structures of a port. Those who originated from the principal ports of the Italian peninsula appear to have exported expertise in dredging as well as salvage and diving and these skills were highly valued by governments.[8] Some locations appear to have developed specialism, such as the Neapolitan ability to reclaim items from shipwrecks.[9] In addition, once secured, contracts might be passed through the generations and facilitated work across the Ligurian and Venetian states.

In previous chapters we have seen the ongoing efforts to manage the networks of streets and water supply. These activities were costly in terms of time, energy, and money but pale in comparison with the expense incurred by the exceptional interventions considered in this chapter. Dredging in Genoa and Venice involved both proactive, regular activities (supported by the system of patents) and more occasional, large-scale public works.[10] The significant costs of the latter were

hydraulic techniques and equipment. In 1586 two of the expert advisers to the Water Office were arrested and prosecuted for betraying information to Ferrara. See Paolo Preto, I servizi segreti di Venezia (Milan: Il Saggiatore, 1994), p. 449.

[5] Pamela O. Long, 'Hydraulic engineering and the study of Antiquity'.

[6] I broadly adopt Lynton Caldwell's definition of the environment as nature's form after social action and technology as the application of the mechanical arts for practical purposes. By distinguishing between the environment and technology here, I am not intending to suggest that the natural environment is 'untouched' or 'uncreated'. See Barbara Hahn, 'The social in the machine: how historians of technology look beyond the object', Perspectives on History 52:3 (2014), 30–1.

[7] ASV, Comun b.5 [unfoliated] (6 April 1570) (the priest Jacomo Vinello, Benedetto Cangialanza, and Andrea Meira Battista and Jacomo Palavicino all Genoese citizens) and reg 9 (28 November 1570) (Nicolo Gariboldo) and (31 December 1570) (Iseppo Albera and Julio Draganotto).

[8] Davids, Karel, 'On machines, self-organisation and the global travelling of knowledge, c.1500–1900', Isis 106:4 (2015), 866–74.

[9] ASV, Comun b.5 reg 9 [unfoliated] (15 February 1570).

[10] Siltation risked the rising of the seabed in Genoa by a metre every fifty years. Giorgio Doria and Paola Massa Piergiovanni (eds), Il Sistema portuale, p. 147.

justified by the recognition that, unless ongoing interventions in the natural environment were undertaken, previous investment would be wasted.

In 1557, the Padri expressed the vital role played by the city's port. Without its effective conservation, the city would be left like a lifeless body (*come un corpo sensa spirito*). It was said to be the responsibility of the Padri, not simply to preserve the depth of the port but to increase it. The raising of the port bed over the course of many years meant that ships entered with difficulty and also could not shelter from storms without significant risk of damage.[11] The resulting, large-scale dredging works relied in part upon the supply of labour and materials from territorial states.[12] The works are documented in the archive and, for Genoa, in unusual visual records. Three vast canvases depict the dredging of sections of the Genoese port in 1545, 1575, and 1596–7 [Images 4.1, 4.2, and 4.3]. The artists of the latter two are Dionisio di Martino and Cristoforo Grassi and the canvases were commissioned by the Padri to commemorate these public works. The inscriptions note the identity of the Padri at the moments of dredging and are very likely to have hung in the seat of this

Image 4.1 Painting showing the dredging of the Genoese port in 1545: View of Genoa Port. Genoa, Museo Navale di Pegli. © 2014. DeAgostini Picture Library/Scala, Florence.

---

[11] ASCG, PdC, 23-86 (23 October 1557).   [12] ASCG, PdC, 12-6 (13 March 1526).

Image 4.2 Painting showing the dredging of the Genoese port in 1575, Dyonis Martens, 'Escavazione del fondo marino del Mondraccio a Genova'. Tempera su tela del 1575. Genoa, Galata Museo del Mare. © 2020. A. Dagli Orti/Scala, Florence.

government magistracy. As a result they can be considered semi-public images, since this palace was accessed by residents for communication and information on a range of subjects, from objections to building works to the registration of access to water supplies. These images, in combination with archival sources, demonstrate the intensity of the public works to improve port environments as well as contributing insights into the nature of the workforce and practices of dredging.

For the Renaissance, we often lack the completeness of the sources which underpin Seth Rockman's 'Scraping by' on labour and survival in early Baltimore. Rockman pieced together the intense manual nature of dredging on the city's 'mud machine' using a series of payroll records from 1808 to 1820. The machine was generally staffed by immigrants, undertaking largely seasonal work. This was mixed-race, low-wage labour, analysed in his chapter entitled 'Dredging and Drudgery'. Rockman set his account against the aspirations of early American leaders to save and improve their social status as part of the 'American dream' through a combination of public works and use of private contractors. There are many points of continuity between the work analysed in this chapter and that of Rockman's study: the nature of the workforce, the

STEMMING THE TIDE 109

Image 4.3 Painting showing the dredging of the Genoese port in 1597: Genoa harbour. Unknown artist. Genoa, Museo Navale di Pegli. © 2014. DeAgostini Picture Library/Scala, Florence.

important link between civic identity and environmental management, and the combination of private and public initiatives. Each of these themes is explored in this chapter which considers practices relating to salvage, dredging, land reclamation, and the diversion of rivers with regard to both patents and, where relevant, public works.

Salvage and Shipwrecks

One challenge encountered in both Genoa and Venice was the significant damage caused to vessels by storms, which prompted government intervention related to salvage operations. Left on the seabed, shipwrecks and cargo caused obstructions, exacerbated issues of siltation, and compromised the safety of the port in inclement weather. In Venice, the authorities recognized the threat that sunken boats posed to the lagoon and canals and which required intervention despite the significant expense this incurred.[13] In 1460, the year of a severe storm and one

---

[13] ASV, Comun, b.16 reg 36 110v (27 August 1585).

in which the responsibilities and funds of Genoa's Padri were revised, a decree was issued to clear the port of shipwrecks. This was the same proclamation considered in earlier chapters which conceptualized this area as the foundation of the city.[14] The Padri attempted to ensure the viability of the area around the Arsenal and instructed vessels which had been wrecked in that area to be moved to a place where they would not impede the movement of other vessels.[15] In 1512, the Padri noted that several boats of varying sizes had been submerged in the Darsina del Vino for some time and that this was greatly prejudicial to the port and particularly the Darsina itself because of the impediment posed to the ships transporting wine, as well as any other vessel.[16] The Padri were similarly concerned with the blockages in the ports along the Ligurian coast. In 1528, for example, the officials wrote to the Consul of Portofino regarding the need to remove sunken vessels from the port of that town in order to minimize the damage caused.[17]

Demand for workers who could assist with essential operations to clear port areas remained consistently high and Genoese, Neapolitan, and Venetian residents found work in other ports by marketing their skills in raising ships and rescuing cargo. This link with expertise drawn from other ports was also true for the architects who supervised public works. During the 1470s, work on the Genoese breakwater was directed by Anastasio Alexandrano noted as *architectus et magister diversorum operum* from Messina.[18] The Padri reported to the government on the extraordinary skills ('*mirabile ingegno*') of this Sicilian architect who was said to be recently arrived in the city and who they also intended to employ in the works at the port and inner harbour.[19] In 1570, a group of individuals from Naples sent a petition offering an invention to reclaim sunken merchandise in Venice.[20] It was a group of Venetian Southampton-based salvage operators in 1545 who attempted the first recovering attempt of the Mary Rose.[21] Those from Naples, Venice, and Genoa were acknowledged to be experts in this field, in part because they were also accomplished swimmers. Swimming skills are difficult to access in the surviving literature although there was an increasing interest in swimming during the sixteenth century. It was long discussed as a useful skill in the context of warfare. Tommaso Garzoni includes swimmers in his *Piazza Universale*. Garzoni notes that in his own time in Italy it was the Venetians and Genoese who were particularly skilled swimmers ('*portano la palma del nuotare*').[22] He also records stories from the humanist Alessandro d'Alessandri

---

[14] ASCG, PdC, 1-71 (16 May 1460).   [15] ASCG, PdC, 3-56 (1 March 1471).
[16] ASCG, PdC, 10-14 (12 July 1512).   [17] ASCG, PdC, 13-4 (3 February 1528).
[18] Giorgio Doria and Paola Massa Piergiovanni (eds), *Il Sistema portuale*, p. 92.
[19] ASCG, PdC, 3-49 (26 October 1470).   [20] ASV, Comun, reg 9 (15 February 1570).
[21] https://maryrose.org/blog/historical/museum-blogger/the-first-men-who-dived-on-the-mary-rose/ (accessed 14 June 2022).
[22] Tommaso Garzoni, *Piazza Universale*, 'De notatori' discorso 112.

[1461–1523] of two remarkable men: the first, known as the fish Calano was from Catania and the second, from Naples was a boatman (*nocchiero*).[23]

Information on salvage operations using skilled swimmers can be found in a book by the humanist and historian Biondo Flavio [1392–1463]. This topographical work entitled *Italia illustrata* was published in 1453. In the section on Lazio, he included a description of Lake Nemi and noted that:

> Prospero Colonna, the Roman cardinal and patrician who inherited from his ancestors the town of Nemi and the castle of Genzano, once heard the fishermen of Nemi saying that there were two ships sunk in the lake. They were not so rotten that they would be torn apart and come away when ropes were attached to them for the purpose, nor when they happened to become tangled up in their nets. Neither could they be hauled out entire by the main strength of all the inhabitants together. Devoted as he is to the liberal arts, especially history, and being the painstaking antiquarian that he is, the cardinal accordingly applied himself to discovering why those great ships should be found in a small lake completely surrounded by high mountains. My friend Leon Battista Alberti, the great mathematician of our age and author of a graceful work on the art of building, was summoned to help in the task. Leon Battista arranged wine barrels tied together in a number of rows on the lake with the idea of setting up winches on either side, as from a bridge. With these experienced carpenters could use an iron hook suspended from especially thick ropes to catch the ship and draw it up. Some workers—more like fish than men—were hired from the seagoing city of Genoa. It was their job to swim down into the deeper parts of the lake to find out how much remained of the ship and in what state of preservation, and to use the hooks let down on ropes to dig into the ship and grab hold of it.[24]

His account of Lake Nemi continues with a description of the fragments which were gleaned from this salvage attempt in 1446, which was ultimately unsuccessful, as in fact were all attempts until that undertaken under Mussolini between 1928 and 1932.

Similar approaches to the problem of raising ships were described by Niccolò Tartaglia [1499–1557] in his publication of 1551 (the *Regola generale di solevare ogni fondata nave*) in which he describes tethering ships together to act as a bridge, filling the vessels with water in order to lower them, securing ropes to the sunken vessel and then slowly emptying the water from the vessels in order to raise the unit as a whole. Other authors employ a similar technique using stones.

---

[23] The experiences of such men would be of interest to seventeenth-century authors interested in 'submarine knowledge' as discussed in Philippa Hellawell, 'Diving engines, submarine knowledge and the 'wealth fetch'd out of the sea', *Renaissance Studies* 34:1 (2019), 78–94 in which the overlapping 'epistemic and economic motives for venturing underwater' are explored.

[24] Biondo Flavio, *Italy illuminated*, pp. 189–93.

112 CLEANING UP RENAISSANCE ITALY

Tartaglia also imagined making use of the distinctively clear Murano glass—blown into spheres of different sizes—to enable underwater diving. One sphere was designed for protection from monsters of the deep (*bestial pesce*) and was large enough to fit a chair inside! At the start of Tartaglia's second book, he echoed Flavio's emphasis on the abilities of the men working on these projects by noting that Signor Traiano (presumably his editor and publisher Curzio Troiano de Navò) had heard from many sailors that at the present time there were many who, without artificial apparatus, could swim nimbly into the deep and remain underwater for a long time. These men were sometimes called *marangone*—after a cormorant—because of the depths to which they could dive in order to salvage sunken ships or merchandise.

Salvage was generally motivated by economic considerations. In 1460, the owner of a boat which was insured was concerned about the impact on the payment if anyone interfered with the salvage of the ship and the Padri was instructed to oversee the removal of the wreck by the government.[25] In December 1460, the Padri also conducted the sale of a boat which had been sunken in the port close to the Arsenal.[26] Salvage might also enable the discovery of things with a value which was more than material. In Genoa in 1636 a consortium of twenty-seven sailors purchased a shipwreck in the port intending to salvage its cargo of iron. They found, in addition to the anticipated contents, a statue which inspired an extraordinary devotional cult around the figure that became known as the Madonna of the Storm (*Madonna della Fortuna*).[27]

The salvage of cargo was consequently recognized as being a potentially lucrative operation. In Genoa in 1565, the sinking of a ship belonging to Benedetto Rodi (which was carrying grain) led to the employment of several *arcellatori* who agreed to raise the cargo. These *arcellatori* were expert in the construction of the chests for holding grain (*arcile*) rather than in salvage per se. This task was undertaken by Giovanni Pietro de Vivaldo and his company. A few days later, the Padri received a report that other members of the *arcellatori*, beyond those who had been tasked with this work, had taken it upon themselves to try to raise the cargo which was said to be inhibiting the work of Vivaldo. The Padri issued a proclamation that no one other than Vivaldo's company was to access the grain which was inside the vessel or which had been carried beyond the ship by the tides.[28]

Severe storms could damage multiple vessels, such as in Genoa in 1613. This event was represented visually in Joseph Furttenbach's *Newes Itinerarium Italiae* (1627) and also made its mark in the archive. A list of the sunken vessels in the

---

[25] ASCG, PdC, 1-85 (24 October 1460) and 1-86 (22 October 1460).
[26] ASCG, PdC, 1-89 (2 December 1460).
[27] Jane Garnett and Gervase Rosser, *Spectacular miracles*, pp. 73–80.
[28] ASCG, PdC, 27-5 (6 January 1565).

Genoese port was compiled on 1 January, along with a note of the boats which had been damaged. Thirty-nine vessels were said to have been wrecked in the port (nine ships and thirty boats) and the list provided details of the captain's name, the nature of the vessel, its country of origin, and its cargo. Vessels from Flanders, France, and England were wrecked alongside those from the Ligurian coast. The cargo of the ships included timber, salt, wool from Spain, and grain (including some from Tabarca). The smaller boats carried wine, wood, salt, grain, and generic merchandise. Alongside these vessels were smaller boats such as a gondola from Savona and a despatch boat for Naples (*feluca di venturino per Napoli*).[29] Of the ten vessels which had been damaged, four were English and the list included a brief description of the impact of the storm. Half of the damaged boats had a broken '*opera morta*' of the ship (the 'top side' or part above the waterline). The '*opera viva*' referred to the section which was submerged. Others had damage to the '*poppa e prora*' (stern and bow).

In the aftermath of storms, there was an expectation that wrecked and damaged ships would be cleared naturally or be salvaged. There was certainly an expectation that sunken boats would be removed by the original owners, alongside frequent complaints in both Genoa and Venice that this was not happening.[30] Interventions by the Padri were intended to hasten the removal of vessels: in February 1460, officials instructed anyone who owned any sort of vessel which was submerged in the port to ensure that it was removed within fifteen days.[31] The reissuing of this proclamation three months later suggests that the problems caused by these vessels endured.[32] In June and October 1460 owners of sunken ships were instructed to remove wrecks within eight days.[33] In some instances, circumstances required greater urgency. In 1498, those owners of boats and ships which were either under water or on the bed of the port were to ensure that they were removed within five days and repaired so that they were watertight and would not sink.[34] On 8 October the owners of the vessels in the Arsenal which were under water were instructed to remove them within three days and not reintroduce them until the vessels had been caulked so that they were watertight.[35] Such repairs might involve the reuse of flotsam which had washed up onto beaches, such as in Boccadasse.[36] By the sixteenth century, owners were instructed to remove sunken vessels within eight days or face fines. The Padri noted that there were ships and other boats which had remained submerged in the port for a long period and the owners had not made any efforts to remove them, causing considerable damage to the port.[37] In December 1458,

---

[29] ASCG, PdC, 221-490 (1 January 1614).
[30] ASV, Comun b.16 reg 37 28r (18 November 1586).   [31] ASCG, PdC, 1-58 (9 February 1460).
[32] ASCG, PdC, 1-66 (6 May 1460).
[33] ASCG, PdC, 1-74 (19 June 1460) and 1-84 (16 October 1460).
[34] ASCG, PdC, 6-174 (3 September 1498).   [35] ASCG, PdC, 6-180 (8 October 1498).
[36] ASCG, PdC, 29-79 (11 October 1568).   [37] ASCG, PdC, 10-104 (17 February 1515).

114 CLEANING UP RENAISSANCE ITALY

for example, the government noted the presence of a ship which had been on the seabed since summer and in 1504 the proposal of the Padri was made in October, following storms in August.[38] The Padri invited offers from those who would work to remove sunken vessels, inviting them to present themselves to the office.[39]

In 1519, the Padri again drew attention to the number of vessels which had been submerged in the port for varying lengths of time and the number of proclamations which had been issued by their predecessors on the subject. They offered owners the opportunity, again, to raise the vessels within three days and noted that a number of these were located at the Punta del Molo near the church of San Lazaro. Any vessel not removed would be raised by the Padri and owners would lose their claim to the materials and cargo.[40] At other times, owners lost valuable materials from these vessels as a result of theft. On the night of 28 December 1564, three ships were wrecked in the port of Genoa. The following day, the Padri issued a proclamation addressing the theft of fittings and timber—materials which the Padri sought to ensure were returned to the owners.[41]

The devastation of the storm of 1613 prompted the offer of a new method for securing ships in the port.[42] The author described the vulnerability of vessels in times of a tempestuous sea (*procelloso mare*), caused by high winds, and the damage that could occur to the port and by extension the public interest. The severity of the impact of the storm in 1613 was said by the author to have been exacerbated by an inability to secure the vessels adequately with cables (*cavi*). The proposed method was said to be without danger to individuals or the port, cheap and enduring, without the need for maintenance and additional spending. The response of the Padri was that it was not entirely true that the damage inflicted by the storm had been caused by a lack of materials to secure the vessels (*sartie et ormeggi*) but instead was, in part, because the equipment for these purposes was damaged and had not been properly maintained. As a result, the proposal was felt to be unlikely to bring about the promised effects. Nevertheless the process by which this environmental challenge was observed, recorded, and responded to was representative of a broader system of inventions, petitions, and patents utilized in both cities during the Renaissance. The enduring challenge of keeping waterways accessible (whether as a result of siltation or storms) was partly met through a system which was designed to encourage the application of new technologies to enduring environmental issues.

---

[38] ASCG, PdC, 1-15 (1 December 1458) and 8-14 (2 October 1504).
[39] ASCG, PdC, 5-118 (7 August 1465).   [40] ASCG, PdC, 11-29 (9 March 1519).
[41] ASCG, PdC, 26-167 (29 December 1564).   [42] ASCG, PdC, 221-495 (1 January 1614).

Petitions and Patents

As the architect Domenico Ponzello walked to work in 1558, his mind was said to be occupied by issues of the Genoese port. He had observed the raising of the seabed and wrote that ships were no longer able to enter the port.[43] He claimed to have designed an invention which would enable five or six thousand boatfulls of rubble to be extracted from this area. Whether on the basis of his reputation as an architect within the city or his confidence in his own invention, Ponzello requested a privilege not for twenty or thirty years, as was more common in petitions of this type, but a perpetual privilege for his lifetime and that of his descendants. He requested a plot of land near the port on which he might build a house. He also requested a one-off payment. As George Gorse has established, the Ponzelli were an important family of Genoese architects. Domenico (active in Genoa and Savoy, 1548–71) and Giovanni (active Genoa, 1549–96) worked on prominent public and private commissions and contributed to the 'development of Genoese architecture and urban planning during the second half of the sixteenth century'.[44] Domenico was elected *Console dell'Arte dei Maestri Antelami Genovesi* (the prestigious guild of master-masons) in 1550 and his brother held this office twice in 1557 and 1572, which Gorse notes as being an unusual achievement. Domenico worked alongside the better-known Galeazzo Alessi on the church of Santa Maria di Carignano and was also sent to Corsica in 1560 to strengthen the fortifications at Recco and other Genoese outposts.[45] His prominent status in the community, however, was not representative of that of the cross-section of people who offered inventions for environmental management in Genoa and Venice.

The Padri del Comune received supplications during the late fifteenth and sixteenth century which requested a privilege for dredging machinery ('invention') used for a negotiable period within both Genoa and its territorial state. These privileges remained valid within a specific period as long as the machinery continued to be used.[46] Roberto Berveglieri has carried out a survey of the Venetian Senate records and identified ninety-seven inventions related to land reclamation, canals, the lagoon, and dredging machines.[47] These were not spaced evenly across the centuries: four patents were granted in 1478–1500, fifteen in

---

[43] ASCG, PdC, 23-111 (18 February 1558).

[44] George Gorse, 'Ponzello, Domenico and Giovanni', p. 1. I am very grateful to Professor Gorse for sharing his research into the Ponzello family with me.

[45] Gorge Gorse, 'Ponzello, Domenico and Giovanni', p. 2. His brother Giovanni also held the role of *Architetto Camerale* to the Genoese Republic from Bernardino Cantone's retirement in 1576 until his own in 1596. In this role he was responsible for planning and clearing the Piazza Soziglia and modernizing the Darsena and Molo. See George Gorse, 'Ponzello, Domenico and Giovanni', p. 6.

[46] ASCG, PdC, 31-91 (20 August 1572).

[47] Roberto Berveglieri, *Le vie di Venezia: canali lagunari e rii a Venezia* (Sommacampagna: Cierre, 1999).

116 CLEANING UP RENAISSANCE ITALY

1501–50 and seventy-eight in 1551–1600. For Genoa, twelve privileges specifically relating to dredging machines have survived alongside other inventions. Most of these were approved during the 1550s.[48]

The technology being offered in these environmental petitions varied. In 1573, Donato Martino from Milan offered a number of inventions to the Genoese state, ranging from those applicable to the dredging of the port, making brass, and creating fountains in areas of stagnant water.[49] In 1595, Marco Manera from Palermo offered three inventions: to make a capacious, secure breakwater which would withstand the force of the elements, to excavate the port to a depth of thirty palms or more, and to prevent detriment from entering the port.[50] Bartolomeo Sommarina offered an invention which, he claimed, could protect the infrastructure of the public fountains from being stolen or damaged.[51] In 1572, an invention was offered which pumped water to a great height, which, its authors claimed, would enable the Padri to supply the city and the dominion plentifully (*abondare*) with water.[52] In the same year, Stefano Spinola submitted a mechanism for transporting water.[53] It involved two square containers and two pipes (made of lead or another material) which were connected at an approximately 60-degree angle. Water would flow into the first vessel from the source and then pass into the second vessel. There was an overflow outlet for the second vessel for times of significant flow of water but in times of dearth, the second vessel would not leak and the water level would remain constant between the two vessels, with the pipe that joined the two remaining perpetually full. This system was said to be widely used in Germany and Lombardy. In other instances, designs survive which were submitted to Padri for infrastructure projects, such as that for the marina in Sarzano by the architect Giovanni Aycardo. This survives without a detailed description but on the reverse of the diagram, the model is said to have been designed in order to avoid damage caused by the sea.[54]

In order to offer an invention in either city, a supplication would be sent to the Padri del Comune, Provveditori di Comun, or Savi ed Esecutori alle Acque, often with a model to accompany the text.[55] A privilege for using the machine or technology would be requested for a set time.[56] Individuals were then required to build their inventions within a stipulated period (which, in Genoa, generally ranged from three and twelve months) and then to begin to use this equipment. Projects could take much longer to bring to fruition, however. The German Pietro Basso devised a machine to dredge and clean the canals of Venice. He was granted

---

[48] ASCG, PdC, 22-188 (1 July 1556) and 22-224 (21 August 1556).

[49] ASCG, PdC, 32-42 (20 May 1573).   [50] ASCG, PdC, 2-142 (1 January 1595).

[51] ASCG, PdC, 32-78 (18 September 1573).   [52] ASCG, PdC, 31-85 (5 August 1572).

[53] ASCG, PdC, 31-109 (18 September 1572).   [54] ASCG, PdC, 63-138 (5 December 1605).

[55] Sometimes the notary recorded that the supplicant had not wished to provide such a model. See for example ASV, Comun b.5 [unfoliated] (12 October 1569).

[56] Models were commonly produced during the Renaissance to support the construction of machinery as well as architecture.

STEMMING THE TIDE 117

his privilege in 1570 but ended up reapplying for an extension to the deadline for building the craft in 1576 because of the difficulties he had encountered in bringing the project to fruition.[57] In addition to ensuring that the inventions represented something genuinely original, government officials considered it their responsibility to monitor the potential economic and social impact of innovation.[58]

Inventions related to environmental management were strongly encouraged. In Genoa, the format of surviving records is standard and the scribe would note the role of the Padri to conserve as well as purge the bed of the port, so that the highest volume of water was retained and ships could pass and remain without hindrance. For that reason, it was noted that all those who offered assistance in this sphere were received by the government. The intended depth of the port varied but the most common articulated aim was a depth of twelve palms (*parmi*) from the harbour front to the Arsenal.[59]

In both cities this system was one way in which technology passed into the city since supplicants could be both residents and outsiders.[60] In June 1563, Guglielmo Fidens from Mechelen (Mechlinia) in Flanders used his invention for excavating canals to support his attempt to settle in Venice with his wife and children. His invention was said to enable fifty boatloads of material to be extracted every day using only three men. It was said to be equally effective in areas of deep and shallow water. His request for a privilege extended to himself and his heirs and encompassed Venice and its *stato da mar*. Such machines were in demand and the response of the Venetian authorities was that this was an invention which should be embraced as potentially very useful.[61] The patent system was also a way in which technology passed through the state, since individuals often stipulated in their supplications that the privileges should apply in specific cities and areas of wider territory. In Genoa, a number of supplications made reference to the Ligurian state and, in one instance, an application also stipulated that any privilege should include Corsica.[62] Technology also came into Genoa from territorial cities,

---

[57] Roberto Berveglieri, *Inventori stranieri (1474–1788): importazione di tecnologiea e circolazione di tecnici artigiani inventori: repertorio* (Venice. Istituto Veneto di scienze, lettere ed arti, 1995), p. 63.

[58] ASV, Comun b.5 [unfoliated] (11 March 1570).

[59] ASCG, PdC, 22-207 (13 November 1557). In 1601, *capitoli* for the excavation of the port were issued. The intention was to create a depth of twenty *palmi* within the port. ASCG, PdC, 221-22 (s.d.) and 221-163 (23 September 1602).

[60] Petitioners in Genoa came from Piacenza, Milan, Lucca, Palermo, and Germany. Giuseppe Feghiano Forlano di Luca in ASCG, PdC, 22-188 (1 July 1556). Berveglieri classified seven of the environmental patents he located for Venice as belonging to foreigners, all of which were placed between 1551 and 1600 in Berveglieri, *Inventori stranieri*, p. 61.

[61] ASV, Comun b.5 17r (20 June 1563).

[62] ASCG, PdC, 2-99 (22 October 1570) contains an example which includes Genoa and its dominion. 31-85 (5 August 1572) references the inclusion of Corsica for a water pump. On Corsican ports during the Genoese occupation see Maria Pia Rota, 'L'apparato portuale della Corsica "Genovese": una struttura in movimento' in Giorgio Doria and Paola Massa Piergiovanni (eds), *Il Sistema portuale*, pp. 297–328.

118   CLEANING UP RENAISSANCE ITALY

such as Savona. In 1589, the Podesta of Savona sent a description and model of a machine which, he noted, had been adopted in that city's Arsenal to clean it. It was said to clear 1,500 units (*cantara*) of rubble and was operated by ten men.[63] Being from outside the city could, however, pose practical problems. In 1609, Giulio Martelli from Padua offered an invention for clearing the Genoese port in the most difficult places which, until now, had remained untouched. He promised a depth of twelve palms but described the problems of finding men to work on the machine, particularly as a foreigner, at anything less than an 'excessive' rate. Martelli requested eighteen galley-slaves from the ships of the Republic.[64]

A significant number of the inventions related to dredging machines. Most were equipped to remove shingle and soil and reclaimed (*resalvato*) larger stones. Sometimes vessels were expected to work in parallel. Different mechanisms were utilized to extract material from the seabed: the apparatus might be shaped like a cup (*la tazza*), a spade (*vanga*), or a spoon (*cucchiaia*) amongst others.[65] The supplications occasionally included brief mention of the details of the building materials, although more commonly it was assumed that the model would be demonstrate the design.[66] In 1495, a petition from Alvise Zucarin included an unusual level of detail regarding his machine. He noted that it was a long, low, caulked barge with a platform for the workers and some of the iron scoops were perforated to allow for the drainage of water.[67] Most descriptions, however, focused upon the qualities of the new machines—especially speed and efficiency—rather than their technical details. In 1571, Tommaso Lercaro Camilla offered an invention 'completely different and opposite (*contrario*) from all the others' and was issued with a standard set of conditions.[68] Unusually for these petitions, a design survives (separately from the text in the archive) with a name on the reverse attributing it to Camilla.[69]

In Venice, Piero del Lorenzo devised a machine which, he claimed, dug canals quickly and with great saving of time and money, without the need to build *palificade* (the screens of piles which were used to make an area watertight).[70] The latter task was, according to supplicants, one which absorbed considerable amounts of time and money.[71] In December 1561 Simon di Nicolo of Zara submitted for approval a number of barges (*burchi*) for transporting mud out of the city and depositing it at sea. This was sent in alongside another which was said to transport fish long distances alive and fresh.[72] Such vessels were designed to

---

[63] C. Assereto, 'Porti e scali minori della Repubblica di Genova in età moderna', in Giorgio Doria and Paola Massa Piergiovanni (eds), *Il Sistema portuale*, p. 240.

[64] ASCG, PdC, 67-97 (1 December 1609).

[65] For descriptions of the machines see Roberto Berveglieri, *Le vie di Venezia*, pp. 39–43.

[66] ASCG, PdC, 2-84 (16 September 1569) mentions that the invention is made of wood.

[67] Roberto Berveglieri, *Le vie di Venezia*, p. 44.   [68] ASCG, PdC, 2-171 (7 May 1571).

[69] ASCG, PdC, 2-105 (23 April 1571).   [70] ASV, Comun b.5 25r (25 August 1563).

[71] ASV, Comun b.5 29r (1564).

[72] ASV, Comun b.5 17v (29 December 1561). Boats for transporting such material were a popular focus for inventions. See also ASV, Comun b.5 23r (25 August 1563).

STEMMING THE TIDE   119

operate in Genoa and Venice on an ongoing basis to prevent siltation and the build-up of problems in the port. Ultimately, however, these efforts remained insufficient to the scale of the task. At these times, therefore, civic schemes of public works were required in the form of large-scale dredging.

Dredging

In 1490, the Venetian government expressed that nothing was more essential to the cleanliness of the air and public health of the city, than keeping the canals clean and clear (*netti et cavadi*) so that water could enter into channels and flow freely (*universalmente*) throughout the city.[73] At that time, however, the city's canals were filthy and required both intervention and additional funding. The necessary intervention, of course, was dredging, on a scale which required considerable quantities of labour. Sometimes the period between dredging works could be surprisingly short. In 1513 part of the port in Genoa was excavated to a depth of nineteen *palmi*.[74] Three years later the Darsina was repaired and excavated to a depth of eighteen *palmi*.[75] The works were often undertaken during the season with the lowest risk of storms and floods, between March and mid-July. They were laborious interventions and, despite their frequency, frequently disorganized. In 1589, the Water Office noted the disorder with which the excavation of the Grand Canal and lagoon had proceeded.[76] They were also, however, essential for reasons which have been outlined in previous chapters: the ebb and flow of the water was known to be essential for the quality of the air and health.[77]

Dredging was perceived as a public work, coordinated by the government but paid for, and with labour contributed in part, by residents. In San Remo (Liguria), from 1435, the statutes required each citizen annually to contribute to the cleaning and dredging of the port and to repair the breakwater.[78] In Genoa in 1505, the government instructed all citizens who employed servants to make these individuals available to assist with the work of dredging the port until the end of the project.[79] In 1466, it was decreed that all men between the ages of twenty and sixty needed to give a day's work per week on the Genoese port since 'everyone gained advantage from the activity of the port' (*tutti traggono vantaggio dale attivita*

---

[73] ASV, Comun, b. 1 (*Della cavation delli canali et conzar le fondamente*) 105v.
[74] Agostino Giustiniano, *Castigatissimi Annali . . . della Eccelsa et Illustrissima Repubblica di Genova*, cclxx.
[75] Agostino Giustiniano, *Castigatissimi Annali*, cclxxii.
[76] Roberto Berveglieri, *Le vie di Venezia*, p. 314.
[77] Roberto Berveglieri, *Le vie di Venezia*, p. 281.
[78] R. Stilli, 'Un porto per Sanremo: difficoltà tecniche e problemi politico-finanziari' in in Giorgio Doria and Paola Massa Piergiovanni (eds), *Il Sistema portuale*, p. 263.
[79] ASCG, PdC, 8-44 (13 June 1505).

120   CLEANING UP RENAISSANCE ITALY

portuali).[80] The use of labour from both the city and the wider territory continued through dredging works of the sixteenth century.[81] In Venice, in 1531, one thousand men were requisitioned from the *terraferma* in order to assist with the excavation of the canals. They were instructed to come equipped with shovels and spades.[82] In 1560 two or three thousand men were said to be required from the *terraferma* because of the miserable state of the lagoon, particularly around the *lidi*.[83]

Although conceptualized as being in the public good, the interventions were not necessarily welcomed or appreciated; indeed, individuals carrying out the back-breaking labour were not always celebrated by the wider population: in 1545, the Padri felt it necessary to issue a decree which forbade all citizens of whatever age or gender from troubling or impeding the men working at the harbour. Residents were also asked not to throw dirt or stones at these individuals.[84] The reasons for this behaviour were not articulated but concerns about unwelcome disruption and the release of miasma as a result of works which were intended to improve the environment and health of the city may also have played a part in shaping the response of the populace.

Stages of the dredging works can be identified in surviving visual and archival records. First, all vessels needed to be removed from the area and so, in June 1516, for example, owners of vessels in the Genoese port were given notice that boats had to be removed from the harbour by the following Monday.[85] A screen (*palizzata*) of planks and bricks would then be constructed in order to seal off the area to be dredged. In Genoa, mechanisms known as *cicogne* (swans) were used to extract water. These worked on a pivot motion, had vessels for scooping water at either end and were each operated by two men. During the large-scale dredging works in Genoa, there were up to 150 *cicogne* in use at a time and these had to be operated both day and night. Once water had been removed from the dredging site, any drains were repaired and waste material removed.

In Genoa, workers from different locations were organized into companies. Giovanni Rebora has suggested that 'exiles', 'vagrants', slaves, and the 'wretched poor of all sorts' were recruited, alongside men from the territory.[86] Rebora has written a chapter on the 1545 excavation and compares it with an ants' nest:

---

[80] P. Massa Piergiovanni, 'Fattori tecnici ed economici dello sviluppo del porto di Genova tra medioevo ed età moderna (1340-1548)' in Giorgio Doria and Paola Massa Piergiovanni (eds), *Il Sistema portuale*, p. 92.

[81] G. Rebora, 'I lavori di espurgazione della Darsena del porto di Genova nel 1545' in Giorgio Doria and Paola Massa Piergiovanni (eds), *Il Sistema portuale*, p. 209.

[82] Roberto Berveglieri, *Le vie di Venezia*, p. 266.   [83] Rompiasio, p. 141.

[84] G. Rebora, 'I lavori di espurgazione della Darsena del porto di Genova nel 1545' in Giorgio Doria and Paola Massa Piergiovanni (eds), *Il Sistema portuale*, p. 214.

[85] ASCG, PdC, 10-150 (6 June 1516).

[86] Giovanni Rebora, 'I lavori di espurgazione della Darsena del porto di Genova nel 1545' in Giorgio Doria and Paola Massa Piergiovanni (eds), *Il Sistema portuale*, pp. 199–220.

incredibly busy, involving thousands of workers and hundreds of mules.[87] The paintings of dredging in Genoa enrich this picture. The depictions include both male and female workers. Some prominent figures are shown drumming, presumably to provide pace to the work. Although archival records do not survive for any of the periods shown in the canvases, rich documentation is extant for the 1583 excavation of the harbour area. Documents provide details of the numbers of workers sent from elsewhere in the territory. Daily lists of workers survive which record names, daily rate of pay, and the days worked. Overall, salaries ranged from 4 to 38 *soldi*. Heads of companies received a daily rate of 20 *soldi* and the operators of the 'swan' units were given 19 *soldi*. The company of German workers ('*tudeschi*' or '*todeschi*') included the lowest paid workers on site. The male workers were paid a daily rate of 12 *soldi* and their head of company received 16 *soldi*. There was a long-standing German community in the city, which dated back to the twelfth century but it is not clear why this particular company was employed and at a lower daily rate.[88] At the lowest end of the payscale were the women on site. They were paid 4, 6, or 8 *soldi* per day for their work. Women are only included in the lists of the German company. More generally we know that women were involved in heavy lifting and played an important role in the building trades but their roles in Genoese dredging works were not specified.[89]

Venice too required large-scale dredging works during the sixteenth century, most notably for the city's Grand Canal, described as the principal ornament of the city. In 1520, the dredging of the Grand Canal, into which all other canals flow, was said to be laudable and necessary.[90] Work was undertaken to repair the *fondamente* and dredge the canal beds so that the water would pass with its fullest and freest course, purifying the air and protecting the health of inhabitants. The most substantial period of dredging during the sixteenth and seventeenth centuries took place between 1536 and 1542.[91] Sections were repeated in 1569 and dredging was also undertaken in the lagoon. Indeed, the relationship between the two bodies of water was clearly recognized. In 1569, part of the motivation for dredging the Grand Canal was said to be to protect the lagoon.[92]

In addition to the obvious significance of the Grand Canal, other bodies of water were identified as 'principal' canals of the city. The nomenclature of waterways provides an indication of their size and significance. Canals were the largest and most strategic, followed by *rii* and then by *rielli*. The connections between these bodies of water were clear. In 1553, the significance of the

---

[87] Giovanni Rebora, 'I lavori di espurgazione della Darsena del porto di Genova nel 1545', p. 220.

[88] There was a '*habitatione de todeschi*' near the gateway of San Tomaso. ASCG, PdC, 222-202 (1 January 1620).

[89] Maria Ågren, *Making and living, making a difference: gender and work in early modern European society* (Oxford: Oxford University Press, 2017).

[90] ASV, Comun, Atti b.1 246v (3 November 1520).

[91] Roberto Berveglieri, *Le vie di Venezia*, p. 138.

[92] Roberto Berveglieri, *Le vie di Venezia*, p. 296.

122 CLEANING UP RENAISSANCE ITALY

excavation of smaller bodies of water, on which depended, in part, the excavation of the Grand Canal was stated as being known by everyone. In the early fifteenth century, some of these principal canals included Santa Maria Zobenigo and San Moisè.[93] In 1538, San Trovaso was described as one of the principal waterways of the city because of the frequency with which boats used it.[94] In 1546, the Rio della Tana was said to be almost entirely silted up. Only small and shallow boats were able to pass through it and that did not include the boat of the Council of Ten which, at night, was unable to patrol, leaving the Arsenal without protection and guard.[95] This area required urgent attention given that the Arsenal was essential to the reputation and conservation of the state.

The ongoing problem of siltation is obvious from the archives. In 1578 most of the channels in Venice were described, yet again, as so severely silted up that it was almost impossible to navigate them. Inhabitants were severely inconvenienced and the disgusting, unbearable smell was injurious.[96] In 1582, it was said to be essential to expedite the vital and necessary task of excavating all canals of the city in the interests of the beauty and wellbeing (*bellezza et comodità*) of the city as well as the salubrity of the air. The work should be done, the Comun were instructed, with the greatest possible brevity and speed.[97] In this vein, the office should ensure that the *sestieri* were cleared one or two at a time, in line with the advice of the experts as to which were the most pressing. The work was to proceed from those districts which faced the sea (Castello and Dorsoduro) and then continue to San Marco, San Polo, Santa Croce, and Cannaregio. All households in the city were to contribute to the cost, without exception. This included properties on the Grand Canal and all manner of property, including gardens and boatyards. The government emphasized that all sites would be included, whether developed or vacant, rented or rentable.[98]

The large-scale excavation of the Grand Canal was funded through payments from all those whose homes or properties bordered the watercourse, as well as those who lived in streets or squares which intersected with the canal. The payment was calculated in relation to their *decima* payment (*grossi doi duc'to per quanto le hanno alle decime*) if someone owned and inhabited a building. If they rented it, then the payment was split between the owner of the property and the tenant.[99] It was recognized that the contributions of religious and charitable institutions might be complicated by their proximity to a number of canals and the Comun was asked to develop a system to make allowances for this. The

[93] Roberto Berveglieri, *Le vie di Venezia*, p. 22.
[94] Roberto Berveglieri, *Le vie di Venezia*, p. 274.
[95] ASV, Comun, Atti, b.2 124r (18 January 1546).
[96] ASV, PC, Atti b.1 402v (20 September 1578). On stench see Joseph Wheeler, 'Stench in sixteenth-century Venice' in Alexander Cowan and Jill Steward (eds.) *The city and the senses*, pp. 25–38.
[97] ASV, Comun, b.1 417r (18 March 1582).
[98] This rich and detailed entry is reprinted in Roberto Berveglieri, *Le vie di Venezia*, pp. 306–10.
[99] ASV, Comun, Atti, b.1, 292v (23 December 1535).

government also sought to limit the possibility of individual households having to make multiple payments, for example in the case of moving house, and so legislated that four years had to pass between contributions to the schemes to excavate canals in different parts of the city. The contributions from residents were coordinated in Venice by the *cassa del cavation*, which had been established as part of the Comun in 1517. A nominated official, known as the *cassier alla cavation*, was required to keep a register of the payments made. Contributions could include money and pawns or pledges.[100]

The basic principle remained that households should contribute financially to the work being undertaken in their vicinity. Indeed, sometimes the impetus for interventions might come both from the government and local residents, as was the case with the Rio di San Trovaso in 1538 when the need for this work had been recognized both by the Comun and the nobleman Alvise Caravello who had a house nearby.[101] Sometimes occupational groups were also targeted, particularly if their work was seen to have exacerbated environmental issues in a district. Dredging at Santi Giovanni e Paolo was said to have become necessary in part because of the storage of timber in this area. The timber merchants were required to contribute to the costs, as was the nearby Scuola di San Marco.[102]

The Venetian authorities were also involved in projects on and around the islands of the lagoon. In 1559, the community of Murano wrote a supplication to the Venetian government regarding the dredging which needed to take place in the canal of the island. It was said that the island was a community of fishermen and the poor, with large families, who could not fund such initiatives. The community was already said to be in debt for the works on the *fondamente*, the construction of the large bridge across the island's main canal (in 1545) and other infrastructure initiatives.[103] The Comun helped to coordinate and encourage the contributions for the dredging of the canal in Murano in 1559 when the work was part way through and funding was obviously running low.[104] In 1562, the Comun noted that great need of the office in Murano because of the programmes that had been undertaken to construct wells, bridges, and *fondamente* meaning that there was little money left to cover significant expenses.[105]

In part the size of the workforce was responsible for the high cost of these public works. In Genoa, the dredging of the Mandraccio in 1576 and Ponte Spinola and Ponte Calvi in 1596–7 were two of the most expensive works undertaken and costed over 90,000 lire each.[106] The funds for such projects were provided by the Padri and the bank of San Giorgio. Funding was supplemented through a variety

---

[100] ASV, Comun, b.13 reg 31 140v (12 February 1559).
[101] ASV, Comun, Atti b.1, 299r (13 April 1538).   [102] ASV, Comun, Atti b.1, 320v (s.d.).
[103] ASV, Comun, b.11 reg 24 9r (4 March 1545) and b.13 reg 31 unpaginated (14 June 1559).
[104] ASV, Comun, Atti, b.1 368v (16 December 1559).
[105] ASV, Comun, b.14 reg 32 176v (14 March 1562).
[106] Giorgio Doria and Paola Massa Piergiovanni (eds), *Il Sistema portuale*, p. 147.

124 CLEANING UP RENAISSANCE ITALY

of means. Additional money was sometimes received through charitable bequests from individuals. In 1585, Pietro Bon left 25 ducats in his will as a contribution to the excavation works.[107] Fines for transgressions were also used to support such works. The dredging of bodies of water could also be couched in charitable terms. In 1561, a consortium of nobles sent a supplication regarding the canal at the Convertite on Venice's Giudecca. It was noted to be necessary to dredge the body of water in the interests of the public good, particularly for the poor and the residents of the institution, so that they would continue to be provided for. The consortium offered to take the mud extracted from the *rio,* possibly for use in gardens as considered in more detail in the next chapter.[108]

The blame for the poor condition of the canals might also, however, be cast in ways which were distinctly uncharitable. In 1517, the canals in Venice were in such a severe state that if action was not taken, it was thought that it would soon prove impossible to excavate them. Particularly culpable were said to be the many boatsheds of the city (*squeri*), which were causing considerable siltation, and the Jewish community in the Ghetto which threw rubbish into the canals because of the lack of communal rubbish container. It is notable that the Ghetto had been established without consideration for this essential element of the urban infrastructure. This was subsequently to be provided at the cost of the community.[109] Furthermore the Jewish community was compelled to take responsibility for dredging the body of water surrounding the Ghetto from 1517.[110]

The problems of funding investment in infrastructure were acute and continuous.[111] In January 1461 the Padri announced that a new intervention to clean the port was necessary and officials invited suggestions as to how to fund this exercise the following month.[112] By the sixteenth century in Genoa, many of the initiatives were paid for using lotteries.[113] These games were coordinated by the Padri as a way of raising funds for various infrastructure projects, including the construction of the choir at the city's cathedral and repairs to the city's aqueduct. In 1527, the Padri noted that these games had been interrupted by periods of plague and warfare but were, in December of that year, at a stage of being reintroduced

---

[107] ASV, Comun, b.16 reg 36 124v (24 September 1585).
[108] ASV, Comun, b.14 reg 32 180 r–v (23 February 1561).
[109] ASV, Comun, b.3 reg.5 38r (7 March 1517).
[110] Ivone Cacciavillani, *Le leggi ecologiche veneziane* (Padua: Invicta, 1990), p. 45.
[111] ASV, Comun, b.1 369r (19 December 1559).
[112] ASCG, PdC, 1-92 (9 January 1461) and 1-96 (23 February 1461).
[113] These were lotteries of the form known as 'the Dutch lottery' rather than that known as the 'Genoese' game. In the former, individuals would purchase tickets at a set price and these would be drawn to determine the winner. In the latter, players try to guess the outcome of a draw. Giovanni Assereto, *Un giuoco così utile ai pubblici introiti: il lotto di Genova dal XVI al XVIII secolo* (Rome: Fondazione Benetton studi ricerche, 2013) explores the '*Seminario*' as it developed in Genoa and notes pp. 9–21 various points of confusion in the historiography regarding the history of the lottery in Genoa. The lottery in Genoa has been widely recognized for its political and economic significance and across premodern Europe betting on elections developed as described in Jonathan Walker, 'Gambling and Venetian noblemen *c.*1500–1700', *Past and Present* 162 (1999), 31.

because the city had been returned to a good, peaceful, and healthy state. In December 1540, the lottery was said to have been halted because of a period of famine in the city. An announcement just a few days before Christmas noted that the game would be restarting because the concerns around food supplies had abated.[114] Two tables were to be situated in the city (in the Piazza di San Lorenzo and the other near to the church of San Pietro). These would be manned daily by officials and scribes. In return for the sum of 20 soldi, players could enter the game. Names would be recorded and a ticket provided.[115] By 1535 the usual places for the playing of the lottery were described as the Piazza de Marini, the Piazza of San Lorenzo, and the office of the Padri and it became customary to draw the lottery in the cloister of San Domenico.[116] Tickets were drawn from morning to evening, until they had all been shown. An entry from March notes the names of those participating in the lotteries 'sub nomine dio'. There were fifty-seven tickets and the majority of these were purchased by individuals as whole entries (36) but other players purchased multiple or fractional tickets. The smallest fraction was a quarter of a ticket (2 units split between eight players) and ten people also purchased a half ticket each.[117]

Lottery announcements encouraged all people to take part, whether Genoese or foreigners.[118] The authorities were keen to emphasize the morality of playing. The end of the lotteries sometimes coincided with a feast day, such as Christmas day in 1535 (for the September lottery), Easter 1536, and the feast day of St Sebastian in 1538, perhaps to further reassure the conscience of players as well as provide a date which was easy to remember.[119] The drawing of the lottery in 1536 was planned for the day of the conversion of St Paul on 25 January.[120] Some games were recorded with phrases that indicate the perceptions of the players: 'if God wills it', 'to get a cockerel', 'I'd like a new shirt'.[121] The perception of the government was clear: this was a vital source of funding for public works. It stressed that players should participate with an easy conscience (*liberamente et da bono animo*) because, beyond the good fortune (*bona sorte*) which might result, the money would be used for praiseworthy and excellent public works.[122] In January 1534 the Padri noted that it was necessary to increase the number of lottery games being played to raise funds for work on the aqueduct. The situation had become so severe that, without the repairs, it was said that by the summer it would be impossible for water to be transported into the city. A copy of the lottery announcement was to be pasted to the door of

---

[114] ASCG, PdC, 16-81 (20 December 1540). [115] ASCG, PdC, 12-78 (10 December 1527).
[116] ASCG, PdC, 14-151 (12 February 1535). [117] ASCG, PdC, 15-16 (11 March 1536).
[118] ASCG, PdC, 12-78 (10 December 1527).
[119] ASCG, PdC, 14-198 (8 September 1535) and 15-168 (18 December 1538).
[120] ASCG, PdC, 15-5 (21 January 1536). [121] ASCG, PdC, 15-242 (s.d.).
[122] ASCG, PdC, 12-78 (10 December 1527).

126 CLEANING UP RENAISSANCE ITALY

the Church of San Lorenzo and one of the columns in the Banchi to be as visible as possible.[123]

The Padri struggled to retain control over lottery games in the city. In 1532, it was requested that unofficial games should be reported and that citizens should be vigilant in ensuring that lotteries, whether for money or goods of whatever quality or quantity, did not take place. Those presenting information about lotteries were supposed to present written evidence about the games.[124] Officials threatened severe penalties for residents who sought to organize unofficial lottery games.[125] In 1550, the success of unofficial lotteries was threatening the state's use of these games for fundraising and the Padri outlawed all games which had not been licensed by their office.[126] In Genoa, then, the difficulty for the government was in maintaining control over the lottery in order to ensure that the funds raised assisted the public purse. Evelyn Welch has characterized the playing of the lottery in Venice in similar terms where money was used to fund the Arsenal and other enterprises but does not seem to have been used for dredging.[127]

Repair and Reclamation

In parallel with the dredging of principal bodies of water, the authorities in both cities demonstrated their concern for the elements of the built environment which were designed to separate land from water. In Venice these discussions focused particularly on the city's *fondamente*—the paved streets which adjoined canals. In 1531, it was clear that many of the sites around the city were lacking these essential structures, meaning that in times of storms (which, the entry of November noted, had occurred in recent days) soil was carried away and deposited in the canals, with obvious impact on the lagoon.[128] All land, secular or ecclesiastical, was to be reinforced within a period of three months. In 1569, the Savi noted the need to construct *fondamente* at the margins of the city's territory and 'open locations of the city' (*luoghi aperti della città*).

During the sixteenth century, these vital constructions of wood, brick, or stone were said to be lacking in too many sites.[129] In 1519, the Comun noted that the *fondamenta* of the rio Sant'Isepo (San Giuseppe), which was constructed of wood, had become damaged and ruined. As a result, the canal water continuously eroded the ground, causing serious damage to the structure of the church. Recently the

---

[123] ASCG, PdC, 14-82 (1 January 1534). For info on pasting such print see Rosa Salzberg, *Ephemeral city: cheap print and urban culture in Renaissance Venice* (Manchester: Manchester University Press, 2014).
[124] ASCG, PdC, 13-201 (27 November 1532).   [125] ASCG, PdC, 15-126 (7 March 1538).
[126] ASCG, PdC, 20-159 (18 July 1550).
[127] Evelyn Welch, 'Lotteries in early modern Italy', *Past and Present* 199:1 (2008), 71–111.
[128] ASV, Comun b.1 '*de fondamente*' 284r (6 November 1531).
[129] ASV, Comun, Atti b.1 284r (6 November 1531) and ASCG, PdC, 19-7 (10 February 1545).

façade was said to have opened up (*aperta*).[130] A continuation of the problems can be seen in the supplication from the convent in Castello where, in 1558, the new church was still in the process of being constructed. The building was said to be ready to have the roof added so that Mass could be celebrated within. The obstacle, however, was the *rio*: wooden and badly degraded, so that the movement of the water carried away the soil of the *campo*. This was causing damage to the church because of the subsidence of the ground. The *palificate* were intended to provide a firm and secure boundary between the water and the land in a city in which the dividing line was rarely fixed or secure.

These concerns also applied to religious institutions situated on islands of the Venetian lagoon. The monastery of San Giorgio Maggiore along with communities on San Giorgio d'Alga, Santo Spirito, San Clemente, and San Antonio were instructed to construct stone *fondamente* in 1546.[131] In 1571 the Savi paid for the stone *fondamenta* around the island of San Cristoforo della Pace and the institution was required to repay the money.[132] Religious institutions located at the edges of Venice also developed initiatives to extend their space by undertaking land reclamation, for example at Santa Giustina.[133]

Fondamente were considered to fall within the oversight of the Savi ed Esecutori alle Acque. In 1519, the *fondamenta* which ran from Santa Marta to the Dogana da Mare was constructed. In 1536, substantial work was undertaken to build and mend these structures on the canal of the Giudecca, Canareggio, San Gerolamo, Santa Maria dell'Orto, San Alvise, San Simion to San Andrea and on the Rio di San Domenico.[134] The value of *fondamente* for protecting the built environment of Venice was perhaps articulated most clearly by Cristoforo Sabbadino. His plan of the city in 1557 proposed new areas of land reclamation on the Giudecca and western edges of the city. In addition, he proposed strengthening and smoothing the edges of the city with a circular *fondamenta* of stone to ameliorate the problem of siltation. This would have required thirty-six new bridges over the existing canals. Only the Fondamenta Nuove would realize part of Sabbadino's vision. The maintenance of these structures also required intervention so that they were not damaged through use. In 1590, eight iron rings were added to the Fondamenta della Croce so that they could be used by boats without damage to the structure itself.[135]

There were enduring efforts to raise the level of the land too. Land reclamation took place at a number of sites described as swampy and low-lying in Venice, including at the 'ramo del Paludo' at SS Giovanni e Paolo and the 'paludo di Sant'Isepo' during the 1520s. In 1516, the Water Office had instructed boatmen and *cavacanali* to transport waste and mud to this area in order to build up the

---

[130] ASV, Comun reg 1 364r (13 May 1559).   [131] Rompiasio, p. 185.
[132] Rompiasio, p. 186.   [133] Ennio Concina, *Venezia nell'età moderna*, p. 111.
[134] Rompiasio, p. 185.   [135] Rompiasio, p. 186.

128   CLEANING UP RENAISSANCE ITALY

ground. By 1533, it had been reclaimed and the government sent materials to smooth out the uneven levels.[136] This was not an area of high population density. The religious community of San Giuseppe had taken up residence in this poor district in 1512 and much of the surrounding territory remained empty. By the 1520s, the development of a canal as part of the reclamation works meant that some houses, albeit often poor wooden structures, had been developed.[137] Some artificial islands in Venice—denoted with the name *sacca*—were also built up over time as a result of rubbish disposal, such as Sacca Fisola on the Giudecca.[138]

In addition to the work to reinforce (and, in some cases, extend) the boundaries of the city, care was also taken over the use of this land. Early instructions related to the care of the banks (*argini*) in the lagoon, including that of 1346 which forbade individuals from grazing animals on these areas.[139] From 1502 it was made clear that spaces adjacent to the lagoon were not to be cultivated but should remain grassland (*prati*).[140] Serious penalties were threatened to anyone who cut or reduced or damaged these areas and incentives used to encourage denunciations of the perpetrators.[141] Through the 1530s, numerous attempts were made to prohibit ferry boats from accessing these sites and animals from grazing there.[142]

In 1485, a piece of legislation regarding the excavation of the raised *dossi* (humps/piles) in the lagoon noted that the accessibility of the lagoon was essential for the health of the city and the comfort of mariners and traders of all kinds.[143] In 1525, the muddy islands in the lagoon which were submerged at high tide, known as *velme* were said to have increased considerably in size with consequences for the salubrity of the air.[144] The quantity of material being excavated was significant, running into the hundreds of boatloads every week.[145] In 1546, the Water Office ordered fifty pontoons (*zattere*) and 100 small boats (*burchielle*) from the Arsenal.[146] In 1565, a further order was made for forty *zattere*, 150 *burchielle*, and eighty large shovels (*badili grandi*) for the dredging of the *barene* and *velme* around the city.[147] In 1578, in addition to identifying a need for additional funds to support the work, the government also recognized the lack of boats available to undertake the excavation. The numbers had been limited in 1510, since which time the population of the city had increased in size considerably. The office suggested increasing the number in order to assist with the urgent task of dredging.[148]

---

[136] Paola Pavanini, 'Venezia verso la pianificazione?', p. 497.
[137] Paola Pavanini, 'Venezia verso la pianificazione?', pp. 499–500.
[138] Roberto Berveglieri, *Le vie di Venezia*, p. 266.
[139] Roberto Berveglieri, *Le vie di Venezia*, p. 269.
[140] Roberto Berveglieri, *Le vie di Venezia*, p. 138.   [141] Rompiasio, p. 260.
[142] Rompiasio, pp. 260–1.   [143] Roberto Berveglieri, *Le vie di Venezia*, p. 238.
[144] ASV, Sanità reg 12 42r (9 October 1525).
[145] Roberto Berveglieri, *Le vie di Venezia*, pp. 282–3.
[146] Roberto Berveglieri, *Le vie di Venezia*, pp. 279–80.   [147] Rompiasio, p. 231.
[148] Boats were recorded at Santa Maria del Giglio (3), Santa Sofia (5), Barileri [barrel-makers] (3), Rialto bridge (2), S Stae (8), the flour warehouse at Rialto (3), San Barnaba (4), Ghetto vecchio (4),

STEMMING THE TIDE   129

Regulating Rivers

The health of both Genoa and Venice relied indirectly on the condition of some of the principal rivers which passed through the wider territory. In Genoa, the Bisagno river to the east of the city and Polcevera to the west were sizeable and the principal focus for government activity.[149] For Venice, the interventions in those rivers that flowed into the lagoon have been widely considered by Ciriacono, amongst others.[150] In order to address the problems of siltation, for example, a channel was made between Mestre and Dese in 1525, known as la Destina. The diversion of the Brenta and Bacchiglione rivers was also intended to protect the balance of the lagoon. In Genoa, in contrast, there were no major interventions in the course of the rivers of the territory. Instead, throughout this period, the Padri had to deal with the impact of these bodies of water on the surrounding areas.

Embankments were also constructed to provide a degree of protection around rivers and repaired or reinforced when necessary. The Valpolcevera is one of the two principal valleys adjacent to Genoa and lies to the west of the city. A plot of land owned by the Incurabili hospital near the Polcevera river was said to be protected from the river by an embankment of one hundred palms length. At the beginning of the seventeenth century, the force of the river had caused about one half of the structure to become ruptured and, as a result, the river waters were able to flow onto land owned by the hospital and others nearby.[151] In 1560, property owners in the Valpolcevera sent a supplication to the Padri concerning necessary repairs to be made around the Polcevera river.[152] The river was said to have caused considerable damage and threatened to have a greater impact if repairs were not undertaken on the breakwater (*molo*) in order to reduce the force (*l'impeto*) of the water. The nobles argued that any damage caused by the river was common to all those whose properties were in the vicinity and therefore the benefit would be felt equally. The Padri were requested to undertake an assessment of the necessary repairs and allocate the costs accordingly.

In 1546, the manner in which the health of the Venetian lagoon and that of the canals of the city were inextricably linked was articulated, as was the relation of both to the security and health of the city.[153] The systems in place to prevent and respond to environmental problems were broadly similar in Genoa and Venice although the specific areas for intervention differed in line with the distinct environments of the two port cities. The development of petitions and patents

---

Parto Gruer b'ch p'le 2, San Tomà (3), Santa Maria della Carità (4), San Benedetto (4), Trinità (2), San Marcuola (4), Lizzafusina (4), San Domenico (12), and San Marco (4) in ASV, Comun reg 1 402v (20 September 1578).

[149] Biondo Flavio, *Italy illuminated*, p. 29.

[150] Salvatore Ciriacono, *Building on water: Venice, Holland and the construction of the European landscape in early modern times* (Oxford: Berghahn Books, 2006).

[151] ASCG, PdC, 67-66 (9 September 1609).   [152] ASCG, PdC, 247-114 (25 June 1560).

[153] ASV Comun b.2, 124r (18 January 1546).

to encourage environmental innovation and new technology played an important role in the ongoing regulation of the environment. Despite the use of these machines and the efforts considered in previous chapters, however, siltation was an enduring problem in both cities. As a result, dredging works, as well as measures to reinforce the boundaries of bodies of water, were viewed as costly but necessary. In both contexts, the priority was to maintain and improve upon the natural balance of the elements in the two environments. In order to attain this, governments had to confront the challenge posed by significant quantities of waste material and also the impact of natural disasters—both of which are the focus for the chapters that follow.

PART TWO

BODIES: CONCEPTS OF BALANCE AND BLAME

5

Working with Waste

Space, Reuse, and the Urban Body

In 1516, the Venetian government ordered the city's Jewish community to live within the confines of one of the cityscape's small islands: somewhere which could be guarded and monitored and was surrounded by water. Officials selected a site that had previously been used for the disposal of waste products from the foundries located in the district of Canareggio.[1] This literal place of thrown-away things (the 'geto' from the verb *gettare* meaning to discard) was appropriated as a space which anticipated potential tensions between residents of the Ghetto and their Christian neighbours. It was, until the Jewish community was moved there, a wasteland. In English, the etymology of the word 'waste' can be traced to the medieval Latin word *vastum* meaning land which had been devastated (during periods of warfare, for example) or that lay uncultivated.[2] Only later, did it take on its meaning of 'neglected value or unrealized productive force' in relation to materials and energy, as well as places. Inherent in the concept of waste is a sense of unrealized value, although this certainly does not preclude connotations of dirt or pollution. From the outset, the notion of waste in English has been linked to that of place and this can also be seen in some of the Italian terms: *immonditie*, associated with immorality as well as dirt and filth, is the most common term used for waste material. It is often employed as a catch-all (in phrases such as 'all other types of "*immonditie*"') and literally refers to things left on the ground. Other terms used in more specific contexts, often with interesting etymology, include *fanghi* (mud or sludge), *letame* (filth), *rovinazzi* (rubble), *rumenta* (rubble), *scarichi* (something dumped), *scovazze* (something dislodged), *terreni* (soil), and *zetti* (rubble).

For both Genoa and Venice the available archival material reveals more about the management of such rubbish and rubble than it does of sewage. Some evidence remains regarding the place of public latrines including at Genoa's Ponte dei Calvi.[3] In the mid seventeenth century, a bank of public latrines ('*il luogo*

---

[1] Ivone Cacciavillani, *Le leggi ecologiche veneziane*, p. 123. The waste products from metal foundries (in this case lead) had been recognized to pose a significant risk to health as a result of noxious by-products causing air pollution in October 1294 by the city's Maggior Consiglio (see p. 128).

[2] Tim Cooper, 'Recycling modernity: waste and environmental history', *History Compass* 8:9 (2010), 1116–17.

[3] ASCG, PdC, 1-129 (14 January 1465).

Cleaning Up Renaissance Italy: Environmental Ideals and Urban Practice in Genoa and Venice. Jane L. Stevens Crawshaw,
Oxford University Press. © Jane L. Stevens Crawshaw 2023. DOI: 10.1093/oso/9780198867432.003.0006

134 CLEANING UP RENAISSANCE ITALY

commune delle commodità necessarie') was located at the base of the Ponte de Chiavari towards the site where a new warehouse was being constructed. The latrines were to be transferred to the other side towards the Ponte de Cattanei and reconstructed according to the design provided. A bank of twenty-two latrines is shown in a rectangular formation (two rows of eleven spaces).[4] When latrines needed to be opened in order to be cleaned, it was noted that this should be done when the risk of rainfall was low to avoid the contents leaking into the surrounding area and, once cleaned, they should be closed up promptly, presumably in the interests of ensuring that the materials and stench were contained.[5] The government also intervened with regard to private latrines when they were seen to impact upon public spaces. In 1471, for example, the rector at the Church of the Crociferi in Bisagno was reprimanded for having constructed a latrine which was causing excrement and rubbish (*stercora et imondicie)* to pass onto the public street.[6] Beyond such specific examples, in this chapter waste is largely synonymous with discarded materials.

Tim Cooper has noted that the categories of waste and dirt are often conflated in scholarship but argues for an analytical distinction to prevent the former concept from 'becoming a one-dimensional analysis of "discipline"'.[7] In addition to the insights derived from Mary Douglas's *Purity and Danger*, the work of one of her students, Michael Thompson, on waste can be instructive.[8] Thompson emphasized the role of visibility in propelling an object (or category) from what he termed one of 'transient' value (one which decreases with time) to that of durable value (which increases with time) mediated by this analytical category of rubbish: 'the discarded but still visible, because it still intrudes, forms a genuine cultural category of a special type—a rubbish category'.[9] Within this, the setting or location for materials becomes significant, as does the process by which they are discarded in a public or private setting.[10] This chapter considers the cultures or systems in place to deal with waste in Genoa and Venice. These operated at the level of the household, workplace, parish, city, and the broader state although the emphasis here is on the handling of waste in public space and the changing practices, people, and places associated with waste, its disposal and reuse.

The population growth and urban development of the fifteenth and sixteenth centuries meant that increased quantities of sewage, rubbish, and rubble were

---

[4] ASCG, PdC, 224-68 (13 April 1643).

[5] Leges Genuensis, *Historiae patriae monumenta* vol. 18 [96].

[6] ASCG, PdC, 3-67 (20 September 1471).   [7] Tim Cooper, 'Recycling modernity, 1116.

[8] On Mary Douglas see the introduction pp. 5–6. Michael Thompson, *Rubbish theory: the creation and destruction of value* (London: Pluto Press, 2017).

[9] Michael Thompson, *Rubbish theory*, p. 101.

[10] For a study of the management of waste and agricultural productivity in premodern Europe see Marc Conesa and Nicolas Poirier (eds), *Fumiers! Ordures! Gestion et usage des déchets dans les campagnes de l'Occident médiéval et moderne. Actes des XXXVIIIes Journées internationals d'histoire de l'abbaye de Flaran* (Toulouse: Presses universitaires du Midi, 2019).

produced in both Genoa and Venice. The systems which had been designed to manage and clear these materials required augmentation in response. In the mid seventeenth century, the Venetian Health Office reminded the city's inhabitants that the vast quantities of rubbish which filled the streets of the city posed a serious threat to *'salute universale'*: the health of all. These materials could rot and produce an intense stench which, in addition to disgusting the senses, could generate serious illnesses. In 1539 in Venice's Calle della Stimaria there was reported to be an enormous quantity of sludge and other rubbish which was giving off a stench so intense and disgusting that it risked contaminating the air and causing an outbreak of epidemic disease.[11] As we saw in chapter two, corruption was associated with heat and so this risk was particularly acute during the summer, meaning that, yet again, there was a seasonality to concerns about health and the environment: omnipresent but intense at particularly moments in the year.[12] Rubbish could also block streets, canals, and drains: threats to those free-flowing channels which were seen in previous chapters to be vital to the wellbeing of the city.

The importance of circulation, reuse, and the retention of energy are all evident in premodern handling of waste. Emily Cockayne has effectively dismantled the image of the early modern period as an idyll of recycling and reuse.[13] During the fifteenth and sixteenth centuries (as before and since) many materials were reused because of the cost and inconvenience of sourcing new ones. This was particularly true for building materials. In 1492, for example, permission was given for timber from a shipwrecked vessel in Genoa to be used in the construction of the city's fortress in the district of Castelletto.[14] In 1521, the rebuilding of the Campanile of San Lorenzo in stone prompted the Padri to arrange for the reuse of the material from a tower which was to be demolished in the district of San Giorgio.[15] Waste materials were utilized in these two port cities for ballast or flood defences in ways which were coordinated by the government.[16] In Venice, dredged sludge was applied to gardens or to reinforce dykes. Early in the sixteenth century embankments on the Botenigo and Brenta rivers and at Lizzafusina in the Veneto were also strengthened using dredged material.[17] Although some schemes were coordinated by the government, the market for these materials was widely known and individuals also requested such materials, as well as responding to notifications of upcoming sales.

---

[11] ASV, Sanità 728 7r (28 August 1539).   [12] ASV, Sanità, 740 10v (30 April 1643).

[13] That sense of value has been a focus for study (as in the current project on trades and the recycling, reuse, and upcycling of objects and materials in medieval England by James Davis, Catherine Casson and John Lee https://blog.history.ac.uk/2021/02/recycling-and-upcycling-waste-in-the-late-medieval-urban-economy/) [accessed 15 June 2021].

[14] ASCG, PdC, 6-60 (10 April 1492).   [15] ASCG, PdC, 11-92 (29 May 1521).

[16] See Pamela O. Long, 'Hydraulic engineering'.

[17] Roberto Berveglieri, *Le vie di Venezia*, p. 254.

136 CLEANING UP RENAISSANCE ITALY

Many premodern manufacturing and artisanal processes used waste materials, including ash for lye in washing and rags for papermaking.[18] In providing an explanation for this repurposing of materials, Carlo Cipolla argued that dearth and poverty were the principal impetus.[19] That, of course, may well have been the case for cultures of reuse and recycling in the domestic sphere—a subject which warrants further attention. In the public space of the ports under consideration here, it was instead the risks to the accessibility and cleanliness of the streets that were principal motivations. Governments employed officials to walk and inspect the streets to ensure that waste was passing to the correct destinations and handlers. The locations in which waste was deposited, and even the purposes for which it was used, changed over years, decades, and centuries—not in a linear fashion towards some sort of efficient ideal, but in response to broader environmental changes and challenges.

Identifying Waste

In both cities, the ownership of materials left in public spaces was a point of contention. Both governments bemoaned the theft of building materials in the streets that were intended for public works on the Genoese aqueduct and breakwater or the wood and stone procured by the Provveditori di Comun in Venice for the 'ornament and comfort' of the city through the construction of bridges, wells, streets, and *fondamente*.[20] Following the demolition of two houses in Sant'Agostino in Genoa, those in the vicinity were reported to have taken timber, tiles (*mattoni*), stone, and other materials illicitly.[21] Sometimes these actions were premeditated and planned. In 1514, the Padri reported with disgust on the lack of respect that had been shown to their office by those who had gone well equipped to take iron and lead from the ruined lighthouse as well as other materials belonging to the Padri on the nearby pontoon. There was clearly a market for these materials since the proclamation addressed both those who might have removed them and those could have been offered them for sale.[22] At other times, such actions may have been more opportunistic. In 1559, a proclamation was issued in Genoa which instructed anyone who had carried away the timber drawn by a recent storm onto the harbourfront to return it.[23] The potential value

---

[18] Heidi Craig, 'Rags, ragpickers and early modern papermaking', *Literature Compass* 16:5 (2019), e12523.

[19] Carlo Cipolla, *Before the Industrial Revolution* cited in Donald Woodward, '"Swords into ploughshares": recycling in pre-Industrial England', *The Economic History Review* 38:2 (1985), 176.

[20] ASCG, PdC, 12-8 (9 April 1526) and ASV, Comun, reg 1 119v (2 March 1495). Severe punishment was threatened to those who stole materials intended for use on the breakwater in Genoa in 1469 in ASCG, PdC, 3-8 (29 April 1469).

[21] ASCG, PdC, 20-113 (29 January 1549).   [22] ASCG, PdC, 10-97 (17 August 1514).

[23] ASCG, PdC, 24-51 (11 September 1559).

WORKING WITH WASTE   137

of these materials, seemingly lying on the streets unrealized, often proved too much to resist.

There were also points of tension relating to the right of residents to utilize the elements of the natural environment for their own purposes. Some of the regulations regarding the removal of materials from coastlines were clearly intended to maintain these areas as a form of protection for the city and wider territory. In 1549, the Padri described the various boatmen and other people who had been taking stones from the area along the coast near the lighthouse. This was said to be very damaging and prejudicial to the port and was outlawed.[24] A related and significant issue in both port cities was the manner in which maritime vessels obtained their ballast. Sand and rock were generally used for this purpose and both governments sought to regulate where this material was procured from and how it was deposited after a journey.[25] In the case of the latter, concerns about placement related to issues of contamination and filth: having spent weeks or months in the hold of a ship, the sand and stone might be polluted, stinking, and noxious.[26] In the previous chapter, we saw the way in which governments regulated the supply of water to vessels to balance the needs of the city with those of the trade economy, as well as undertaking efforts to keep pollution out of the public water supply. The handling of ballast was approached with similar concerns.

In 1471, the Genoese government reminded the community that no one was permitted to help themselves to the rubble on the Ponte Calvi for ballast.[27] More frequently mentioned was the removal of sand and stones from the beaches along the Ligurian coastline, including Carignano, Albaro, Sampierdarena, Cornigliano, and Sestri.[28] Cases were brought against those who took sand from the beach at Nervi (to the east of the city).[29] In 1547, residents were reminded not to remove ballast or sand from there without replacing the materials with an equivalent quantity of stone.[30] In 1557, the beach at Boccadasse was said to have been badly reduced in size, as reported by residents, because of the boats which went there to load up with ballast. The Padri pronounced that this was not permitted and the proclamation was particularly directed towards boatmen and muleteers (who, presumably, were taking this material in order to sell it on)[31] In 1567, the Podestà of Rapallo and the Padri issued a joint announcement that it was prohibited for anyone to remove material from the beach at Rapallo for ballast.[32]

---

[24] ASCG, PdC, 20-69 (5 September 1549).
[25] At times in Venice salt and heavy cargo were used to replace the sand and rock. See Frederic C. Lane, *Venice and history: the collected papers of Frederic C. Lane* (Baltimore MA: Johns Hopkins University Press, 2019).
[26] I am grateful to Claire Weeda for drawing my attention to this aspect of the handling of ballast.
[27] ASCG, PdC, 3-59 (21 May 1471).   [28] ASCG, PdC, 1-75 (23 June 1460).
[29] ASCG, PdC, 15-89 (11 June 1537), 22-8 (4 April 1554) and 22-88 (16 January 1555).
[30] ASCG, PdC, 19-155 and 156 (1 October 1547).   [31] ASCG, PdC, 23-89 (29 October 1557).
[32] ASCG, PdC, 28-31 (3 March 1567).

138 CLEANING UP RENAISSANCE ITALY

Since the fourteenth century it had been forbidden for individuals to remove sand from Venice's Lido. This was reiterated in the early sixteenth century.[33] This area was a vital one for protecting the city against the water. It had an extended *palificata*, or barrier of wooden piles with the spaces filled with large stones. Joseph Wheeler has noted that excavated sludge was reused to reinforce these dikes.[34] It was, therefore, considered vital that material was not taken from this area since this would weaken the location's ability to act as a barrier against the force of the sea.

In Genoa in 1566, the Padri illustrated the way in which the practices of the port could be used to maintain balance within the environment. Some beach areas between the lighthouse and the city were said to have grown considerably in size and vessels in the port which needed to load up with ballast were directed to these sites. The location for ballast in Venice was more consistent. The Punta di San Antonio, which has been characterized by Danielle Abdon as an important place of arrival and transit, was also significant for the management of the city's environment. In addition to the roles considered in later sections, it was the principal location for sourcing and loading ballast in the city.[35]

The unregulated transportation of ballast could be as damaging to the environment as illicit sourcing. Loading ballast at night, for example, was strictly forbidden in Genoa because of the potential damage to the port if materials were dropped (or dumped).[36] The Padri stipulated that this work should not be done between the hour of the Ave Maria in the evening until the clear light of day ('*giorno chiaro*'). The penalty for contravention was the burning of a vessel.[37] Even with these risks and regulations, the Padri received denunciations about the offloading of ballast beyond allotted areas of the port.[38] In 1463, the problem caused by the disposal of ballast in Venice's Grand Canal was also highlighted.[39] This was more commonly an issue in the lagoon where individuals presumably felt that they were less likely to be observed. Penalties were imposed on all those who discarded material from ships or any other boat into the water or onto the *velme* (the mudflats of the lagoon which are often exposed by the tides).[40]

Improper disposal of ballast was just one way in which waste materials might pass into bodies of water. Environmental management also necessitated the regulation of behaviour and customs. In 1538, the Padri noted with dismay that every Sunday and feast day, from the arsenal or breakwater, small boats would set out to race (*regatando*) within the Genoese port. These races may well have been

---

[33] Rompiasio, p. 270. [34] Joseph Wheeler, 'Stench in sixteenth-century Venice', p. 36.
[35] Rompiasio, p. 257. [36] ASCG, PdC, 20-64 (26 August 1549).
[37] ASCG, PdC, 20-92 (16 November 1549).
[38] ASCG, PdC, 20-146 (17 June 1550). This was a cause for concern elsewhere because of the pollution caused by the release of ballast in the port in Den Briel (Maerlantse) during the fifteenth century. Guy Geltner and Claire Weeda, 'Underground and over the sea', p. 142.
[39] ASCG, PdC, 6-17 (9 July 1490) and Roberto Berveglieri, *Le vie di Venezia*, p. 235.
[40] Rompiasio, p. 258.

WORKING WITH WASTE   139

associated with factionalism within the city since, between them, the crews were said to have arguments to the end that they threw stones at one another's vessels. These invariably ended up in the water thereby exacerbating the problem of siltation and causing enormous damage to the port. The Padri instructed that in the future, no one should rent boats to youths or those who were looking to engage in such behaviour, nor engage in such behaviour themselves, under threat of penury or corporeal punishment.[41] Elsewhere on the Italian peninsula, 'since at least the tenth century, rival bands of youths had battled for supremacy in open fields with fists or stones, or wooden swords and shields' and equivalent behaviours seem to have manifested themselves in Genoa and Venice on or over the water.[42]

There is no doubt that cleanliness was seen to have important religious implications. The environment often featured in miracle narratives or hagiographical tales as, sometimes, did cleaning.[43] Fabrizio Nevola's work on fifteenth-century Siena describes a process by which 'devotional images and dedications to the Virgin Mary were instrumental to the urban improvement of semi-derelict or marginal sites'.[44] Dennis Romano has highlighted similar issues during the medieval period when the government in Pistoia forbade tethering pack animals near the grain market 'out of reverence for Saint James the Apostle and Saint Zeno the Confessor' and passed a law against 'encumbering or fouling any piazza in front of any church in the city' which was done 'to the honor of omnipotent God and of his saints'.[45] In the context of Italian Renaissance piety, the connections between sanctity and cleanliness were particularly evident in the regulation of public space. In Venice during the sixteenth century, it was noted by the Health Office that the disposal of rubbish in Piazza San Marco was prohibited, as was urination or the production of any other filth (*fare altre immondizie*) in front of the Church of

---

[41] ASCG, PdC, 15-132 (27 April 1538).

[42] For Venice, Robert Davis has explored the 'quasi-ritual brawls' which filled bridges in the city such as San Barnabà in *The war of the fists.*

[43] For an outstanding study of Ligurian miracle stories and their visual manifestations see Gervase Rosser and Jane Garnett, *Spectacular miracles.* Cleaning also features prominently in the miracle narrative of Santa Maria delle Carceri in Prato when an image steps down off the wall to clean an abandoned prison. See Caroline Walker Bynum, *Christian materiality: an essay on religion in late medieval Europe* (New York: Zone Books, 2011) p. 106. Molly Morrison has explored the associations between holiness and filth in hagiographic accounts of female saints eating filth or licking wounds: 'Strange miracles: a study of the peculiar healings of St Maria Maddelena de'Pazzi, *Logos* 8 (2005), 129–44. Such behaviour featured in the story of St Catherine of Genoa. Ellen Arnold has documented the role that the environment played in miracle stories of the medieval Ardennes in, 'Engineering miracles: water control, conversion and the creation of a religious landscape in the medieval Ardennes', *Environment and History* 13 (2007), 477–502.

[44] Fabrizio Nevola, 'Surveillance and control of the street in Renaissance Italy', in 'Experiences of the Street in Early Modern Italy', *I Tatti Studies in the Italian Renaissance* 16 (2013), 98 and Niccolo Machiavelli, *Mandragola* Act five, scene one, cited in Gervase Rosser and Jane Garnett, *Spectacular miracles*, p. 109.

[45] Dennis Romano, *Markets and marketplaces*, p. 137.

140   CLEANING UP RENAISSANCE ITALY

San Marco.[46] In Genoa in 1567, it was noted to be important that neither rubble or any other sort of rubbish was placed at the side of the Ducal Palace in Piazza Nova at the side of the Church of Sant'Ambrogio up to the railings of the palace, or around the church. The fine in this instance would be 20 soldi as well as the loss of equipment (*bochali delli muli*) and other items for collecting rubbish.[47]

The most pressing issue to emerge in Genoa and Venice, however, in terms of civic regulation was the disposal of building rubble. In 1467, the Genoese Padri reminded inhabitants that they were prohibited from obstructing (*ingombrare*) the port with these things, including stones, marble, tiles/bricks (*mattoni*), or lime (*calcina*).[48] In Venice, the work of the building trades was carefully monitored. In theory, one of the officers of the Comun was supposed to be notified about any planned building works so that they could measure the depth of nearby watercourses at the outset and return at the end to ensure that the level of the canal bed remained unaltered.[49] In practice, when removing sections of walls to create balconies, chimneys, and other structures, artisans were said to deposit the rubble in the canals. Similar materials were dumped in streets and squares. In 1566, the Comun noted that builders were failing to take away rubble and rubbish after finishing their work. The consequences were that either these materials passed into watercourses as a result of rainfall or they were thrown by children and damaged the public wells.[50]

The disposal of building materials was carefully regulated because of the recognized impact that large quantities of rubble could have on the locality. In 1586, concern was expressed by the Venetian procurators that stone, rubble, mud, and other rubbish were being dumped on the *fondamente* and other public places. Over time, these materials would pass into the canals. This was said to be particularly damaging (and presumably frustrating) given that a general excavation of the canals was being undertaken at that time. Within three days, it was said that any such material must be taken away and these spaces left clean and clear. Any stone which had not been removed in this time would be taken and utilized for repairs to the *fondamente*.[51] Similarly in 1547 Stephano Zaraboto was instructed to remove timber which he had left on the campo of Sant'Antonio within three days; he was informed that anything left beyond this period would be taken to the Arsenal for use.[52]

In 1551 the Padri issued regulations regarding the disposal of materials produced by the trades of the city.[53] Four years later, officials noted that these

---

[46] Gianpietro Zucchetta, *Una fognatura per Venezia: storia di due secoli di progretti* (Venice: Istituto veneto di scienze, lettere ed arti, 1986), p. 13.
[47] ASCG, PdC, 28-114 (7 October 1567).   [48] ASCG, PdC, 1-191 (1 June 1467).
[49] ASV, Comun, Atti, b.2 223v (23 January 1585).
[50] ASV, Comun b.14 reg 33 151v (7 March 1566).
[51] ASV, Comun, b.16 reg 36 176v–177r (4 June 1586).
[52] ASV, Comun b.11 reg 25 17v (13 August 1547).   [53] ASCG, PdC, 21-50 (27 August 1551).

instructions seemed to have been forgotten and required revision and reissue. Any workers who needed to leave building materials, soil, or other materials (*immonditie*) in squares or streets were required to leave a pledge with officials, which would be noted by the scribe and not returned until the materials had been removed. Piles were intended to be marked with two flags (*bande*) and a light (*lume*) so that pedestrians would be aware of the obstacle and materials were not permitted to be left in times of rainfall.

The various building projects of the 1550s in Genoa, including the city's famed Strada Nuova generated large quantities of rubble and rubbish which needed to be disposed of. This period of urban redevelopment involved demolition as well as construction.[54] Areas of the city which were being rebuilt also attracted illegal rubbish dumping. In 1557, for example, the Padri particularly highlighted that rubble and rubbish may not be left in the site of the redeveloped Strada Nuova or in the nearby district of San Francesco and the Amarosa fountain.[55] Wastelands in general were recognized to become dumping grounds for rubbish and owners of nearby properties petitioned for permission to incorporate these sites into their ownership to avoid insalubrious spaces developing in their vicinity.[56]

There were issues of waste materials which related particularly to the equipment utilized within ports. In Venice, for example, there were concerns about the disposal of oak apparatus used by fishermen (*fassinazze con le foglie per pigliar con quelle delli gambari*).[57] In Genoa, the Church of San Marco at the port was said to be surrounded by timber, anchors, and artillery in 1549, which was creating an obstruction near the church and there was concern that these materials would enter and obstruct the port.[58] As noted in the previous chapter, sunken boats were thought to cause significant damage. Inhabitants were also repeatedly reminded not to thrown rubbish into the port directly, either in general terms or with reference to particular locations. In 1532, for example, those who inhabited houses between the Arsenal and the Molo were reminded not to throw rubbish into the water from their balconies or out of windows.[59]

Trades were regulated to minimize their impact upon the environment. In Genoa, sculptors and stonemasons with workshops facing the water were expected to ensure that they had an iron grill fitted to the windows and doors of their shops in order to prevent chips and other small pieces of stone falling into the water. For shops facing onto the streets, similar structures were to be introduced in order to prevent chips of marble and other stones from hitting passers-by, an event which was described as happening '*di continuo*'.[60] Leonardo da Vinci's much-quoted observation that a 'sculptor's face is pasted and smeared all over with marble

---

[54] ASCG, PdC, 13-153 (30 January 1532).   [55] ASCG, PdC, 23-57 (17 July 1557).
[56] ASCG, PdC, 30-1 (5 January 1570).   [57] *Antichi scrittori* vol. III, p. 41.
[58] ASCG, PdC, 20-42 (31 May 1549).
[59] ASCG, PdC, 10-56 (4 October 1513) and 13-157 (4 March 1532).
[60] ASCG, PdC, 29-43 (10 July 1568).

142 CLEANING UP RENAISSANCE ITALY

powder making him look like a baker, and he is covered with minute chips as if coming from a snowstorm, and his dwelling is dirty and filled with dust and chips of stone' may well reflect something of the reality of many of these workshops.[61] Skinners and tanners were also expected to remove the potentially polluting waste materials of their work.[62] Sellers of vegetables were instructed not to throw the pods of beans and peas or the remnants of lettuce onto streets or into fountains to prevent them from passing into the port and causing stench.[63] In 1565, the Venetian *vignaroli* on various islands were forbidden from throwing plants into the lagoon.[64]

The illicit disposal of rubbish, however, was thought to be a problem caused by those across the social spectrum. In Venice in 1516, a proclamation—which was repeated in the coming decades—noted the bad habits (*pessima consuetudine*) of the families and wives of gentlemen, citizens, and many other individuals. People were said to be throwing rubbish and waste into the canals.[65] This was being done publicly—with the implication being that it was being done shamelessly—and with real detriment to the city's canals. In 1558, it was clear that the problems endured: rubbish was being thrown into the canals and streets by women, children, and servants (amongst others) instead of being taken to designated areas. These materials were causing blockages in the canals as well as striking people who were moving through the city by canal or by street on the back.[66] Details were provided about how fines would be issued for transgressions, including the note that if the culprit was a minor then the head of household would be held culpable. Significant concern, therefore, was raised by government authorities in both cities regarding the collection and disposal of waste. As a result, considerable effort was made to clarify the nature of materials left in urban spaces through the specification of clear locations for waste.

Placing Waste

The streets of both Genoa and Venice included communal rubbish areas or containers known as *caselle de lo scovaze*.[67] These were generally square structures

---

[61] Cited in Paula Hohti Erichsen, *Artisans, objects and everyday life*, p. 112.
[62] ASCG, PdC, 3-40 (18 June 1470) and 5-6 (7 March 1481).
[63] ASCG, PdC 6-92 (7 May 1494) on the '*bucce di fave piselli avanzi di lettuga*'.
[64] Rompiasio, p. 271. Roberto Berveglieri, *Le vie di Venezia*, p. 289.
[65] ASV, Comun b.3 reg.5 36r (1 August 1516).   [66] ASV, Comun, b.1 359v (18 August 1558).
[67] For example, the *casela* in Santa Maria Formosa is referred to in ASV, Comun b.10 reg 21 153v (26 May 1536) and there is a depiction in Giudici del Piovego, disegni, b.23 reg 13 misure c.21 dis 16 (21 September 1634) which shows the rectangular structure in the corner of the campo next to the *rio*. An eighteenth-century image of a rubbish container in San Nicolò with a brick wall can be seen in SEA, Disegni, Atti, b.58 dis 3 (1760).

which were used to store waste before it was collected for transportation.[68] These structures were above ground but elsewhere in Venice there were subterranean rubbish units, as at the Pescaria in Rialto in order to protect the Grand Canal from the rubbish produced within the fish market and, from 1609, on the Fondamenta Nuove.[69] The openings of the rubbish containers were not supposed to face onto public streets.[70] Nevertheless they had a clear impact on nearby dwellings. In 1537 in Venice, in San Giovanni in Bragora, a building was described as old and in poor condition. It was noted that it would be difficult to rent because of the rubbish container (*caxella da scovaze*) beneath the balcony.[71] In Genoa in 1574, the doctor Giovanni Battista Giustiniano described the effects of having one of these receptacles close to his property.[72] He described it as disgusting to see, something that offended the sight of the house and those of others in the vicinity. Such structures affected the value of property and those which developed illicitly often did so in the ruins of derelict houses.

The square *scoazzere* of Venice often gave their name to the areas in which they were situated, such as a small street at San Apollinare.[73] The importance of these units was recognized in 1622 when the officials of the city's Water Office reflected on the fact that, contrary to the government's instructions, some of these rubbish containers had been removed under 'various pretences' and not replaced. This was said to have happened at San Mauritio, Sant'Aponal, San Severo, San Martino, San Leonardo, San Stefano, and Sant'Angelo. This must have been particularly problematic in the case of the latter since the *scoazzera* of San Mauritio had previously been incorporated into that of Sant'Angelo, meaning that two districts were left without this repository. The consequence, the officials noted, of the absence of rubbish containers was that residents had liberally thrown their rubbish into the surrounding canals causing them to become clogged and swampy.[74]

Not all areas of the city were provided with equal access to these rubbish containers, however. When the Jewish Ghetto was first established, it was done so without such a structure and this was only introduced in 1517 and at the cost of the community.[75] In 1540, the only rubbish container remained that of the Ghetto Vecchio and residents of both that area and the Ghetto Nuovo were reminded to treat it with care.[76] In 1548, a proclamation was made to remind those within the Ghetto that they were forbidden from throwing rubbish from their balconies or into the canals.[77] In 1587, the *proto* was sent to the Ghetto Nuovo to inspect

---

[68] In 1589, the Monache di Santa Croce requested a section of public land *verso la scoazzera* in order to develop the choir of their church ASV, Giudici del Piovego, b.21 7r.

[69] Rompiasio, p. 252.   [70] BMC, Dona delle rose 466 (22 February 1530).

[71] Ennio Concina *Venezia nell'età moderna*, p. 16.   [72] ASCG, PdC, 33-56 (15 July 1574).

[73] Giuseppe Tassini, *Curiosità veneziane*, p. 661.

[74] Ivone Cacciavillani, *Le leggi ecologiche veneziane*, p. 53.

[75] ASV, Comun b.3 reg 5 38r (7 March 1517).

[76] ASV, Comun b.11 reg 24 83v (26 June 1540).

[77] ASV, Comun b.11 reg 25 155r (4 August 1548).

144 CLEANING UP RENAISSANCE ITALY

diverse roof terraces (*altanelle*) which had been constructed facing the canal, which were said to have caused considerable damage to the siltation of the canals. It was determined that the drainage holes should be covered with a mesh to prevent anything other than water passing through them. This was an area of the city which the authorities monitored particularly closely with regard to the disposal of rubbish.

Despite the provision of communal rubbish containers, it is clear that the dumping of rubbish in the streets continued to be a problem. From there, materials made their way into bodies of water which, in turn, became clogged. In the previous chapter, we considered the dredging that was required to clear these. The authorities then sought to oversee processes of reappropriation and reuse of dredged material. In Venice, materials were transported to various sites around the city and the lagoon. This was a long-standing practice. In 1306, permission had been given for Lorenzo Sagredo to use the excavated mud from the canals to raise the level (*levandum*) of his garden.[78] Two years later, the Maggior Consiglio set out the principle that dredged material could (and preferably should) be allocated to nearby residents rather than transported elsewhere in the city.[79] It might be utilized to improve the quality or the quantity of land. In February 1560, for example, Jacomo Badoer offered to receive the rubbish (*scovaze*) from an empty plot at San Giacomo dall'Orio as well as 600 boatloads of mud (*fango*) from whichever *rivi* were being dredged for his garden at San Zuane Evangelista.[80] The entry in the archive notes the financial benefit which would be derived from transporting the mud to this garden rather than out into the lagoon. A further environmental benefit would come from the removal of the rubbish from the empty plot of land: the Comun expressed that the cost would be balanced out by the positive impact that this would have on the health of the city and particularly on the area surrounding this plot because the rubbish was emitting an unbearable stench, which threatened to be highly dangerous for health (*nocivissimo alla vita*).

Dean Ferguson has suggested that European cities did not develop the specialized attention to nightsoil collection and use which characterized Asian cities between the sixteenth and twentieth centuries.[81] He refers to Fernand Braudel's assertion that beyond a few exceptions beyond the Italian peninsula, 'European agriculturalists rarely took advantage of the accumulation of human waste to improve soil fertility on their farms'. It is notable that the dredged material that

---

[78] Roberto Berveglieri, *Le vie di Venezia*, p. 216. Particularly renowned gardens included that of the Erizzi family at San Canciano, of the Michieli at SS Gervasio e Protasio, and of the Buoni family at San Angelo according to Giuseppe Tassini, *Curiosità veneziane*, p. 519.

[79] Roberto Berveglieri, *Le vie di Venezia*, p. 216.

[80] ASV, Comun b.14 reg 32 74r (7 February 1560).

[81] Dean Ferguson, 'Nightsoil and the "great divergence": human waste, the urban economy and economic productivity, 1500–1900', *Journal of Global History* 9:3 (2014), 384.

was applied to gardens in Venice would have been a mixture of dirt and human waste since domestic drains emptied directly into the city's waterways.

This dredged material might be requested by individuals or institutions. In 1562, the nuns of San Cosmo and Damiano on the Giudecca sent a supplication which referred to the need they had of the material extracted from a canal for their vineyard in which many trees were said to have died and others were continuing to wither.[82] In 1586, the mud which was removed from a canal at Sant'Andrea was requested by Francesco Bernardo and Leonardo Mocenigo for their land.[83] It was noted earlier in the sixteenth century that those who received the sludge and mud from public excavations onto their low-lying ground were required to take care over its handling and ensure that it was smoothed out to the satisfaction of the government.[84] Naturally once these materials had been transported to these sites it was important that they were protected with secure foundations and walls in order to ensure that the material did not simply pass back into the surrounding bodies of water.[85]

Dredged materials from canals were also used to raise the level of land at the edges of the city in Venice. In 1592, the mud from the Rivo di Santa Giustina was taken from the *sacche* (areas used to deposit excavated materials) to the area between San Francesco (presumably della Vigna) and Misericordia.[86] Requests for such interventions were made by individuals but were more commonly directed by coordinated government efforts.[87] Dredged material was frequently transported to the Punta di San Antonio in the 1550s.[88] It was also utilized in public construction projects such as in 1570 when the Council of Ten instructed the Water Office that all of the mud and dirt should be taken to San Nicolo del Lido to the place identified for the construction of the fort.[89] In 1574, material excavated from the *barene* (the shoals in the lagoon which are submerged at high tide) was taken to the same place.[90]

At other times dredged materials were used to enlarge the area of usable land on lagoon islands. Particular attention was paid to San Giacomo in Paludo, so named because the first convent there was said to have been developed out of a 'large marsh'. Originally the site of a hospice for travellers and pilgrims caught in bad weather, it developed into a site for religious communities.[91] Excavated materials were deposited elsewhere too.[92] In 1520, the material from the Grand Canal was to be transported to Sant'Andrea della Certosa and the vineyard of the patriarch.

---

[82] ASV, Comun b.14 reg 32 217v (31 August 1562).
[83] ASV, Comun, b.16 reg 36 181v (26 June 1586). [84] Rompiasio, p. 249.
[85] *Antichi scrittori* vol. III, p. 42. [86] Rompiasio, p. 168. [87] Rompiasio, p. 252.
[88] Rompiasio, p. 257. [89] Roberto Berveglieri, *Le vie di Venezia*, p. 301.
[90] Rompiasio, p. 142.
[91] Giorgio and Maurizio Crovato, *Isole abbandonate della laguna veneziana: com'erano e come sono* (Venice: patrocinio Associazione Settemari, 1978), pp. 146–60.
[92] Roberto Berveglieri, *Le vie di Venezia*, p. 229.

146 CLEANING UP RENAISSANCE ITALY

Both sites were said to be particularly low-lying.[93] Substantial amounts were taken to island vineyards (from Malamocco to San Francesco dal Deserto), although problems came when workers came to cultivate the land. In particular, these workers were reprimanded for sifting out the stones and bones within the deposited materials and then throwing them back in the lagoon.[94]

This concern that dredged materials might pass back into the water was also clearly articulated in Genoa. Here there was an ongoing debate as to the safest place to deposit rubble and dredge materials in order to prevent this from happening. The Padri consulted experts as part of these discussions. One of the best-documented periods of consultation came in 1557 when the Padri held a meeting intended to identify the least damaging site for the disposal of rubble. The options were at the Bisagno river (to the east of the city) or at Sanpierdarena to the west.[95] The Padri emphasized there were no other sites suitable for discussion beyond those two (although one of the men interviewed expressed the sentiment that neither site was ideal but that he was unable to suggest a better one).[96] Twenty men were consulted. The Padri considered this group to be constituted by 'citizens and mariners, knowledgeable and expert in the effects of the tides'. Most discussed the issue in person (although two contributions were added after the session). Seven of the men were noted as being sailors. The views of thirteen figures were recorded in summary. It was noted that the remaining seven men agreed with the others. The group was unanimous in recommending that the material produced by building works in the city should no longer be taken to the banks of the Bisagno, as had been done for many years. Instead it was felt that it would pose far less damage to the port to return to the traditional method ('*modo antiquo*') of carrying the rubble by boat beyond the lighthouse at Capo di Faro to the west. One of those interviewed noted that this was a topic which had been the subject of discussion for many years amongst those who were well informed and that all felt that the site to the west was preferable.

The reasons for preferring the site to the west of Genoa varied. Many of those interviewed reflected on the torrential nature of the Bisagno and its propensity to flood. They explained that when the river swelled it dispersed the rubble from the location in which it had been deposited and a significant quantity was then carried to the port. The sailors noted the prevailing winds and current along the coastline. Domenico Bonasola explained that the current of a *lebecchio* wind would carry materials west but never easterly. Another sailor observed the same and described having seen two anchors become detached from a ship in the Genoese port and carried by a strong current; these were recovered west of where they had fallen.

---

[93] Roberto Berveglieri, *Le vie di Venezia*, pp. 260–1.   [94] *Antichi scrittori* vol. III, p. 42.
[95] ASCG, PdC, 23-71 (1 September 1557).
[96] For comparative discussions of maritime and hydraulic expertise see Philippa Hellawell, '"The best and most practical philosophers": seamen and the authority of experience in early modern science', *History of Science* 58:1 (2020), 28–50 and Pamela O. Long, 'Hydraulic engineering'.

WORKING WITH WASTE   147

Battista Pariscone recalled the loss of the ship of the *Imperatore* when many things were recovered from the west and none in the east. He also described the effects of storms, claiming that nine times out of ten a storm would begin with a *scirocco* wind (with the remaining one caused by a *lebecchio*). During the storm the current would be more vigorous underneath the water than above it and the impact of this in Genoa was to carry materials westwards. These individuals used their experience of storms and salvage to inform their assessments of appropriate environmental management.

This understanding of the tides, and the design of policies in the light of this knowledge, was also reflected in discussions of new elements of infrastructure. In 1602, Raffaele Raggio assessed the viability of constructing a second breakwater for the port at the lighthouse. His view was that this was unnecessarily costly, precarious because of the exposure of the works to the unpredictable force of the sea, and would make it difficult to defend the city. It would also be damaging to the port. The construction of a barrier on that side of the port would risk extensive siltation of the area because it would inhibit the principal current which was responsible for removing most of the rubbish and soil.[97]

The transportation of materials by boat was not without its disadvantages, which were recognized both by the experts and by the Padri. First, the risks of carrying the material by boat could be partly mitigated through the use of a cloth known as a *stuole* or *veroni* in order to keep the materials on board. Second, the boatmen should be supervised by an official so that they did not deposit the rubbish in the wrong place. Those who travelled to the lighthouse at Capo di Faro could use the guardian of the lighthouse to witness and record the disposal.[98] There were also issues relating to the seasonality of transportation by boat. In 1533, it was noted that it was difficult for Venetian boatmen to dispose of mud and materials on the Lido in the winter; the wind caused the material to end up in the water, if not the boat to capsize. In Genoa, in times of inclement weather, operators of dredging machines were permitted to leave materials in the ditches at the Ponte di Spinola as long as they informed the officers of the Padri.[99]

The Padri issued new instructions regarding the removal of rubble from the city in the light of the 1557 consultation. Materials were to be taken outside the port to the lighthouse and deposited using the boat which belonged to the Padri (flying the flag of St George to indicate that it was being used for government purposes). Only authorized boatmen were permitted to carry rubble and permissions had to be renewed annually. Both property owners and boatmen were responsible for ensuring that the streets of the city remained clean and clear on a daily basis and a financial penalty would be issued for transgressions. Severe penalties were issued for those who deposited rubble beyond the place identified as safest for the port:

[97] ASCG, PdC, 221-150 (1 January 1610).   [98] ASCG, PdC, 30-19 (12 May 1570).
[99] ASCG, PdC, 22-224 (21 August 1556).

148 CLEANING UP RENAISSANCE ITALY

the loss of their vessel, financial or corporal according to the adjudication of the Padri. An official was appointed to accompany the transportation of the rubble and who was responsible for reporting any misdemeanours. Finally some provision was made for those who were building at a substantial distance from the shore. In these circumstances, the Padri could authorize the transportation of rubble overland. It is clear that materials continued to be transported to the Bisagno, since close attention was also paid to the gateways and roads as the route for this material.[100]

The use of local, expert knowledge was also evident within the broader Ligurian state. In 1567 it was referenced by the Podestà of Voltaggio as having informed a report made to the Padri relating to the diversion of rainwater from a street to the nearby river. The views of old men and experts of the area were said to have been solicited.[101] In Venice, the insights of experience were utilized to inform government decisions on the lagoon and other matters relating to the water. Eight of the most judicious and experienced (*sensati e prattici*) fishermen were appointed to advise the government.[102] There was an important focus on the area in which these men lived in order to provide an insight into different localities and trades: two were to derive from San Niccolo, two from Chioggia, two from Burano, one from Sant'Agnese, and one from Murano. As required, they were asked to give their opinions to the government either verbally or in writing. The only other stipulation was that the individuals should be older than thirty-five.[103] Numerous men, then, were involved in identifying and depositing waste materials, as well as providing evidence to inform practices of waste management. This variety widens further when we consider the civic structures in place to move and handle waste.

Handling Waste

Once waste materials had been left outside a domestic or occupational setting, it passed through multiple pairs of hands. The systems for moving waste intersected and overlapped with those already in place to support life in the early modern city. Reflecting on an outbreak of plague in sixteenth-century Venice, the notary Rocco Benedetti observed how life changed in times of disease and observed, with regret, the absence of porters around the city, as well as chimney sweeps and *curacondotti*. The consequence of this was that people were forced to do these jobs for themselves ('*di sua mano far li servigi*') which seemed to the writer to be extremely

---

[100] ASCG, PdC, 27-46 (5 July 1565), 29–103 (2 December 1568) and 29-159 (26 May 1569).
[101] ASCG, PdC, 28-97 (8 August 1567).   [102] ASV, SEA, 343, 71v (5 September 1536).
[103] Rompiasio, p. 139.

strange ('*molto strana*').[104] As we will see, each of these groups—alongside others—had some responsibility for handling waste.

The work of porters could be wide-ranging and a number of names were given to these men, who were known as *bastazi* or *fachini* in Venice and *camalli* in Genoa.[105] Their services were not only essential within the city but also in the particular spaces of the port. These workers carried items as individuals or in teams, with forms of cranes utilized for the heaviest loads. In Genoa these seem to have been largely located on floating platforms (*pontoni*) rather than fixed on the portside as with the treadwheel crane shown in a 1515 map of Antwerp.[106] The responsibilities of porters in both Genoa and Venice ranged beyond this core work, however. In Venice, they might be tasked with cleaning wells.[107] In January 1560, porters and their supervisors were instructed to clear snow from the bridges and principal streets of the city and deposit it at twenty-five nominated places.[108] This system endured until the eighteenth century, when the public responses in times of severe weather made clear that workers at the level of the parish were responsible for clearing snow and depositing it in the nearest canal.[109] Given the changes in climate of this period, this role became increasingly significant. Other episodes of extreme cold were recorded in 1432, 1442, 1491, 1549, 1581, 1594, and 1603.[110] During these periods, heavy snowfall would seriously disrupt passage through the city on foot. As a result, porters were in some ways responsible for the accessibility of the streets, as well as the transportation of goods and materials through these spaces.

Working in these jobs on behalf of the state might be temporary or form just a small part of the work of these groups, such as with Genoa's *mulattieri* who

---

[104] Rocco Benedetti, *Relatione d'alcuni casi occorsi in Venetia al tempo della peste l'anno 1576 et 1577 con le provisioni, rimedii et orationi fatte à Dio Benedetti per la sua liberatione* (Bologna, 1630), p. 22.

[105] Giorgio Costamagna (ed.), *Gli statuti della compagnia dei caravana del porto di Genova* (Turin: Accademia delle scienze, 1965).

[106] *Salve felix Andwerpia* reprinted in Frederik Buylaert, Jelle de Rock, and Anne-Laure van Bruaene, 'City portrait, civic body, and commercial printing in sixteenth-century Ghent', *Renaissance Quarterly* 68:3 (2015), p. 805. Anna Boato and Anna Decri reference the *ruote* (wheels) set up at the port for lifting large stones. These would be operated by one or more men inside the wheel and were used during the fifteenth century during work on the port area under the direction of Anastasio Alessandro. Anna Boato and Anna Decri, 'Archive documents and building organisation. An example from the modern age' in S. Huerta (ed.), *Proceedings of the first International congress on construction history* (Madrid, 2003), p. 386.

[107] Giuseppe Tassini, *Curiosità veneziane*, p. 252.

[108] ASV, Comun b.14 reg 32 68v (22 January 1560) notes that the places are: on the wooden bridge in Canareggio, at the Rio Terra, on the *ponti di morti*, at Santi Apostoli, on the bridge at San Felice, by the pharmacy and where they sell *fassine* at Santi Apostoli, on the square at San Canciano and San Zuan Grisostomo, at the crossing at Santi Giovanni e Paolo, in the square at San Lio, Santa Maria Formosa, San Moisè, Santa Maria Zobenigo, Santo Stefano, Sant'Aponal, San Polo, Sant'Angelo, San Luca and San Bartholomeo, on the bridge *di fra menori*, San Pantalon, at San Stae near the baker (*pistor*) by the crossing, at San Cassiano and on the square of the meat market at Rialto.

[109] ASV, Comun b.46 (January 1757).

[110] Dario Camuffo, Chiara Bertolin, Alberto Craievich, Rossella Granziero, and Silvia Enzi, 'When the lagoon was frozen over in Venice', *Journal of Mediterranean Geography* (2017), 1–59.

150 CLEANING UP RENAISSANCE ITALY

transported waste materials from the city out to the vicinity of the Bisagno river, or the boatmen in both cities who transported waste materials. For others, such jobs might constitute the focus of their working lives, such as with Venice's *cavacanali* who were responsible for digging and dredging canals. There were also dedicated cleaners appointed in Venice ('*nettadori*' or '*conduttori de' sestieri*') to serve each district. They were expected to clean ('*nettar*') on a weekly basis. The roles associated with urban cleanliness became increasingly specific in Venice over the course of the sixteenth century, with the role of the cleaning of drains (undertaken by *gattolieri*) being separated from that of cleaning of the streets, which remained with the *nettadori*. In 1485, the poor state of the *gattoli* had been described as one of the principal causes of the siltation of canals and increased corruption of the air in the city.[111] In theory residents were responsible for clearing these, as well as cleaning the areas of the streets in front of their homes or workshops. In Genoa it was recognized that the streets required regularly cleaning although, as noted in chapter two, this responsibility was placed at the door of residents.[112] The government's role was one of oversight (through walking the streets to ensure that regulations were adhered to) and the removal of rubbish from designated sites to spaces beyond the city.

As elsewhere in the premodern world, many of the occupational groups employed in handling waste materials would have been considered as dishonourable trades.[113] Dealing with vile but essential tasks, both these workers and the materials they handled were essential to the management of energy and waste in the early modern city.[114] Disposal of urban waste 'included sanctioned and legally recognized workers as well as workers with a decidedly irregular and sometimes uncertain legal status'.[115] Cleaning jobs could be difficult to recruit to. In 1646, the Venetian Health Office recognized the need for rubbish to be removed from the city's plague hospitals and sought four cleaners for the job. They asked the head of the company of *scoacamini* (chimney sweeps) to find suitable individuals but he said that he would be unable to, suggesting instead the use of those who cleared out latrines (*fosse*), which included a number of men from the Ghetto.[116] The

---

[111] Roberto Berveglieri, *Le vie di Venezia*, p. 241. The *gattoli* were drains which took waste from homes into the canals, as well as those which formed part of well structures.

[112] ASCG, PdC, 13-112 (4 June 1531).

[113] Kathy Stuart, *Defiled trades and social outcasts*. Donald Reid, *Paris sewers and sewermen: realities and representations* (Cambridge MA: Harvard University Press, 1991), p. 92. Douglas Biow discusses perceptions of laundry women and latrine cleaners in *The culture of cleanliness* recognizing similar ambiguities of status.

[114] Donald Reid, *Paris sewers and sewermen* and Roberta J. Magnusson, *Water technology in the Middle Ages* p. 21 on workers including Sienese workmen who dug the city's *bottini* (subterranean filtration conduits).

[115] Dean T. Ferguson, 'Nightsoil and the "great divergence"', p. 381.

[116] ASV, Sanità 740 66r (15 February 1646).

communication with the chimney sweeps may well have been, as Tassini suggests, because these workers also, at times, dug out latrines.[117]

Many of those responsible for the transportation of waste were male although it is clear from regulations of domestic and occupational practices that both men and women were involved in the initial identification and separation of waste. In a number of proclamations relating to the disposal of waste in the streets and squares, women are specifically mentioned, indicating the perceived relevance of this group to effective adherence to the rules. Other environmental proclamations tended to be addressed to 'everyone regardless of state or condition' and did not make specific mention of gender.

In specific instances, the ideas about waste, gender, and pollution were brought together, for example in the language used to describe the sex trade. St Thomas Aquinas (1225–74) used it to encapsulate St Augustine's view of this work and in 1585 Fray Francisco Farfan reiterated such long-established assumptions vividly:

> The brothel in the city then, is like the stable or latrine in the house. Because just as the city keeps itself clean by providing a separate place where filth and dung are gathered, so neither less nor more, acts the brothel; where the filth and ugliness of the flesh are gathered like the garbage and dung of the city.

A petition from the friars of San Francesco di Castelletto in Genoa, considered in chapter three, alleged that the prospective move of the city's municipal brothel to their district would transform the existing healthy hillside into a forest of gloom (*selva oscura*).[118] Indeed, the whole area would soon be transformed into a den of treachery and fraud (*tradimenti and habitation mariolesca*). The concern of the friars was that the pimps, prostitutes, and other shady characters would frequent the neighbourhood as well as the churches. Indeed the friars protested that the holy and blessed churches themselves would degenerate into latrines and sinks of foul vices (*et cosi di chiese spirituali et sante saranno cloache et sentine d'ogni piu vicio nefando*), portraying vividly some of the ways in which groups of people were seen to affect space and why the zoning of cityscapes was seen to be justified.

A number of workers were used to keep thoroughfares and waterways clean in a more literal sense. In 1493, the volume of rubbish being thrown into the canals caused the Venetian Senate to instruct the Comun to provide two boats per district, each with one or two men, in order to collect the rubbish and remove it to locations as instructed.[119] These twelve rubbish disposal boats were used to clean the city four times per month. The district street cleaners were required to

---

[117] Giuseppe Tassini, *Curiosità veneziane*, p. 660.

[118] Reprinted in Ennio Poleggi, *Strada nuova: una lottizzazione del '500 a Genova* (Genoa: Sagep, 1968) p. 407 and discussed in greater detail in Jane L. Stevens Crawshaw, 'Cleaning up the Renaissance city'.

[119] ASV, Comun b.3 reg. 5.

152 CLEANING UP RENAISSANCE ITALY

present a signed attestation that they had cleared the streets as well as the drains which carried waste from homes to canals (*gattoli*) every eight days.[120] These individuals would have been known, and were supervised, at a local level. Indeed, they only received payment if they had in their possession an attestation from a local parish priest or official of the district. This responsibility could be delegated to a local artisan if the government was informed.[121] Concern about fraud and deception on this front clearly endured, since in 1598 officials reiterated this need for a signed statement that the work had been completed and, indeed, added that it should state that the person in question had seen 'with their own eyes' (*ocularmente veduta*) that the area had been cleaned, and was clear of rubbish (*netta d'immondizie*).[122]

In a series of prints from the mid eighteenth-century, Gaetano Zompini depicted the trades of the streets of Venice. These included the *cura gatoli* (of whom it was said they walked throughout the city from dawn to deal with dirt and keep the streets clean); the *cava rii* ('we drain the water and remove sludge from the waterways and transport it away in boats'); and the *scoazer* ('to help gardens and vineyards to grow, I myself am dirty and in rags and carry away the filth and keep houses and palaces clean').[123] These figures were also expected to remove filth and rubbish from the communal rubbish bins. In 1487, however, the government assigned boats with three men in order to undertake a city-wide exercise. They were equipped with large and small shovels and other unspecified items in order to clean streets and drains, remove domestic rubbish and dig out the edges/ridges (*i dorsi*) of the canals so that the city would remain clear and clean (*libera et netta*). They were to work through the city by *sestiere*, beginning with San Marco and then taking each in turn before repeating the process.[124]

In Genoa, all inhabitants were reminded that rubbish should be placed in a corner or at the side of the street so that the muleteers could collect and carry it beyond the city.[125] These individuals worked within and beyond the city walls and were responsible for the transportation of materials between urban and rural settings. This was recognized to be a dangerous occupation, which often involved extensive amounts of night-time working.[126] The muleteers would have been familiar figures in the streets—wandering in search of work and often transporting large items and quantities of goods between as well as around cities. To facilitate

---

[120] ASV, Sanità, 740 10v (30 April 1643).   [121] Rompiasio, p. 251.

[122] Rompiasio, p. 251.

[123] *Le arti che vanno per via nella città di Venezia* (1753) 'Co xe l' Alba per tute le Contrae/I gatoli curemo dal sporchezzo;/E se mantien le strade ben netae); 'Sechemo l' acqua, e prima la se ferma;/Da i rii cavemo el fango col bail,/E in burchiele el portemo in tera ferma); 'A ingrassar orti, e vigne schena, e brazzi/Me sporco, e stracco; e porto via scoazze:/E sta nette per mi case, e palazzi.'

[124] Roberto Berveglieri, *Le vie di Venezia*, p. 246.   [125] ASCG, PdC, 20-54 (13 July 1549).

[126] Cited in Trevor Dean 'Eight varieties of homicide in Renaissance Bologna' in Trevor Dean and K. J. P. Lowe (eds), *Murder in Renaissance Italy* (Cambridge: Cambridge University Press, 2017), p. 100 n. 26.

WORKING WITH WASTE 153

building projects in the city of Genoa, with its steep terrain, substantial digging work was often required in order to prepare the site (whether excavation or flattening of the ground) and remove the superfluous materials and this often involved muleteers.[127] These figures were associated with strength, manual labour, sweat, and dirt. Douglas Biow cites Aretino's *Dialogues* when 'lascivious nuns, thrilled at the unexpected presence of a filthy muleteer in their midst, promptly sat the man down and proceeded to clean him off' with a freshly laundered towel.[128]

The physical strength required for this role was also recognized by the Padri. In 1516, it was noted disapprovingly that a number of the muleteers had sent their animals into the city under the control of young boys and rubble was being dispersed throughout the city as a result of the lack of control being maintained over the animals. The muleteers were commanded not to send mules loaded with materials under the control of young men less than fifteen years old in the interests of preserving the condition of the streets.[129]

Mulattieri in Genoa had to be licensed by the Padri.[130] At various points they were required by the government to contribute to public works, such as work in 1466 on the city's aqueduct.[131] In 1473 all muleteers and cart drivers (*vetturanti*) were required to transport one load of the material removed from the sewers at the Banchi and Soziglia.[132] Similar expectations were articulated to the city's boatmen to support work on the breakwater in 1484 and 1491.[133] More regularly, however, the muleteers removed building materials and other rubbish from the streets of Genoa on a daily basis. A list of the muleteers registered with the Padri survives from 1571. In it, each individual is listed along with the number of mules he owned. In the introductory note, the scribe recorded that the responsibilities of the muleteers included the transportation of stones, mortar, sand, bricks, and rubbish (*inmonditia*).[134] This list of names from 1571 recorded forty-six *mulattieri* who owned 107 animals between them. Each person's herd ranged from one to six mules. Across the entries, ten of the *mulattieri* had just a single animal. There are six families which had multiple members listed (the largest of which was the Machiavelli family with six members and twelve animals).

The *mulattieri* were instructed to ensure that their carts were equipped with large cloths (known as *zerbini*) which would be used to ensure that the waste materials, once collected, did not fall out onto the streets of the city over the course of the bumpy journey to the allotted sites for disposal.[135] It is clear that this was a common problem and the Padri intervened on a number of occasions, stipulating the minimum size of this cloth.[136] In 1547, for example, the impact of the rubble,

[127] Anna Boato and Anna Decri, 'Archive documents and building organisation', p. 382.
[128] Douglas Biow, *Culture of cleanliness*, p. 15.   [129] ASCG, PdC, 11-25 (26 January 1516).
[130] ASCG, PdC, 1-171 (25 June 1466) and 11-88 (12 April 1521).
[131] ASCG, PdC, 1-174 (19 July 1466).   [132] ASCG, PdC, 3-106 (12 August 1473).
[133] ASCG, PdC, 5-88 (16 June 1484).   [134] ASCG, PdC, 30-145 (7 August 1571).
[135] ASCG, PdC, 19-92 (7 September 1546).   [136] ASCG, PdC, 25-32 (8 July 1561).

154   CLEANING UP RENAISSANCE ITALY

sand, and other rubbish being dropped from carts and spread throughout the city was described and concern was raised that, in times of rainfall, these materials would be carried into the port. Individuals were instructed to ensure that the coverings over their carts extend beyond the mound of materials by half a palm on every side.[137]

Fabrizio Nevola has noted that muleteers, with their carts and animals, could pose a real hazard to the safety of the streets in Renaissance Italy.[138] In 1523, the Genoese Padri also observed the disorder being caused by these men and their animals passing through one of the streets of the city in both directions. The resulting aggression and violence posed a threat to the safety of children who might be present at the same time. The Padri intervened to try to establish a one-way system of sorts whereby all muleteers who were leaving from Ponte degli Spinola in the port were permitted to use the street in question with their animals but those who wished to return were required to take a longer route round to avoid the encounter '*l'uno cum l'altro*'.[139] Concerns were raised not only about the routes for these journeys but also their destinations. In 1565, the Padri expressed concern that some muleteers, for greater ease and their own financial gain, were transporting rubble to archways and other sites within the walls rather than outside them to the allotted places.[140] Even if they did take the rubble to the Bisagno, it is clear that some did not use the allocated areas and complaints survive from members of the city's elite complaining that material had been dumped outside their doors.[141]

There were concerns too about the work of boatmen in both cities and their potential for fraud or transgression. In Genoa, the conduct of the boatmen was a cause for frustration and disgust amongst the officials of the Padri. The rubble and rubbish produced by the citizens was said to be dumped in places extremely damaging to the port. The behaviour of the boatmen was described as disrespectful and demonstrating a concern solely for their own interests. Boatmen were paid on a weekly basis at a set rate according to the number of boatloads they excavated from the port. There was understandable concern regarding the ability for payments to be calculated fraudulently—as noted in 1633 in Savona individuals could simply circulate around a port area, clocking up payment, with the same material in their boat.[142]

In Venice, boatmen were instructed to work during the day and not by night.[143] Nevertheless there is evidence of contravention of regulations. In 1522, Zuan

---

[137] ASCG, PdC, 19-165 (1 December 1547) and 29-206 (23 September 1569).

[138] Fabrizio Nevola, *Street life*, pp. 76–7.   [139] ASCG, PdC, 11-144 (27 June 1523).

[140] ASCG, PdC, 27-42 (2 July 1565).

[141] ASCG, PdC, 15-187 (6 March 1539) and 20-73 (11 September 1549).

[142] C. Assereto, 'Porti e scali minori della Repubblica di Genova in età moderna' in Giorgio Doria and Paola Massa Piergiovanni (eds), *Il Sistema portuale*.

[143] Rompiasio, p. 254.

WORKING WITH WASTE   155

Ballocho, a boatman, had disposed of rubble by dumping it in the Venetian lagoon, beyond the allotted place, and was obliged to remove, at his own expense, thirty boatloads of mud from within the lagoon.[144] More generally, in 1586 it was observed that the boats which were intended to carry waste materials to the appointed locations were not doing so but instead that these materials were being strewn around the canals. The Venetian procurators reiterated that no boatman, *cavacanalo*, or anyone else should behave in that manner and that they would not have the excuse of being ignorant of the law.[145]

The *cavacanali* of Venice were involved in a variety of different tasks associated with the environment of the city. Principally, as their name suggests, they were responsible for digging canals and had a vital role to play in the construction of new buildings or repairs to existing structures. There are suggestions in the archival records that the role of *cavacanalo* may have been one which was undertaken by those who migrated into the city, including Antonio Cremonese and Battista d'Asola.[146] Payments to the *cavacanali* are recorded frequently in the records of the Comun and Water Office in different infrastructure and dredging projects across the city.[147]

The *cavacanali* were responsible for draining sections of canals so that they could be excavated or the foundations of nearby buildings repaired.[148] Some of this work was intended to be preventative but the *cavacanali* were also employed to deal with emergency situations, such as in 1547 when a house had collapsed at Santa Maria dei Miracoli and the canal needed to be cleared.[149] In 1548 an official was elected to accompany the scribe of the Comun to oversee the allocation of payments for the excavation of the canals in place of his deceased predecessor. One of his responsibilities was also to inspect the quality of the *pallade* (screens made of posts or piles) which the *cavacanali* constructed. These were intended to stay in place until canal beds could be inspected to ensure that a sufficient quantity of material had been excavated.[150] The entry noted that these often broke so that the areas were flooded by the canal water prematurely and the work was not completed properly.[151] In 1560 Andrea Bertolin had worked on the canal of Santa Maria Mazor near Ca' Bernardo but his credit was withheld because he had taken away the *pallade* before being given permission to do so, meaning that it was not possible to see the excavated area.[152]

Cavacanali were also given the responsibility of transporting the materials extracted in the course of their work, cleaning areas of rubbish within the city

---

[144] Roberto Berveglieri, *Le vie di Venezia*, p. 263.
[145] ASV, Comun b.16 reg 37 28r (18 November 1586).
[146] ASV, Comun b.12 reg 27 23v (7 June 1550) and b.14 reg 32 74v (5 February 1560).
[147] ASV Sanità 734 32r (8 February 1577).   [148] ASV, Comun b.11 reg 24 54v (13 March 1542).
[149] ASV, Comun, b.11 72r (30 January 1547).   [150] ASV, Comun, b.14 74v (5 February 1560).
[151] ASV, Comun b.11 99v (s.d.)   [152] ASV, Comun, b.14 reg 32 unpaginated (22 April 1560).

156 CLEANING UP RENAISSANCE ITALY

and transporting waste.[153] In 1565, for example, construction work in the church of San Simon on part of an altar paid for by the wool guild (*scuola di tesseri dl panni d'lana*) prompted Marcilian *cavacanalo* to be paid to carry away the materials removed in the course of the building work.[154] In the same year these workers were instructed to take away the bricks, wood, and other things which were on the *fondamenta* and to reclaim the bricks which had fallen into the canal.[155] In 1585, *cavacanali* were noted as assisting with the measurement of all of the dredged canals by the *proto* of the Water Office.[156] The *cavacanali* worked throughout the city and were also sent into Venetian territory in service to the state, for example to Crete at the end of the sixteenth century.

The *cavacanali* had a *scuola* which was based in San Andrea de Zirada and established in 1503.[157] This area also appears to have been the district in which many *cavacanali* were resident. Records survive of the brothers Ferramondo and Angelo Cavacanali living in Santa Croce in 1515.[158] In 1548, Zuan Maria de Vidal was noted as living in Sant'Andrea in the '*Rio di Cavacanali*'.[159] The church of Sant'Andrea della Zirada in Santa Croce has a fourteenth-century depiction of the calling of Peter and Andrew on its façade. This shows the two apostles stepping out of their fishing boats into the water, guided by the hand of Christ. In 1565, Stephano, Agustin, and Francesco *cavacanali* were said to be living at the canal of the *burchielle* at Tre Ponti, also in Santa Croce.[160] There are also, however, records of *cavacanali* living elsewhere in the city. In 1566, Andrea Cavacanali rented a house from the physician Nicolò Massa in San Pietro di Castello. Located close to San Domenico, it was described as 'old' and cost 6 ducats a year in rent.[161] Ennio Concina has noted that the poor in the city could pay 4 ducats per year for rent and boatmen commonly paid between 3 and 12 ducats.[162]

It is notable that in a will made on the city's *lazaretto vecchio* on 19 July 1523 Nadalin (son of Nicolo) Cavacanali left the equivalent sum of nearly a month's rent for Mass to be said for his soul to the Madonna and San Gregorio. The money for this had been left with the prior of the *lazaretto nuovo*. Presumably Nadalin had been sent initially to this latter institution and then transferred to the *lazaretto vecchio* when he became unwell. He had also left two silver *pironi* (a type of crank

---

[153] ASV, Comun b.14 reg 32 75r (7 February 1560).
[154] ASV, Comun b.14 reg 33 50r (29 June 1565).
[155] ASV, Comun b.14 reg 33 44r (14 June 1565).
[156] ASV, Comun, b.16 reg 36 63r (16 March 1585).
[157] E. A. Cicogna, *Corpus delle iscrizioni di Venezia e delle isole della laguna veneta* (Venice: Biblioteca Orafa di Sant'Antonio abate, 2001), p. 135.
[158] ASV, Dieci savi alle decime in Rialto, Deputazioni unite, Commisurazione delle imposte, Condizioni di decima, Filze. Redecima 1514 b.28 S Croce 76 and 78.
[159] ASV, Comun b.11 reg 25 146r (19 July 1548).
[160] ASV, Comun b.14 reg 33 44r (14 June 1565).
[161] Richard Palmer, 'Nicolò Massa: his family and his fortune', *Medical History* 25 (1981), 408.
[162] Ennio Concina, *Venezia nell'età moderna*, pp. 74–5.

or peg which may well have been occupational tools similar to those used in construction) and two silver *zenture*.[163]

Both the people and places associated with waste were closely regulated in Genoa and Venice because of the importance of preventing siltation and reusing materials effectively (for flood defences, soil enrichment, or land reclamation). Both governments attempted to regulate the removal and disposal of environmental material in order to ensure the uninhibited flow of water. This necessitated systems for the removal of urban waste as well as its transportation and safe disposal. Although there was greater direct control over the workers handling waste material in Venice than Genoa, both cities saw a wide variety of occupational groups involved in this work. Systems for managing waste were strained during the premodern period and prompted governments to reflect on the natural, valuable, or useful materials which belonged within the city and those which needed to be removed. These adjudications of what belonged and what was external to the city intensified in many of the contexts which are the focus for the final chapter: that of natural disasters.

---

[163] ASV, Sanità 726 94r (11 February 1524).

6

Dealing with Disasters

Environments, People, and Piety

In this beautiful earthenware panel (Image 6.1) from the early sixteenth century, the Madonna and Christ Child are flanked by two plague saints (Sebastian and Roch). The setting here is richly resonant: piety, health, and wellbeing are aligned with beauty, order, and cleanliness. The specific context of the creation of this panel is not known but the general intention was to depict vividly the splendour and advantage that could be gained when religious, architectural, and environmental ideals were aligned. As we have seen in previous chapters, communities engaged with these ideals both constructively and subversively, in ways which complicated the governance of health and the environment. Objects such as this certainly impressed upon the viewer the virtues of cleanliness. The inclusion of the period's most significant intercessors against the plague, however, also whispered a warning. The beauty and order celebrated here were fragile and precious, easily shattered by events which exerted a heavy social and environmental toll: natural disasters. Many of the environmental problems outlined in previous chapters developed incrementally over time. What was staggering and terrifying about natural disasters was the rapid devastation, which could overtake a city within minutes and from which it might take decades to recover.[1]

Distinct in their manifestations, and with geographical variation, premodern natural disasters can nevertheless be considered as a set of circumstances which prompted common assessments of causation and response.[2] Changes in the environment could be interpreted as expressions of divine blessing and approval, as in the Mass of dedication of Santa Maria Maggiore which commemorates miraculous snowfall in August 358 on the site, or could convey the fiercest and most brutal judgement of nature. Of bodies of water, for example, it was written that 'the wrath of the sea can never be underestimated' and that it should be seen as 'an enemy [that] does not sleep . . . but comes suddenly like a roaring lion,

---

[1] See the helpful discussion in Peregrine Horden and Nicholas Purcell, *The corrupting sea: a study of Mediterranean history* (Oxford: Wiley-Blackwell, 2000), p. 180.

[2] Michael Matheus, Gabriella Piccinni, Giuliano Pinto, and Gian Maria Varanini (eds), *Le calamità ambientali nel tardo medioevo europeo: realtà, percezioni, reazioni* (Florence: Firenze University Press, 2010) and Domenico Cecere, Chiara De Caprio, Lorenza Gianfrancesco, and Pasquale Palmieri (eds), *Disaster narratives in early modern Naples: politics, communication and culture* (Rome: Viella, 2018).

Cleaning Up Renaissance Italy: Environmental Ideals and Urban Practice in Genoa and Venice. Jane L. Stevens Crawshaw, Oxford University Press. © Jane L. Stevens Crawshaw 2023. DOI: 10.1093/oso/9780198867432.003.0007

Image 6.1 Tile panel, earthenware; The Virgin and Child between Saint Sebastian and Saint Roch. Central Italy, probably Pesaro; about 1500–1510 © Victoria and Albert Museum, London.

seeking to devour the whole land'.[3] Similarities of scale and devastation prompted writers to draw comparisons between different types of disaster. The Venetian notary Rocco Benedetti, for example, compared the plague of 1575–7 to a tempest, writing that just as storms do not abate without a dying-down of the winds, so too the fury of the plague would not be contained without a placation of the wrath of God.[4] The association of natural disasters with sin (whether general or specific) was, of course, the most obvious and widespread connection. For some premodern observers, the most effective preventative measures throughout this period remained spiritual and specific cults developed in many parts of the Italian peninsula including the Madonna of the Earthquake.[5] Both Genoa and Venice

---

[3] Raingard Esser 'Fear of water and flood in the Low Countries' in William Naphy and Penny Roberts (eds), *Fear in early modern society* (Manchester: Manchester University Press, 1997), p. 73.
[4] '*perche si come non si vede cessar la fortuna del Mare se prima non cessa il furor de venti, cosi non sarebbe cessata la furia della peste se prima non fosse placata l'ira della sua divina giustitia*', in Rocco Benedetti, *Relatione d'alcuni casi occorsi in Venetia al tempo della peste l'anno 1576 et 1577 con le provisioni, rimedii et orationi fatte à Dio Benedetti per la sua liberatione* (Bologna, 1630).
[5] Fabrizio Nevola, *Street life*, pp. 92–7.

160 CLEANING UP RENAISSANCE ITALY

developed significant cults related to 'Madonnas of the sea'.[6] In this chapter, we will consider such connections in more detail before examining the practical and symbolic measures which were intended to prevent and alleviate the effects of storms, floods, and plague in Renaissance Genoa and Venice.

Despite the catastrophic scale of many of these events, scholars have asserted that 'the memory of natural disasters is, in contrast, to the memory of war, markedly short-lived'.[7] This chapter will also, therefore, consider the efforts of governments to mark or commemorate natural disasters in both textual and material ways. Maartje van Gelder and Filippo de Vivo have demonstrated efforts to disrupt official remembrance through archival suppression in response to political unrest.[8] This chapter explores the ways in which official remembrance was constructed in relation to disruptive environmental events.

By the sixteenth century, efforts to measure the impact of natural disasters were well developed, whether through the use of the official hydrometer located at the Porta di Ripetta in Rome to measure the height of floods or the large bureaucratic exercise undertaken during the plague of 1575–7 in Venice to collate and analyse statistics for infection and mortality. Some natural disasters were recorded with 'writings on walls'. In cities such as Verona the levels reached by flood waters were etched in the stones of the city.[9] In Venice, the *'comune marino'* (the line of algae which represented the average level of high tides) was sometimes etched into the stone of buildings with a straight line and the letter 'C' with the date. Some of the earliest surviving examples date back to the sixteenth century.[10] The same city contains the sotoportego di Corte Nova which accommodated an image of the Madonna with saints Roch, Sebastian, and Justina. This was said to have been painted by one of the residents of Castello named Giovanna in order to invoke protection for the neighbourhood. The image was believed to offer protection from epidemics (plague and then cholera) until the nineteenth century and it is still commemorated today. A red slab of marble was also inserted in the pavement to mark the point at which the plague was stopped in its tracks as a result of the protection of the Virgin.[11]

---

[6] For Genoa and Liguria see Jane Garnett and Gervase Rosser, *Spectacular miracles*, particularly pp. 254–8.

[7] Christof Mauch, 'Introduction' in Christof Mauch and Christian Pfister (eds), *Natural disasters, cultural responses: case studies towards a global environmental history* (Lanham MD: Lexington Books, 2009) p. 3.

[8] Maartje van Gelder and Filippo de Vivo, 'Papering over protest'.

[9] For Rome, see Katherine Rinne, *The waters of Rome*, p. 123. On writings on walls see Fabrizio Nevola, *Street life*, pp. 199–204.

[10] Dario Camuffo, 'Analysis of the sea surges at Venice', 4.

[11] Sheila Barker, 'Miraculous images and the plagues of Italy, c.590–1656' in Sandra Cardarelli and Laura Fenelli (eds), *Saints, miracles and the image: healing saints and miraculous images in the Renaissance* (Turnhout: Brepols, 2017) and https://www.savevenice.org/project/sotoportego-di-corte-nova (accessed 18 June 2021).

DEALING WITH DISASTERS   161

Other reflections were made in material culture, including paintings, buildings, and objects like the panel with which this chapter began. In numerous paintings commissioned in times of plague, the saints and the Virgin are depicted interceding on behalf of communities who are represented visually by images of the cityscape or collected groups of men and women. One of the earliest forms of these paintings, showing the Madonna della Misericordia sheltering members of the community from the arrows of plague, was produced in Genoa by Barnaba da Modena in the 1370s.[12] Publications were also composed, retained, and republished that described the cause, progression, and end of natural disasters.[13] Each of these might seek to explain the onset of the disaster as well as celebrate retrospectively the institutions and interventions which were seen to be instrumental in bringing about the end and recovery.

Diverse measures were introduced to prevent natural disasters or lessen their impact. This could include the dredging works explored in chapter four but also informed the use of specific materials or motifs in urban and domestic design. As we saw in the context of the ideal cities, the materials utilized for construction and decoration were held to be deeply significant. Scholars of jewellery and clothing have demonstrated that the symbolic and physical properties of materials could exert a tactual impact on the wearer. From the jewels embedded in wedding rings to the coral which became such a feature of Genoese visual culture, many materials were celebrated for their talismanic, as well as aesthetic, qualities.[14] In Andrea Vendramin's 1627 De mineralibus, coral was noted as having a protective purpose for people on land or at sea. It was believed to drive away evil spirits, bad dreams, high winds, storms, and attacks by wild animals. It was also, however, thought to protect urban infrastructure, by safeguarding homes from lightning.[15]

More commonly, such objects exerted agency through their imagery and text. In 1470, Pope Paul II proclaimed that the Agnus Dei was beneficial in a wide variety of contexts, protecting both people and places. It could safeguard parturient women as well as combat natural disasters including fires and floods.[16] The

---

[12] Louise Marshall, 'Manipulating the sacred: image and plague in Renaissance Italy', *Renaissance Quarterly* 47:3 (1994), 512. Marshall notes that this was likely commissioned by the city's Consortia de li forestèri de la Madonna de Misericordia in the context of the plague of 1372 although the specific purpose as a petition or representation of votive thanks is not clear.

[13] Samuel Cohn Jr., *Cultures of plague.*

[14] Sara Matthews-Grieco, 'Marriage and sexuality' in Marta Ajmar-Wollheim and Flora Dennis (eds), *At home in Renaissance Italy* (London: V&A Publications, 2006) p. 110. Jacqueline Musacchio, 'Lambs, coral, teeth and the intimate intersection of religion and magic' in Sally Cornelison and Scott Montgomery (eds), *Images, relics, and devotional practices in medieval and Renaissance Italy* (Temple AZ: Arizona Center for Medieval and Renaissance Studies, 2006), pp. 139–56. For religious images in the streets see Edward Muir, 'The Virgin on the street corner: the place of the sacred in Italian cities' in Steven Ozment (ed.), *Religion and culture in the Renaissance and Reformation* (Kirksville MI: Sixteenth Century Journal Publishers, 1989), pp. 25–40.

[15] Cited in the 'Introduction' to Marta Ajmar-Wollheim and Flora Dennis (eds), *At home in Renaissance Italy*, p. 15.

[16] Jacqueline Marie Musacchio, 'Lambs, coral, teeth', p. 144.

162 CLEANING UP RENAISSANCE ITALY

exhibition catalogue *Madonnas and miracles* demonstrated the ways in which paintings, woodcuts, plaques, and texts might be displayed or touched in order to preserve domestic spaces and their inhabitants.[17] Some forms of protection were also rendered as part of buildings. Many Italian homes had IHS incorporated above doorways, encouraged by the preaching of San Bernardino of Siena. In Genoa, a number of properties had slate lintels over the main entrance, showing scenes such as the Annunciation or St George and the Dragon. Many of these also contained a square projection with the monogram of Christ.[18] The iconography of these elements was designed to have a prophylactic effect on people and place alike. Nevertheless, despite these preventative efforts, natural disasters affected Genoa and Venice in repeated and diverse ways which prompted efforts to explain these events and imbue them with meaning and purpose.

Stories of Natural Disasters

The earthenware panel with which this chapter began represents the centrality of the Virgin and Child within devotional responses to the plague. Both acted as intercessors through whom vows were made to alleviate the worst plague outbreaks of the premodern period. Such intercession was often credited with the alleviation of the strain of natural disaster and, on the Italian peninsula, might prompt the construction of votive churches, often designed with a strong sense of architectural balance and proportion. In a panel from Arezzo in 1479 which showed St Roch praying for the city, one of his feet rests upon fragments of stone which litter the colour paving—a sense of the manifold ways in which natural disasters wreaked a destructive force from which only divine intervention might rescue a city.[19]

Explanations of the cause of the disease, as with other natural disasters, however, tended to include a different cast of characters. One such account of the outbreak of plague of 1575 concentrated on the identification of portents of the impending epidemic. On 26 March 1575 at 4.53pm, conjoined twins were said to have been born within the Jewish Ghetto.[20] The author of a printed account of the birth claimed to know not only the precise time of their delivery but also the

---

[17] 'Protecting the home and family' in Maya Corry, Deborah Howard, and Mary Laven (eds), *Madonnas and miracles: the holy home in Renaissance Italy* (London: Philip Wilson Publishers, 2017), pp. 114–16.

[18] Hanno-Walter Kruft, *Portali genovesi del Rinascimento* (Florence: Edam, 1971) and Luciana Müller Profumo, *Le pietre parlanti: L'ornamento nell'architettura genovese 1450-1600* (Genoa: Banca Carige, 1993).

[19] Cited in Fabrizio Nevola *Street life*, p.169.

[20] Robert Jütte, 'Im Wunder vereint: eine spektakulaere Missgeburt im Ghetto 1575' in Uwe Israel, Robert Jütte and Reinhold C. Mueller (eds), *Interstizi: culture ebraico-cristiane a Venezia e nei suoi domini dal medioevo all'eta moderna* (Rome: Edizioni di storia e letteratura, 2010), vol. 5 pp. 517–40.

DEALING WITH DISASTERS   163

moment of conception: 2.48pm on 7 September 1574. Once these calculations had been established, it became possible to assess the celestial alignment of those moments and draw interpretation through astrological insights. These assessments were believed to tell only part of the story, however. In a pamphlet describing the birth and its significance, the anonymous author referred to the view of experts on the causes of birth defects: excess semen, lack of semen, or filth (*sporcitie*) of the same.[21] Unclean semen could be the cause of so-called 'monstrous births' which produced creatures believed to be part animals, part humans. In the preface to the publication, Giovanni Giuseppe Gregorio from Cremona included an image of the children in question and noted that they each had two arms and two legs and all necessary parts of the body except the private parts (*le vergognose*). They shared a channel for defecation. The notoriety of this birth was exacerbated by the space of their birth and residence in the Jewish Ghetto. An account from 1575 included a hand-tinted image of the children with their parents in which the only colour to have been added was yellow in line with premodern distinguishing signs.[22] This account was intended to emphasize the otherness of the conjoined twins across every aspect of their identity. Natural disasters more generally have been seen to intensify as well as illustrate social and religious tensions of the period. It was a similar symbolic association with impurity which determined the Jewish prohibition on handling Catholic objects as part of their work in the second-hand and lending trades at the end of a plague outbreak in 1558.[23]

This event in 1575 was not the only portent or sign associated with the impending epidemic. A broadsheet published that year described the aforementioned conjoined twins alongside conjoined puppies (*cagnolle*), conjoined chickens, a fish out of its usual waters (seen in the lagoon the previous summer and known as a Phisertera), a bright light in the night sky, and two earthquake tremors.[24] A unifying frontispiece image was provided to the text, intended to illustrate the intensity of the signs or warnings. A failure to heed these warnings underscored the role of the natural disaster as an episode of judgement.[25] These events were seen to have a social cause and environmental consequence.

---

[21] The pamphlet is published first as *Discorso sopra il significato del parto mostruoso nato di una Hebrea in Venetia nell'anno 1575 adi XXVI di Maggio* (Venice, 1575) and then twice in the following year as *Discorso sopra gli accidenti del parto mostruoso nato d'una hebrea nel ghetto di Venetia nell'anno 1575 a di XXVI di Maggio. Dove si ragiona altamente del future destino de gli hebrei. Di novo ristampato* (in Bologna and Venice). This case is discussed in David B. Ruderman, *Kabbalah, magic, and science: the cultural university of a sixteenth-century Jewish physician* (Cambridge MA: Harvard University Press, 1988), chapter five: 'Out of the mouths of babes and sucklings' and is contextualized in relation to R. Abraham Yagel's [1553–1623] later exploration.

[22] *Nova et Ridicolosa Espositione del Mostro nato in Ghetto, con il Lamento di suo Padre per la Morte di Quello* (Venice, 1575).

[23] ASV, Comun reg 1, 362v '*Li hebrei non possino impostar sopra cose sacre*' (26 November 1558).

[24] *Mostri e segne che si sono veduti in Vinegia nell'anno 1575* (Venice, 1575).

[25] Raingard Esser, 'Fear of water and floods in the Low Countries'.

164 CLEANING UP RENAISSANCE ITALY

Many of these characteristics of natural disasters are expressed in an account by the Venetian diarist Marin Sanudo of an earthquake in Venice in 1511. He recorded the scale of the impact and the omens which were interpreted:

> It seemed as though the houses were collapsing, the chimneys swaying, the walls bursting open, the bell-towers bending, objects in high places falling, water boiling, even in the Grand Canal, as though it had been put on fire.'[26]

The sensation, though intensely felt, did not result in widespread collapse of buildings. Instead, the structural impact was more localized. This led to a sense of symbolism in the damage inflicted and political interpretations to be made of the parts of buildings which did fall, including the marble statues of four kings at St Marks and the high ridge of the roof above the great balcony of the Great Council chamber in the city's Ducal Palace.

The Venetian patriarch, Don Antonio Contarini, was said to have explained the earthquake as a sign from God, caused by sin. When he spoke to the Venetian College (the part of the Venetian Senate which controlled the proposals made and topics discussed) he identified particular moral problems:

> Venice is full of these, especially of sodomy, which is recklessly practised everywhere. The female prostitutes have sent to him to say that they cannot make a living because no one now goes to them, so rampant is sodomy: even the old men are getting down to it. He has heard from confessors that fathers are interfering with daughters, brothers with sisters, and so forth. And the city is becoming irreligious...We are now halfway through Lent. In other years the confessors would have heard the confessions of half the Venetians by this time; but now they have heard no one but the female tertiaries and a tiny number of others.

The patriarch proposed processions at St Mark's for three days, and processions in the parishes in the evenings, and three days fasting to appease the wrath of God. Sanudo concluded his account by noting, 'I applaud these things as an aid to piety and good conduct; but as a remedy for earthquakes, which are a natural phenomenon, this was no good at all...'. Despite Sanudo's scepticism, many believed that the unnatural events resulted from the behaviour of certain groups within Venetian society. Sanudo recorded over the following days that sermons were preached against the city's Jewish community as well as acts of blasphemy, sacrilege, and sodomy. Often, human sin was to blame not only for the start of the natural disaster but for its severe progression. In his account of the fire at

---

[26] Reprinted in translation in David Chambers, Brian Pullan, and Jennifer Fletcher, *Venice: a documentary history*, pp. 188–90.

DEALING WITH DISASTERS   165

Rialto in 1514, Sanudo recalled that people were more focused on rescuing merchandise from the buildings than putting out the fire, meaning that the flames continued to spread, exacerbated by the strong winds.

A lesser-known earthquake occurred in Genoa in April 1536, the events of which were recorded in a pamphlet of the same year printed (it is presumed) within the city.[27] The author described himself as sleeping at the time the earthquake began and related that, within his home, the building, chests, benches, the bed, and roof shook as though the devil himself had arrived with all of his minions to carry the observer off to hell. The earthquake was said to have ruined houses, palaces, towers, and the social toll was even more severe: pregnant women miscarried and many people were killed. The event was also said to cause numerous other ills, of which, the author commented, not even a single per cent could be described. On looking out of the window, it seemed like the Day of Judgement, with the streets filled with people crying out to God. This is reminiscent of an account of a devastating earthquake in Naples in 1456 for which the Sienese ambassador recorded the cries of the people walking through the streets, lost and distraught. The noise was so great 'that it seemed the stones were crying'.[28] In the case of the Genoese author, however, he also despaired that Christian society cried out to God during times of persecution but, as soon as the moment had passed, returned to their sinful ways of living.

The reason for the earthquake, for the pamphlet's author, was clear: the widespread gambling which was taking place in Genoa and the resulting offences caused to God, the Saints and the Virgin Mary through blasphemy. He described many taverns and gaming houses within the city and wrote that three of these gaming houses (*barratterie*) were destroyed in the earthquake, which he took to be a sure sign that the gambling was the cause of the event, because it was in these localities that people carried out all sorts of scandalous behaviour which 'stank to high Heaven'. Genoa was famous for gambling and was the home of one of the earliest lotteries, as explored in chapter five. The connections between gambling and blasphemy have been widely recognized: Federico Barbierato has explained that gambling was feared as a way of testing and commanding God.[29] Javier Villa-Flores has considered the connections in detail in a chapter of his book Dangerous Speech in the context of early modern Mexico.[30] This association, then, was held broadly in the early modern Catholic world and was observed acutely in both Venice and Genoa.

---

[27] What follows is taken from the reprint of the tract in V. Promis, 'Descrizione sincrona del terremoto di Genova, seguito il 10 aprile 1536', *Atti della Società ligure di storia Patria* x (1874).

[28] Fabrizio Nevola, *Street life*, pp. 92–3.

[29] Jonathan Walker, 'Gambling and Venetian noblemen', p. 46.

[30] Javier Villa-Flores, *Dangerous speech: a social history of blasphemy in Colonial Mexico* (Tucson AZ: The University of Arizona Press, 2006).

166 CLEANING UP RENAISSANCE ITALY

In 1571, a statement from the Venetian Council of Ten described men who left

their wife and children left to die of hunger in the house to satisfy their immoderate appetites, because in these conventicles of drinkers, they speak without respect of any quality of persons, they blaspheme, gamble and finally they luxuriate and indulge in every sort of depravity.[31]

In both cities, taverns and guesthouses were closely regulated and clear instructions were issued on a regular basis which identified illicit activities within these spaces, such as providing lodging for sex work or permitting gambling.[32] The connections between gambling, blasphemy, and bad behaviour, with an added sprinkling (or handful) of filth can be seen in the well-known case of Antonio Rinaldeschi from Florence in 1501. Rinaldeschi lost money and clothing whilst gambling at a tavern called the Fig Tree. Whilst crossing a small *piazza* in front of the church of Santa Maria degli Alberighi, he stooped to gather a handful of dry horse dung and threw it at a tabernacle with a fresco of the Virgin Annunciate, known as the Madonna de'Ricci. Rinaldeschi was hanged as a result of the offence.[33] One account of these events noted that a priest was sent to detach the offending substance (*'spichare el detto stercho dalla detta Nostra Donna'*). More generally Catholics did not wash their religious statues but would instead have brushed or dusted them clean.

This story about the consequences of immoral acts is reminiscent of the lesser-known tale of Antonio Schiaffino from Camogli in Liguria. In 1558, the forty-year-old blind man was said to be outside the chapel dedicated to the Madonna del Boschetto. He was accompanied by a group of youths, who challenged him to throw a stone through the doorway of the chapel. He accepted the dare and told them to put a stone at his feet. He threw it and it went not only through the doorway but also past the wooden grating which protected the chapel's miraculous image. The stone struck the image and ripped it. The youths fled, terrified. Antonio remained as if stupefied and immediately his foot began to swell up and his leg developed wounds from which putrid blood began to seep. The effect was agonizing pain and the miserable man ended his days wounded and maimed.[34] It is interesting to note that the origin of the cult of the Madonna del Boschetto lay in

---

[31] Cited in Jonathan Walker, 'Gambling and Venetian noblemen', p. 33.

[32] ASCG, PdC, 13-39 (9 November 1529).

[33] William J. Connell and Giles Constable, 'Sacrilege and redemption in Renaissance Florence: the case of Antonio Rinaldeschi', *Journal of the Warburg and Courtauld Institutes* 61 (1998), 53–92.

[34] A painted image of this event was produced in 1558 and includes an inscription https://www.beweb.chiesacattolica.it/benistorici/bene/6082867/Scuola+ligure+%281558%29%2C+Castigo+subito+da+Antonio+Schiaffino#reg_pol=&provincia=&comune=&denominazioni_adv=Castigo&nomi_correlati=&oa.tipo=&oa.sgti=&abstract=&oa.insieme=&secoloRomano=&anno_min=&anno_max=&dominio=1&ambito=CEIOA&advanced=true&view=griglia&locale=it&ordine=&liberadescr=&liberaluogo=&action=ricerca%2Frisultati&highlight=Castigo.

a series of visions of the Virgin Mary by a twelve-year-old peasant girl called Angiola Schiaffino in 1518 who, presumably, was a relation of Antonio.[35]

Numerous accounts of sin and natural disaster included prominent mention of filth and stench. In the reflection on the Genoese earthquake, the idea that gambling and blasphemy 'stank to High Heaven' was not simply a convenient turn of phrase. Devotions might include or be envisioned as sweet scents ascending to the heavens. Prayers offered to the Virgin Mary were 'visualised as verbal roses that could be woven together to form a crown—hence the use of the word *corona* in Italian to describe rosary beads'.[36] The association between stench and immorality (as well as the converse between sweet smells and devotion) was, therefore, well established.

Communities recognized and responded to the threat or incidence of natural disasters in a myriad of ways. Previous chapters have explored the many forms of environmental management which were directly intended to reduce the risk or impact of natural disasters. The associations between piety and the cleanliness of the environment, retold in hagiographical literature, offered examples of miraculous interventions that changed the environment. One example comes in the stories told of St Isidore of Chios. This saint's body remained in Chios until 1125 when it was brought to Venice under the supervision of Doge Domenico Michiel (1118–30) on his return from Jerusalem. According to an eye-witness account of the translation of the relics by Cerbano Cerbani, the original intention had been to construct an ex voto chapel in the vicinity of San Marco to house St Isidore's relics but this was never realized and so the body of the saint languished for two centuries before Doge Andrea Dandolo decided to commission a beautifully decorated (and recently restored) chapel within the Basilica of San Marco. This was completed in 1355, the year after Dandolo's death.[37]

Within the chapel's iconography St Isidore is depicted alongside St Mark, St John the Baptist, and St Nicholas worshipping Christ and the Virgin. The three latter saints are also shown on St Isidore's tomb, above which stands a representation of the Annunciation. The mosaics which run down either side of the chapel show scenes from St Isidore's life (on the upper level) and death (on the lower row). The other side of the chapel depicts the stages of the translation of his relics. At the point at which the mosaics were completed in Venice, the story of St Isidore would have been unknown to most Venetians and scenes in the mosaic cycle, as well as narrative elements in a fourteenth-century manuscript in the city's

---

[35] Jane Garnett and Gervase Rosser, *Spectacular miracles*, p. 66.

[36] Maya Corry, Deborah Howard, and Mary Laven (eds), *Madonnas and miracles*, p. 94.

[37] Stefania Gerevini 'Inscribing history, (over)writing politics: word and image in the chapel of Sant'Isidoro at San Marco, Venice' in Wilfried E. Keil and Kristina Krüger (eds), *Sacred scripture, sacred space: the interlacing of real places and conceptual spaces in medieval art and architecture* (Berlin: De Gruyter, 2019) and Michele Tomasi (ed.), 'Il culto di sant'Isidoro a Venezia', *Quaderni della Procuratoria* (2008) and P. Saccardo, *La cappella di S. Isidoro nella Basilica di San Marco* (Venice, 1987).

168 CLEANING UP RENAISSANCE ITALY

Marciana library, place a notable emphasis on the significance of water and cleanliness.[38]

Soon after his arrival on Chios, Isidore was said to have chosen to stay in the home of Afra, a woman of poor moral standing. In the face of Isidore's piety, Afra fell to her knees and declared, 'Sir, my sins mean that I am not worthy to have you under my roof,' to which Isidore replied, 'Our Saviour, detained by wicked and unclean people could not be sullied by their presence. Instead his purity washed away all of their impurities.' Afra asked, 'How can it be that I, so deeply immersed in sin, superstition and sensuous living can cleanse myself?' Isidore replied, 'Believe in Jesus Christ, receive baptism and you will remain clean.' The conversion of the woman prompted an encounter with a demon, who challenged Isidore as to why, since he served a God who loved purity of body and soul, he had chosen to enter into a house of those whose bodies were dirty and souls filthy. Furthermore, the demon complained that if Isidore was going to go around taking away his slaves (the women) then he should be allowed to replace them. To this, Isidore replied, swear to me that you will kill whomever I concede to you as yours. The demon agreed and Isidore instructed him to go to a spring on Chios called Caroht, from which no one could drink because a dragon lived there, whose breath killed those who approached. The demon shouted, 'you Christian deceiver. You have made me promise to kill my friend!' and he screamed with rage before he went and suffocated the dragon. From that moment on, the spring was purified. The story is reminiscent of that of another military saint, patron of both Chios as well as Genoa: according to the legend of St George recorded by Jacopo de Voragine, a dragon had guarded a spring of water in Silena. Once the dragon was slain by Saint George, the spring's water was theurgically cleansed and became a site of healing. San Siro, whose titular church was the original Cathedral of Genoa, was himself associated with the cleanliness and safety of water since was said to have banished a basilisk from a well in Genoa.

The lower row of the mosaics depicts the stages which led to Isidore's death. The third section shows the body of the saint being dragged along the ground, lacerated by stones and thorns. At this moment, the compassionate environment of the island was said to have reacted: the trees began to weep. Their tears became the island's most famous export—mastic (known also as the 'tears of Chios'). The mastic trees feature in the mosaic scene and the sculptural panel on the Saint's tomb. Rudolf Dellermann has suggested that this beautifully carved angel is unusually prominent when compared with other fourteenth-century tombs.[39] She holds, alongside the incense burner, an incense boat which is particularly

---

[38] Cerbano Cerbani, 'Translatio mirifici Martyris Isidori a Chio insula in civitatem Venetam', *Recueil des historiens de Croisades: Historiens Occidentaux*, vol. 5, pp. 321–34.

[39] Rudolf Dellerman, 'I mosaici della cappella di Sant'Isidoro nella basilica di San Marco a Venezia', *Arte veneta* 60 (2003), 6–29.

large. He attributes these elements to the association between St Isidore and mastic (which was used in oral medical treatments as well as incense).

The connection between health and the weeping trees also features on one of the *oselle* produced to commemorate the dogeship of Francesco Erizzo in 1631. The front shows the winged lion of St Mark. The reverse contains a more complex scene with the Virgin Mary holding the Christ Child and the two are suspended above a beautiful depiction of a tree. Large droplets of what is likely to be myrrh are shown dropping from the branches and trunk. Two cherubs, representing the wind, spread the sweet odours. This was clearly intended to be a representation of the restoration of health for the environment and the city. It provides a reminder of the ways in which both pollution and purification might be associated with the symbolic and physical changes in the environment.

St Isidore's healing cult was, then, already established by the time his relics were taken to Venice and the account of their journey by the aforementioned Cerbani also emphasized the protection of health and the environment. Before leaving Chios, the ship was said to have been protected from a devastating plague and the vessel was kept safe on the journey to Venice despite numerous storms.[40] There is no evidence currently of a healing cult associated with St Isidore in Venice itself, however. Instead, the annual procession on St Isidore's feast day became an intensely Venetian commemoration of the Republic's defeat of the overly ambitious doge—Marin Falier—who led a conspiracy in the wake of a defeat at the hands of the Genoese. The plot was discovered by the Council of Ten on 15 April 1355 and the procession of St Isidore's feast day on 16 April was transformed into a Mass in the chapel of St Marks and a ritual re-enactment of the funeral of the disgraced doge. Even before the dramatic events of 1355, Edward Muir notes that the annual procession on St Isidore's feast day had been established as a memorial to Doge Domenico Michiel's triumphs in the Crusades and so lacked any healing or environmental elements.[41] Michele Tomasi has suggested though, the coincidence between the development of the chapel dedicated to St Isidore and the end of the outbreak of the Black Death is striking.[42] Without further evidence, the story remains a vivid depiction of the connections between sin, pollution, and illness as well as piety, purity, and health.

The common, explanatory framework given to natural disasters was that they were caused by sin, whether in a general or highly specific way. The language of disasters, therefore, was often infused with notions of morality, sanctity, and cleanliness. This forms the general backdrop for the following sections, which explore the measures undertaken within Genoese and Venetian communities in the context of plagues, storms, and floods. These responses reinforce that the

---

[40] Philip Argenti, *The occupation of Chios*, p. 368.   [41] Edward Muir, *Civic ritual*, p. 218.
[42] Rudolf Dellerman, 'I mosaici della cappella di Sant'Isidoro', p. 38.

170   CLEANING UP RENAISSANCE ITALY

settings of both cities lay at the heart of economic and social identity and yet posed constant challenges to the health of the inhabitants and their surroundings.[43]

Plagues

Plague devastated Northern Italian cities regularly during the fifteenth century. During this period, the Health Office was founded on a permanent basis in Venice and the manner in which public health officials responded to epidemic disease was codified and recorded. Both Genoa and Venice experienced severe outbreaks of plague during the 1570s: in 1575–7 in Venice and 1579 in Genoa. Mortality in the case of the former outbreak was approximately a quarter of the city's population and that of the latter closer to 13 per cent.[44] Assereto has argued that the plague of 1579 ushered in an important step in the development of the Genoese Health Office by stabilizing the work of this magistracy as it had developed in the previous decades.[45] In both cases, the documentary evidence of strategies for governance during these periods is considerable. Many of the interventions outlined in previous chapters had a role to play in keeping episodes of the plague at bay or under control. In times of plague, it was feared that the clustering of street sellers in squares across cities could cause crowds to build up and so, in Verona for example, these individuals were encouraged to spread themselves through the city and the streets.[46] In public spaces, fires should be burned three or four times per month in order to improve the quality of the air.

In both cities household and district quarantine was imposed alongside the operation of the city's plague hospital (*lazzaretto*). Public health structures relied on officials appointed to oversee districts and the responsibility for monitoring levels of infection and mortality rested with these individuals. In Genoa they were also tasked with ensuring the cleaning of districts. Governments supplemented and amended these measures in the centuries that followed on the basis of observation and expert advice.[47] Spatial and administrative boundaries took on heightened significance, however, during times of plague and the importance of the locality as an administrative unit intensified.

During plague epidemics, the usual channels for communication and access were utilized for vital public health work. In 1576, for example, the Venetian Health Office reflected on the danger posed by burial of the dead within the city

---

[43] For an analysis of water as a polluting, damaging threat see Raingard Esser, 'Fear of water and floods'.

[44] In the case of Genoa the number of deaths has been estimated as 8,500 out of a population of 67,000 and, for Venice, was approximately 47,000 out of 168,000. Giovanni Assereto, '*Per la comune salvezza*', p. 30.

[45] Giovanni Assereto, '*Per la comune salvezza*', p. 36.

[46] Archivio di Stato, Verona, Sanità reg 33 137r.   [47] Samuel Cohn Jr, *Cultures of plague*.

itself and determined that two boats were required to serve the city. One was to travel twice a day to San Marco, Castello, and Canareggio and the other to San Polo, Dorsoduro, and Santa Croce in the allotted locations. The regular journeys were to be made in the morning and also after nine, and more often if required.[48] Accessible waterways were needed to facilitate the movement of the wide variety of boats for the transportation of people to the city's plague hospital islands.[49] Clear streets were required for the journeys of medical personnel and Health Office employees through the city. In 1576, it was stipulated that the death of a number of doctors had prompted the Health Office officials to look to ensure that two would be reserved to treat nobles, citizens, and other 'persons of quality' of the city and not required to travel across the *sestieri* in order to inspect corpses or those infected with the plague.[50]

The threat or development of plague necessitated the control of movement and mobility. In 1582, the Genoese Health Office reminded *mulattieri* coming through the val Polcevera that they were not permitted to transport material into the city without the necessary documentation or inspection and quarantine at the *lazzaretto*.[51] In addition to the widely recognized monitoring of goods and travellers, times of plague also heightened the importance of shared communication between Italian states. A short extract in the Mantuan state archive, said to have been copied from the records of the Genoese Health Office in 1579, provides an insight into the information which was recorded by these government bodies and some of which was subsequently shared with the authorities elsewhere.[52] The series of entries demonstrates the way in which authorities sought to assess levels of infection (and threat) by triangulating sources of information. This included notices from other Health Offices (about plague within and beyond the Italian peninsula) but also reports from local officials with numbers of deaths and cases from the city and the *lazzaretto*. The authorities in Piacenza and Parma were in particularly frequent contact with the office in Genoa. In response to the outbreak of 1579, the doctors of Genoa were said to have met in order to assess the nature of the disease and diagnose its nature. These men attributed the outbreak to the weather over the previous year which had been humid, with a dominant *Austrini* wind, combined with the insufficient diet of the poor.

Plague prompted an acute focus on the minutiae of urban life. In some cities, the cleanliness of homes, as well as the provision of bedding, was observed and recorded by the authorities.[53] The spatial borders of units became deeply significant, whether territorial boundaries, city walls, or the doorways of houses. Each

---

[48] ASV, Sanità, 733 1v (13 July 1576).   [49] ASV, Sanità, 733 2r (13 July 1576).
[50] ASV, Sanità, 733 7v (6 August 1576).   [51] Giovanni Assereto, 'Per la comune salvezza', p. 38.
[52] I am very grateful to Marie-Louise Leonard for sharing this material with me from ASMc, AG, b.2609, 211r–216v.
[53] John Henderson, *Florence under siege* and Nicholas Eckstein, 'Florence on foot: an eye-level mapping of the early modern city in time of plague', *Renaissance Studies* 30:2 (2015), 273–97.

172   CLEANING UP RENAISSANCE ITALY

was addressed in public health and environmental measures. In 1487, a chronicle from Antwerp recorded that almost everyone in the town nailed a devotional print (bearing Jesus's name) to their front door in order to ward off the plague.[54] Movement around the city was carefully monitored, whether that of people, objects, or animals. There was considerable concern about the illicit movement of goods motivated by theft. The Health Office doctor Alberto Quattrocchi in Spalato noted that one of the most important roles of the Health Office officials was to ensure that those in quarantine received all necessary foodstuffs and supplies in a timely fashion since 'need is the mother of theft' (la neccessità è madre del latrocinio).[55]

The flow and balance of the streets were interrupted by quarantine restrictions. As elsewhere on the peninsula, in Venice during the outbreak of 1575–7 the authorities organized an eleven-day lockdown, in which individuals were not permitted to enter the houses of others and women and children could not leave their district of the city. The symbolic resonance of the forty-day period of quarantine illustrates the way in which early modern responses to disease combined medical ideas with religious ones. This symbolic and significant period regularly features in the Bible.[56] It was the period set out for embalming in Genesis, as well as for mourning, repentance, and purification after childbirth and of course is the liturgically sanctioned period for Lent.[57] The forty-day period might be seen as one of repentance more broadly. In premodern Rome a boules player threw a ball at the Madonna della Misericordia. The offender lost his arm, sought mercy, repented, and the arm returned forty days later.[58] The religious significance of the period of quarantine was not coincidental—it was intended to bring comfort to those in need and to encourage those undergoing quarantine to consider themselves as undergoing a period of purification, to be spent in devotion.

Quarantine regulations sought to anticipate networks of sociability in order to limit the spread of the disease. If a suspicious death occurred in Venice, the Health Office doctor would examine the body for signs of plague. If identified, the household would be put into quarantine and all members of the family would be interviewed under oath in order to attempt to trace the source of the infection and identify, in turn, contacts who may have contracted the disease. The Health Office's 1541 regulations are revealing with regard to sociability. The household would be asked whether the deceased had visited the home of anyone who had died, whether foreigners had lodged in the household or whether foreign goods

---

[54] Frederik Buylaert, Jelle de Rock, and Anne-Laure van Bruaene, 'City portrait, civic body', p. 809.

[55] ASV, Sanità 737 200r–202r (30 June 1607).

[56] The Bible, Old Testament, Genesis 7; Exodus 24 and 34; NT Luke 4:1–13 and Acts 1:3.

[57] The Bible, Old Testament, Genesis 50:2–4; Deuteronomy 9:25. For the forty-day period in relation to criminal cases see ASV, Senato Terra, reg 29, 123r (26 May 1537).

[58] Fabrizio Nevola, Street life, p. 220.

DEALING WITH DISASTERS 173

had been received recently, how long the patient had been ill for, how many times the doctor visited, which pharmacy was used for medicines, whether blood-letting was administered, whether the parish priest had visited, whether friends or family had visited (and whether this was at the bedside or in the house), whether any neighbours had come in to help around the house 'as often happens', and whether any items had been removed from the house. Contact between neighbours was recognized in the regulations. Inhabitants living in the same building as a sick or deceased person would be quarantined for twenty-two days but if they shared a kitchen with that individual then they would stay in isolation for forty days.

Although contagion was seen to pass through touch or in the air, the original causation of outbreaks might be seen to originate with the water. Notably, epidemics might be traced back to episodes of flooding. At the end of the sixteenth century, di Zorzi attributed the outbreak of 1575 to the flooding of the waters through the streets and wells.[59] Annibale Raimondo blamed an event in October 1574 when furious winds swept the lagoon water through the streets, cleared out the drains, washed the squares, and cleaned sites of dirt and filth. The *pilelle* of the wells and their surrounding squares became polluted with rubbish and filth and fresh and saltwater mixed with fresh within the wells.[60] This had a particular impact upon the poor, who could not afford to drink wine to satisfy their thirst and were reliant on the water of public wells.

New cults made explicit use of elements of the environment in the context of epidemics. In a manuscript from the Wellcome Library, London, William Schupbach illustrated the significance of water in what became a story of a Venetian plague miracle. Said to have occurred in 1464, the story was revitalized during the plague of 1576 when a broadsheet was published retelling the miraculous immunity of a convent on the Giudecca called Santa Croce.[61] The original story recounted the visit of a young male to the institution who asked to be provided with some water. The *portonera* drew some from the well, gave it to him to drink and he subsequently departed. This water came to be associated with miraculous properties and, during the 1575–7 plague outbreak, people crossed to the Giudecca to consume this water. Eventually part of the wall of the convent was taken down to allow for the construction of a conduit to dispense water to those beyond the institution.[62]

---

[59] F. di Zorzi, *Dell'aria e sua qualità . . . dove specialmente si scuopre quale egli si sia in Venetia; et si leggono altre cose notabili d'intorno cosi potente e maravigliosa città* (Venice, 1596).

[60] Annibale Raimondo, *La viva et vera cagione che ha generato le fiere infermità che tanto hanno molestato l'anno 1575 et tanto il 76 acerbamente molestano il Popolo de l'invittissima Città di Vinetia: Indirizzato à tutti quelli che non sono idioti delle cose naturali de gli accidenti et che molto intendono la prattica della Città di Vinetia* (Padua, 1576).

[61] See William Schupbach, 'A Venetian "plague miracle" in 1464 and 1576', *Medical History* 20:3 (1976) 312–6.

[62] William Schupbach, 'A Venetian "plague miracle" in 1464 and 1576', p. 314.

174 CLEANING UP RENAISSANCE ITALY

Other architectural responses to natural disasters were even more substantial than the addition of a new conduit.[63] In the midst of the plague of 1480–1, a domestic devotional image of the Virgin Mary, which had been displayed by its owner outside the home, was said to be the cause of many cures. A neighbour heard the Virgin ask for an appropriate home for the image and the city's ornate church of Santa Maria dei Miracoli was completed in 1489. As noted in the introduction, the case of the Madonna dell'Orto in Chiavari is one which illustrated the influence of popular piety. An ex voto image, created to give thanks for the survival of Maria de'Guerci from plague in 1493, came to be associated with curative properties. Its reputation developed during the plague of 1528 to the extent that local health officials became concerned about the crowds amassing around the image. In addition, the garden outside the city in which the image was located had previously been used for the burial of plague corpses making it an intensely dangerous site from the perspective of disease and contagion.[64] A wall was constructed around the image which was believed to be the conduit for healing miracles in 1630–3, after which point it was transferred to a church setting.

In times of plague, it was recognized that high standards of cleanliness were essential and many policies which were commonplace within the ports were intensified. In Savona, for example, the Health Office was intended to ensure that in times of war or plague that foreigners and other poor and miserable people were expelled from the city.[65] Attention was paid to the cleanliness of homes. Dirt, filth, and rubbish were removed and the windows were opened to allow healthy flow of air from the winds. The *pizzigamorti* (body clearers) or others who carried out the cleaning were instructed to make sure that they were meticulous in their cleaning and did not leave rubbish, rags, water, or any other materials in the house.[66] Inside, aromatic herbs were used to make sweet smells in a warming pot over a fire including incense, styrax, and ambergris. A mixture of water, warm vinegar, and wormwood was sprayed in the air and on the walls of the building. This herb was used in Galenic medicine to settle the stomach and would be found in later alcoholic drinks including purl, absinthe, and vermouth. In Spalato, Quattrocchi reported that houses should be cleaned by the allotted workers, known as *netesini*. The rooms were perfumed from room to room using a scent sent from Venice. Doors and windows should be kept closed and remain so for one day and one night. The windows could then be opened for four days to allow the air to clean the space before people returned.[67]

---

[63] Sheila Barker, 'Miraculous images and the plagues of Italy, c.590–1656'.
[64] Giuseppe Bontà, *Storia della Madonna dell'Orto* (Genoa, 1847).
[65] *Statuti politici della citta di Savona*, p. 97.   [66] ASV, Secreta MMN b. 95 17r (13 June 1576).
[67] ASV, Sanità, 737 201r (30 June 1607).

DEALING WITH DISASTERS   175

Authorities also sought to ensure salubrious conditions within institutions. In times of plague it was intended that 'those in prison or in monasteries should be exposed to fresh air and their quarters cleaned regularly, their foul odours eradicated'.[68] In sixteenth-century plans for the prison at Rialto, certain cells were to be enlarged and balconies constructed at Leona and other jails to provide relief in the heat of the summer.[69] Concerns about cleanliness also shaped entry procedures for hospital patients. In the Hospital of San Pietro e San Polo in Castello the sick were stripped down so that 'the dirt [could] be taken off them'. They were then given a clean shirt and sheets and put to bed.[70] In times of plague there is no doubt that the cleanliness of the city's plague hospitals was of paramount concern. Medical and secular authorities sought to ensure that these sites remained clear of all putrid, dirty materials and that the beds and sheets were clean.[71]

Numerous advisers applied the same principles to the management of cities and outlined concerns about cleanliness motivated by the idea that filth is 'the mother of infection'.[72] Andrea Gabrielli who was practising as a doctor in Genoa in 1576 recommended that the city should be kept 'free from all forms of putrefaction and fetid smells, by enforced cleaning of stables, latrine and sewers and guarding the city from the importation of bad fruit and vegetables and other foul-smelling substances and chemicals such as sulphur and arsenic'.[73] The burial of the dead was to be carefully attended to and manure was supposed to be kept a safe distance from the city. In the instructions issued in Spalato, the Health Office doctor Alberto Quattrocchi noted that the streets must not be used to dump rags or rubbish and street cleaners should ensure that the streets were maintained and clean. Any rags found in the streets or within properties should be burned at a distance from the centre and in an open place.[74]

Similar items were of concern in the Venetian plague hospitals. In January 1575 the Health Office recorded that a quantity of rags were in the *lazaretto vecchio*, along with other rubbish from the hospital of the sick. The prior had instructed for these to be burned but this had not happened. These needed to be dealt with, along with ropes (*gomene*) from ships, and other rigging and cordage that had been left outside and exposed to the elements. They were to be noted down and valued before being burned, along with four, tied coils of rope, cord, and canvas all of

---

[68] ASV, Sanità, 737 201r (30 June 1607).
[69] ASV, Consiglio dei Dieci, parti comuni, filza 90 (7 April 1564) cited in Brian Pullan, *Rich and poor*, p. 397.
[70] ASV, Sanità 740 118v (26 January 1648).
[71] Nicolo Massa, *Ragionamento dello Eccellentissimo m Nicolo Massa sopra le infermita che vengono dall'aere pestilentiale del presente anno MDLV* (Venice, 1556) 16r.
[72] John Henderson, ' "La schifezza, madre di corruzione": peste e società a Firenze nella prima epoca moderna', *Medicina e storia* 2 (2001), 23–56.
[73] Gabrielli cited in Samuel Cohn Jr., *Cultures of plague.*
[74] ASV, Sanità 737 200r–202r (30 June 1607).

176 CLEANING UP RENAISSANCE ITALY

which had been damaged during the long period in which they had been left on the island.[75] A quantity of sheets which had been cleaned in the *lazaretto vecchio* but remained unclaimed and the owners of which were not known were to be burned because of their low value and the fact that it would be very difficult to return them after two years. It was recorded that many goods had been burned in the interests of protecting the health of the city and that the same should be done here so as not to jeopardize the health of the city.[76]

The value of the elements with regard to disinfection was reiterated by the Health Office doctor Alberto Quattrocchi in Spalato. He recorded that there were four ways to disinfect suspected or infected goods and each made prominent use of the elements of the environment. Quattrocchi listed them in ascending order of effectiveness: first goods could be buried in sand for ten days and cleaned by beating to remove miasmatic air for a further four. Second, they could be kept in the open air, again with regular cleaning by being beaten and fumigated over a period of forty days. Third, they could be submerged in flowing water for four days and then dried and left in the open air for fourteen days. Finally, the goods could be washed and dried and then boiled with lye for two hours. In order to clean mattresses and feather beds, Quattrocchi recommended removing the wool and feathers and cleaning using the fourth method of disinfection.[77] Clear channels of water were used in Venice to disinfect materials. A number of points known as '*chiovere*' where wool was dried beyond epidemics were used to clean the goods from houses in which someone had died of the plague.[78] The doctors who referred to these sites in their report noted that their use was appropriate for many families but not all: nobles, citizens, or merchants tended to live in homes in which objects were infrequently handled by inhabitants and where individual items might have been untouched for months and perhaps years. In these instances, the disinfection of domestic goods was less pressing than for those lower down the social spectrum.

The damage caused to objects and buildings during quarantine could be considerable. During the plague of 1575–7 the Health Office moved from its usual residence in the Terra nova and at the end of the outbreak, the officials reflected on the changes which had taken place to the building during their absence.[79] The offices had been stripped of chair backs (*spalliere*), rugs, cushions, and other necessary things. Some of these had been stolen, others sent to the *lazaretti* and burnt during the contagion and were duly replaced. Hospital buildings were also badly affected. The priors of the two *lazaretti* wrote to the Health Office in December 1581, four years after the severe outbreak of plague. They described the state of the institutions as being ruined: the buildings, hospitals,

---

[75] ASV, Sanità 732 83r (11 January 1575).
[76] ASV, Sanità, 728 92v (2 December 1560).
[77] ASV, Sanità, 737 200r–202r (30 June 1607).
[78] ASV, Sanità, 733 13v (14 August 1576).
[79] ASV, Sanita, 733 190r (14 August 1577).

pilings, canals, walls, apartments, spaces, and rooms were all in this state. One part of the women's hospital had recently collapsed.[80] Nearly twenty-five years later, the state of the buildings on the *lazaretto nuovo* was still causing concern. This time the majority of the doors, balconies, ceilings, and floors of the building where merchandise and people underwent quarantine were all in a poor state of repair.[81] The institutions also required paving. Previously on the plague hospital islands, the lack of paving along the paths which led to the sites of disinfection meant that these thoroughfares were muddy and almost always full of water and filth. The porters found it very difficult to carry the goods and merchandise on their shoulders. The changes to the paving meant that more could be achieved and by a fewer number of porters.[82]

In other instances the Health Office found itself in possession of items which had been sent from the *lazaretti* and Sant'Anzolo dela Concordia two years previously and for which the owners were now unknown. These included silver and other trinkets including rings, coral and paternoster beads, and similar items. Since these were not believed to carry contagion they were to be sold and the money would be used by the Health Office. It was noted that this would recompense the Health Office for the extraordinary efforts they had undertaken, and continued to undertake, in keeping the city clear of beggars ('*tenir netta la cita de furfanti et poveri forestieri*').[83]

In addition to the movement of people, elements, and goods, officials also expressed concern about the movement of animals. In Venice, the Health Office oversaw a '*vespero siciliano*' of the dogs and cats that wandered the city. The government had intended for the animals to be buried immediately because they were believed to carry the plague but ended up having to pay people to remove the animals' bodies from the canals because they were giving off such a foul stench.[84] Concerns too centred around the presence of pigs, pigeons, and chickens which were believed to pose a risk to public health because of their associations with stench and movement.[85]

The disruptive effect of periods of plague, in the light of changes to the rhythms of urban life, shaped a sense of time.[86] In 1609, residents around the Piazza dei Tessitori testified about a small passageway to the brothel.[87] In their accounts, one referred to a wall falling down 'before the plague of 1589'. These events became moments which structured memory. Although those who experienced plague were aware that it might hit regularly during the premodern period,

---

[80] ASV, Sanità, 735 78r (16 December 1581).   [81] ASV, Sanità, 737 170r (20 April 1605).
[82] ASV, Sanità 731 44r (29 July 1567).   [83] ASV, Sanità, 730 293r (2 December 1560).
[84] Rocco Benedetti, *Relatione d'alcuni casi occorsi in Venetia*.
[85] ASV, Secreta MMN b. 95 17r (13 June 1576).
[86] Jane Stevens Crawshaw, 'A sense of time: experiencing plague and quarantine in early modern Italy', *I Tatti Studies in the Italian Renaissance* 24:2 (2021), 269–90.
[87] ASCG, PdC, 67-6 (11 May 1609).

178 CLEANING UP RENAISSANCE ITALY

reference to the seasons was generally made retrospectively as part of explanations of causation. A sense of seasonality was more acute in accounts of other natural disasters, particularly the storms and floods which are considered in the rest of this chapter.

Storms and Floods

Chronicles note the severe loss of life that might occur during an intense storm. In 1471, a storm was said to have coincided with many people taking to the water in Venice on the feast day of St Lawrence and 'more than a thousand people in the lagoon... sank'. In June 1504 a storm in Venice caused numerous boats to capsize causing the death of an estimated five hundred people.[88] Severe sea storms in the Adriatic have been recorded in seven years of the fifteenth century and nine in the sixteenth.[89] In Venice, winter storms threatened to erode the land adjoining canals unless sufficient foundations and *fondamente* were in place.[90]

As discussed in the previous sections, many of the responses to natural disasters brought to the fore a sacred view of the environment. In 1341, for example, a devastating storm was said to have affected Venice.[91] A sixteenth-century painting of this event by Jacopo Palma il Vecchio [1480–1528], *Saints Mark, George and Nicholas save Venice from a storm* was originally created for the Scuola Grande di San Marco.[92] It was completed after Palma il Vecchio's death by Paris Bordone [1500–1571]. The events of that legend brought together the three saints on a journey through the Venetian *bacino* with an old fisherman. In the legend, the fisherman was sheltering from a storm under a bridge. A stranger emerged from the church of San Marco and requested that they go, first to San Giorgio Maggiore and then San Nicolò al Lido. The fisherman made the trip, hesitantly, given the intensity of the weather. At each stop, another stranger joined the vessel and once the trio were on board they encountered a ship with demons as the crew and succeeded in sinking it through prayers and spiritual signs. A companion painting by Paris Bordone shows the final stage of the legend in which the fisherman presents the doge of the Republic with the gold ring of St Mark, received

---

[88] Dario Camuffo, Caterina Secco, Peter Brimblecombe, and Javier Martin-Vide, 'Sea storms in the Adriatic Sea and the western Mediterranean during the last millennium', *Climatic Change* 46 (2000), 213.

[89] Dario Camuffo, et al., 'Sea storms in the Adriatic Sea and the western Mediterranean during the last millennium', 215 records these in 1410, 1413, 1418, 1430, 1455, 1471, 1473, and 1500, 1504, 1521, 1525, 1526, 1530, 1531, and 1550.

[90] ASV, Comun reg 1 (10 September 1551).

[91] Trevor Dean, 'Storm, suicide and miracle: Venice 1342' in Michael Knapton, John Law and Alison Smith, *Venice and the Veneto during the Renaissance: the legacy of Benjamin Kohl* (Aldershot: Ashgate, 2000).

[92] David Rosand, *Myths of Venice: the figuration of a state* (Chapel Hill NC: University of North Carolina Press, 2001), p. 68.

DEALING WITH DISASTERS   179

miraculously in the course of these events. This was the basis for the annual ritual of the Sensa, in which the doge symbolically married the waters.[93]

As well as reinforcing the close association between the patron saint of the city and the environment, the stories of storms also prompted the development of specific devotional cults within the Venetian lagoon. An intense storm in 1508 around the island of Chioggia was said to hit the island with weather so intense that it seemed like the Day of Judgement. Once the weather had calmed, a humble man called Baldassare went to check on the damage. Walking along the shore, he heard his name called out and turned to see a woman dressed entirely in black who was seated on a log which had been deposited on land during the storm. These events were said to have been described in verse in 1535 by Cristoforo Sabbadino as well as numerous other authors in the centuries which followed.[94] The devotional cult developed into a significant focus for devotion in Chioggia and beyond.[95]

As well as being associated with the calming of the seas during particular tempestuous events, religious rites and the cult of saints might also be invoked in order to try to prevent such episodes. At the harbour front of Genoa, the church of San Vittore dei Marinari served the waterfront district and the priest was also responsible for blessing ships and warehouses of the port and administering the sacrament to prisoners on the Republic's ships.[96] The relics of John the Baptist in Genoa were utilized extensively in shaping the city's relationship to the environment. Annually on the saint's feast day, the relics were taken to the waterfront and the harbour was blessed.[97] Carrie Beneš has described the ways in which, in earlier centuries, they were 'credited with converting criminals, healing the sick, preserving the city from earthquakes, calming storms and saving Genoese sailors from shipwreck'.[98] One of the most prized relics of the city of Genoa—the ashes of St John the Baptist—is contained in an elaborate silver reliquary that was paid for in part as an expression of thanks for the survival of ships which were anchored in the port of Genoa during a storm.[99] The intervention of the saint was said to have calmed a storm which had struck violently at a moment when the port was

---

[93] He was said to have sought shelter in Venice and, in a dream, was told by an angel 'Peace to you, Mark. Here is where your body will rest' (*Pax tibi, Marce. Hic requiescet corpus tuum*). See Edward Muir, 'An escaped Trojan and a transported Evangelist: auspicious beginnings' in *Civic ritual*, pp. 65–102.

[94] Antonio Calcagno, *Storia dell'apparizione di Maria Vergine sul lido di Chioggia* (Venice, 1823) p. 19 refers to Coronelli's mention of this text in his *Isolario*, p. 65.

[95] Maya Corry, Deborah Howard, and Mary Laven (eds), *Madonnas and miracles*, pp. 138–9 and undated sixteenth-century print *Come apparse a Chioza la beata Vergine Maria intitolata la Madonna della Navicella*.

[96] Jane Garnett and Gervase Rosser, *Spectacular miracles*, p. 74.

[97] Gervase Rosser, 'The church and religious life' in Carrie E. Beneš (ed.), *A companion to medieval Genoa*, p. 349.

[98] Carrie E. Beneš, 'Civic identity' in Carrie E. Beneš (ed.), *A companion to medieval Genoa*, p. 208.

[99] Giustina Olgiati (ed.), *Genova, porta del mondo*, p. 59.

180 CLEANING UP RENAISSANCE ITALY

crowded with large trading vessels. The sudden nature of the storm prevented interventions to protect the vessels and the water was miraculously calmed when the ashes of the saint were brought to the waterfront.

An awareness of the spiritual setting of natural disasters also infused organizational structures. A beautiful manuscript conserved in the Archivio Storico del Comune in Genoa preserves the fifteenth-century statutes of the city's Compagnia del Mandiletto and situates the organization and purpose of this lay organization overtly and distinctively within the setting of a maritime port.[100] The number of company members was limited to forty. Eight souls had been saved in the Ark at the time of the universal flood, so eight officials were chosen to oversee the organization. The statutes are also saturated with maritime metaphors: life on earth is described as a dangerous sea, for example, and heaven (*beata patria*) a tranquil port; the company itself is described as a boat in which to navigate the choppy waters. As a charitable organization, the function as well as the structure of this group was intended to have a prophylactic effect on its members and the wider community. Storms and floods were often aligned and, indeed, connected both in theory (as here in the statutes) and in practice.

The nature of flooding differed in Genoa and Venice. In the former city, there was a recognition that river flooding within Liguria was something which ought to be anticipated. Premodern authors recognized that it was rare for a river not to flood; in some places annual cycles of such events were essential for creating cultivable land.[101] The range of explanations for floods was broad.[102] The impact of storms and floods, of course, extended beyond the area immediately surrounding the waterways. These events damaged infrastructure and buildings within the city. Walls collapsed and bridges crumbled under the force of the water.[103] Flooding was limited in the city of Genoa because of its topography but, at times, the port was affected badly by intense storms. In Venice, the nature and cause of floods was distinct. That city has experienced flooding as a result of sea surges, known as *acqua alta*, throughout its history. Frequent episodes were recorded in the first half of the sixteenth century and these were one of the motivations for the dredging of the Grand Canal between 1536 and 1542.[104]

In 1547, the Genoese Padri del Comune were involved in discussions about the appropriate response to the significant damage caused by the Bisagno River, which

---

[100] It was named after the large handkerchiefs (*mandiletti*) into which inhabitants would be encouraged to make donations of alms.

[101] Andrea Bacci, *Del Tevere*, p. 214.

[102] John Morgan, 'Understanding flooding in early modern England', *Journal of Historical Geography* 50 (2015), 37–50.

[103] ASCG, PdC, 5-31 (6 November 1481) and 15-171 (6 April 1539).

[104] Dario Camuffo et al. record sea surges of the fifteenth and sixteenth centuries in 1410, 1423, 1429, 1430, 1437, 1440, 1442/3, 1444, 1445, 1464 for the fifteenth century (ten episodes in total) and 1503, 1504, 1511, 1514, 1515, 1517, 1518, 1519, 1521, 1522, 1523, 1525, 1526, 1527, 1529, 1531 (2), 1532, 1534, 1535 (2), 1536, 1539, 1542, 1550, 1559, 1574, 1576, and 1599 (29 events).

DEALING WITH DISASTERS 181

had burst its banks and damaged buildings and gardens in the surrounding valley.[105] The Val Bisagno was a large valley to the east of the city of Genoa. This area was crucial for food supplies. Raffaela Ponte has illustrated that Genoa's environment was prone to conditions of drought followed by flood. The Bisagno river was described in the early fifteenth century as torrential ('*torrente*') and was known for episodes of severe flooding, such as that on 30 September 1452, which badly damaged the important bridge of Sant'Agata.[106] In this instance, the river water had stretched over the public road in that area and the devastation was obviously widespread, stretching from the bridge to the house of Pietro Francesco Cattaneo. It was recognized to be in the 'public good' that repairs should be made and the costs were to be borne by all those who owned land, houses, and possessions in that valley. Previous chapters recorded the way in which building materials might be repurposed for flood defences.[107] In the case of the Bisagno, the placement of rubble was monitored to ensure that it did not impede the flow of the river.[108]

In the management of the rivers, the spaces of the *giara* (which was cultivated land along the banks of the channel) was vital. These spaces were carefully protected and residents and the authorities alike resisted proposals for structures to encroach on them.[109] In 1556, the roads which ran from the *giara* of the Bisagno to the Church of San Siro were completely ruined to the extent that they were impassable by foot and by horse. The intention was that these streets should be made good so that it would be very easy to travel along them.[110] After a flood in July 1570, repair work was required to roads which were described as disordered and damaged. The failure of a tradesperson to supply the necessary materials, despite receiving a down-payment, led to him being incarcerated.[111]

Conventionally, rubble from Genoa had been transported out to allocated sites in Bisagno. In fact, legislation throughout the fifteenth century insisted that the *mulattieri* should deposit rubbish in these sites.[112] In the following century, the Padri specifically instructed the muleteers to take the material they removed from the city to an area at Bisagno to try to combat the problem of flooding.[113] This was done by building up flood defences by using large stones on the banks of the Bisagno. This same material was also deposited close to the piers of the bridge of Santa Zita presumably to strengthen these structures against the force of flood waters.[114]

The Padri also expected owners of houses and land to take their own precautions against flooding. In 1566, they reflected on the damage incurred in

---

[105] ASCG, PdC, 19-160 (4 November 1547).
[106] This was the route taken by travellers going east out of the city from the Porta Aurea.
[107] ASCG, PdC, 22-221 (1 August 1556). [108] ASCG, PdC, 63-49 (14 April 1605).
[109] ASCG, PdC, 1-192 (3 June 1467). [110] ASCG, PdC, 27-118 (2 April 1556).
[111] ASCG, PdC, 30-53 (31 July 1570). [112] ASCG, PdC, 6-101 (26 September 1494).
[113] ASCG, PdC, 22-221 (s.d.). [114] ASCG, PdC, 29-166 (15 June 1569).

182 CLEANING UP RENAISSANCE ITALY

Sanpierdarena during a time of heavy rainfall, particularly on the higher ground. A great deal of water was said to have descended into the streets as well as villas of the citizens, which, in part, occurred because too little care had been taken by inhabitants. They had closed the openings (*pertuxi*) through which rainwater would normally flow. They had also failed to clean (*scurare*) their ditches. As a result, the damage which occurred was described as '*eccessivo*' and posed a 'public danger' to travellers. The Padri issued a proclamation that included repairing damaged walls and opening the *pertuxi* in the streets and houses.[115]

A letter from Francesco Carbonara noted that each time a repair was proposed around Albere that the residents and owners of properties claimed that they should not be responsible for contributing towards the costs because their own buildings were in secure locations, not affected by flooding, and as a result they would receive no benefit from the work—the key criteria for identifying contributors. In addition, though, he said that these families were incredibly poor and, above all else, did not intervene proactively to protect their homes but undertook repairs when necessary. In times of flood, they were accustomed to flee from their homes in Albere.[116] Such records remind us that the impact of natural disasters, as well as opportunities for preventative measures, might fall unevenly across the population.

In Liguria, the construction of embankments was often initiated by the local elites. Antonio Doria purchased a house in Struppa, he requested permission to erect walls in order to repair the area around the Bisagno river and one other (unnamed) river.[117] Doria noted that this work would be of public benefit and also convenient for travellers and those who lived nearby. He requested a stretch of the gravel bank which he noted was particularly wide where the river floods. Officials from the Padri went to inspect the site and report back. One complication in the request was the route of an important public road which, it was noted, must remain unimpeded. The officials instructed Doria that the walls should be of sufficient form and strength (*acomodatus et fortis*) to be able to withstand the force of the flow of the rivers. It is clear, therefore, that these walls were perceived as a form of defence for the town. A district in Struppa still bears the name 'Doria' in recognition of the house and extensive grounds developed in that area close to the parish church of San Siro.

Despite efforts to ensure that sufficient space was provided to reduce the force of the water flowing through these rivers, there were numerous occasions on which the impact of flood waters was recorded. In 1481, the wall next to a dye-house in Bisagno had collapsed as a result of the impetus of the river.[118] The bridge at Cornigliano was destroyed in 1521 and the need for the repair was reiterated the

---

[115] ASCG, PdC, 27-147 (12 June 1566).   [116] ASCG, PdC, 67-65 (23 September 1609).
[117] ASCG, PdC, 23-12 (5 February 1557).   [118] ASCG, PdC, 5-14 (12 April 1481).

following year.[119] In 1555, a street was destroyed by a flood of the Bisagno.[120] In 1556 an embankment on the Polcevera was reconstructed in order to protect the public street which was known as the Rivarolo superior. The previous structure had been destroyed by flood water.[121] In 1563, residents of Varenna reported that the river had destroyed a group of pilings at 3.30am.[122] In 1609, those living close to the Bisagno river were said to have been frightened by the ways in which the river water was moving through channels and streets. Water ran with such fury towards the public street that it reached the church of Santo Spirito. The proposed intervention was the raising of the walls of the channel and the construction of an embankment.

There is little evidence that natural disasters led to a change in approach to the management of the environment and health. Experience and the insights of experts continued to be utilized to develop traditional interventions. There was an expectation of recurrence for floods and storms. Instead the aim was to reduce the intensity and frequency of natural disasters and ameliorate moral, social, and environmental concerns.

---

[119] ASCG, PdC, 2-60 (28 March 1521) and 11-105 (28 January 1522).
[120] ASCG, PdC, 2-131 (6 September 1555).   [121] ASCG, PdC, 22-194 (4 August 1556).
[122] ASCG, PdC, 26-71 (11 September 1563).

Conclusion

Corruptible Cities

The best-known images of the premodern, mercantile centres of Genoa and Venice portrayed these ports as bustling with boats and laden with cargo to supply the Republics' trading economies. At diverse times in their histories, maritime fleets were vital to the security of these cities. As this book has illustrated, however, both places also relied upon a further grouping of far smaller boats (public and private) which worked to ensure the accessibility of the bodies of water which were so vital for life in the maritime cities. These boats dealt with the practicalities of the ports: the wrecked vessels, sunken cargo, and silting seabed or canal beds. They collected the rubbish and rubble which were drawn from the homes, streets, and waterways of the cities and operated as part of a broader network of people and places which were employed to ensure the cleanliness and wellbeing of these ports and their societies.

The environment was actively and ambitiously managed in Renaissance Italy because of the intricate relationship which linked people and place. Many acts of environmental management, traditionally defined as hydraulics or engineering, were also social policies which were intended to improve the behaviour and morality of communities. Environmental management was used as a way of ordering and defining communities, as well as responding to the strains which these groups encountered. Discussions of potentially vulnerable or dangerous social groups underscore the connection between cleanliness, social value, and moral purity which was widely held within this culture and the same is true for the obverse relationship between filth, pollution, and sin. Environmental cleanliness required the regulation of behaviour and was intended to work towards those social and urban ideals articulated clearly in ideal city tracts of the period.

This book has argued that a fruitful comparison of governance can be undertaken between sites with similar settings and political systems, which encountered analogous environmental and social challenges. In order to protect the flow of the streets and waterways, the governments of Genoa and Venice regulated the infrastructure of communication, supply, and waste. The aims and approaches of environmental management differed. The sense of collective interests was portrayed as paramount in Venice and used to justify interventions in the common good. Public health here, as elsewhere in Europe, was an important driver of this work. This language was employed far less frequently in Genoa

Cleaning Up Renaissance Italy: Environmental Ideals and Urban Practice in Genoa and Venice. Jane L. Stevens Crawshaw, Oxford University Press. © Jane L. Stevens Crawshaw 2023. DOI: 10.1093/oso/9780198867432.003.0008

CONCLUSION   185

where, instead, common interests dilated upon the space of the port. The protection of this area was what was seen to bring together the interests of those across the social and economic spectrum and, consequently, it was around this notion that civic identity was developed. The concept of public health remained one of the most important provisions of a state within premodern political theory and, in many places, was central to practice. Nevertheless, the example of Genoa reminds us that, rather than seeking to identify public health work (most notably in a teleological sense of progression towards a modern ideal), historians of the premodern period might look instead for the variety of social and cultural ideas which were used to support interventions in health and the environment.

Genoa and Venice also had different roles for the state in rendering environmental ideals in practice. In both cities, funding combined public and private initiatives. There were differences in the organization of this work. In Genoa, once issues had been raised by individuals, the government would coordinate responses by working through local residents and occupational groups. In contrast to Venice, very few of these workers were employed and paid directly by the state. Instead, greater emphasis was placed upon community members in order to ensure cleanliness and wellbeing across the city. There was no single model for the division of tasks between private and public structures and, indeed, neither emerges as necessarily more effective in achieving the urban cleanliness and wellbeing which was sought. In both settings the important work which took place at the level of the locality brought many schemes to fruition. In both cities, too, the state was successful in coordinating systems for innovation in the technology for environmental management, as well as organizing large-scale public works of dredging periodically through the sixteenth century (and beyond). Other institutions were utilized, of course, particularly for communication. Parish churches were expected to publicize proclamations and to read out reminders to parishioners on a regular basis; in Venice in 1637, for example, it was decided that regulations on the disposal of rubbish should be read out every first Sunday in the month in the parish churches.[1]

An enduring framework for medical understanding (recognized in the use of the term 'premodern' medicine) does not detract from the significant demographic and technological changes of the sixteenth century which had an impact on initiatives relating to health and the environment. This was a period in which agency was attributed to the environment, as was a form of embodiment and emotion.[2] Seasonal changes, combined with the impact of natural disasters, impressed upon premodern observers the significance and precarity of balance and cleanliness in the environment.

---

[1] ASV, Comun, b.46 (Indice, 1637).
[2] Sasha Handley and John Morgan, 'Environment, emotion and early modernity', *Environment and History* 28:3 (2022), 355–61.

186   CLEANING UP RENAISSANCE ITALY

In the eighteenth century, the use of the landscape and environment as a lens for understanding and improving health intensified.[3] By the twentieth century, however, the health and the natural environment were generally separated in organizational terms. Naturally, the history of premodern environmental management does not offer a model to emulate in the present day: too many aspects of the broader context have changed fundamentally. Instead, though, it can suggest 'the memory of possibilities... simply other possible worlds, other ways of living' which challenge us to interrogate our responses to our own enduring challenges relating to social wellbeing and environmental management in the contemporary world.[4]

---

[3] See, for example, the contemporary work by Gaspare Federigo [1769–1840], *Topografia fisico-medico della citta di Venezia* (3 vols) and also secondary studies including Mary Dobson, *The contours of death and disease in early modern England* (Cambridge: Cambridge University Press, 1997) which particularly highlights the significance of the landscape for notion of health in the eighteenth century.

[4] Natalie Zemon Davis, *A passion for history: conversations with Denis Crouzet* (Kirksville MI: Truman State University Press, 2010), p. 12.

Bibliography

Archival Sources

Genoa
Archivio Storico del Comune di Genova
Padri del Comune

Venice
Archivio di Stato
Dieci Savi alle Decime
Giudici del Piovego
Provveditori di Comun
Provveditori alla Sanità
Savi ed Esecutori alle Acque

Verona
Archivio di Stato
Ufficio di Sanità

Primary Sources

Bacci, Andrea, *Del Tevere, della natura et bonta dell'acque et delle inondationi* (Rome, 1558).

Benedetti, Rocco, *Relatione d'alcuni casi occorsi in Venetia al tempo della peste l'anno 1576 et 1577 con le provisioni, rimedii et orationi fatte à Dio Benedetti per la sua liberatione* (Bologna, 1630).

Calcagno, Antonio, *Storia dell'apparizione di Maria Vergine sul lido di Chioggia* (Venice, 1823).

Caniato, Giovanni (ed.), *Metodo in pratica di sommario o sia compilazione delle leggi, terminazioni et ordini appartenenti agl'illustrissimi et eccellentissimi Collegio e Magistrato alle acque, opera dell'avvocato fiscale Giulio Rompiasio* (Venice: Ministero per I beni culturali e ambientali Archivio di Stato, 1988).

Cataneo, Pietro, I quattro primi libri di architettura di Pietro Cataneo.

Cerbani, Cerbano, 'Translatio mirifici Martyris Isidori a Chio insula in civitatem Venetam', Recueil des historiens de Croisades: Historiens Occidentaux, vol. 5, pp. 321–34.

Coronelli, Vincenzo, *Isolario* (Venice, 1696).

Costamagna, Giorgio (ed.), *Gli statuti della compagnia dei caravana del porto di Genova* (Turin: Accademia delle scienze, 1965).

Desimoni, Cornelio, *Statuto del Padri del Comune della Repubblica Genovese* (Genoa, 1886).

188 BIBLIOGRAPHY

Discorso sopra il significato del parto mostruoso nato di una Hebrea in Venetia nell'anno 1575 adi XXVI di Maggio (Venice: Domenico Farri, 1575).

di Zorzi, Filippo, *Dell'aria e sua qualità...dove specialmente si scuopre quale egli si sia in Venetia* (Venice, 1596).

Fioravanti, Leonardo, *Il reggimento della peste dell'Eccellente dottore et cavaliero m Leonardo Fioravanti bolognese* (Venice, 1571).

Flavio, Biondo, *Italy illuminated*, Jeffrey A. White (ed. and trans.) (Cambridge MA, 2005).

Garzoni, Tommaso, *Piazza universal di tutte professioni del mondo* (Venice, 1605).

di Giorgio Martini, Francesco, *Trattati di architettura ingegneria e arte militare*, edited by Corrado Maltese (Milan, 1967).

Giustiniano, Agostino, *Castigatissimi Annali...della Eccelsa et Illustrissima Repubblica di Genova* (Genoa, 1537).

Gratiolo, Andrea, *Discorso di peste* (Venice, 1576).

Massa, Nicolo, *Ragionamento dello Eccellentissimo m Nicolo Massa sopra le infermita che vengono dall'aere pestilentiale del presente anno MDLV* (Venice, 1556).

Mostri e segne che si sono veduti in Vinegia nell'anno 1575 (Venice: Pietro Farri, 1575).

Paschetti, Bartolomeo, *Del conservare la sanita et del vivere de'Genovesi* (Genoa, 1602).

Petrarch, Francesco, *Epistolae familiares*, Ugo Dotti (ed.), (Urbino: Argalìa, 1970).

Podestà, Emilio, *Storia di Parodi Ligure e dei suoi antichi Statuti* (Ovada: Accademia Urbense, 1998).

Poggi, Vittorio (ed.), *Leges Genuensis* in *Historiae patriae monumenta*, volume 18 (Turin, 1901).

Porcacchi, Tommaso, *L'isole piu famose del mondo* (Venice, 1576).

Promis, V., 'Descrizione sincrona del terremoto di Genova, seguito il 10 aprile 1536', *Atti della Società ligure di storia Patria* x (1874).

Raimondo, Annibale, *La viva et vera cagione che ha generato le fiere infermità che tanto hanno molestato l'anno 1575 et tanto il 76* (Padua, 1576).

Ravenna, Tommaso, *Come i venetiani possano vivere sempre sani* (Venice, 1565).

Sanuto, Marino, *I Diarii di Marino Sanuto*, Rinaldo Fulin (ed.) (58 vols, Venice, 1879–1903).

Spencer, John R. (ed.), *Filarete's treatise on architecture* (New Haven CT: Yale University Press, 1965).

Spinola, Andrea, *Il Cittadino della Repubblica di Genova...diviso in 4 tomi* (n.d.).

Statuti politici della citta di Savona: con le sue rifforme et addittioni rimesse a suo luogo, tradotti in linguq volgare (Genoa, 1610).

Vitruvius, *The ten books on architecture*, Morris Hicky Morgan (trans) (New York NY: Dover Publications, 1960).

Zompini, Gaetano, *Le arti che vanno per via nella città di Venezia* (Venice, 1753).

Secondary Sources

Abdon, Danielle, 'Sheltering refugees: ephemeral architecture and mass migration in early modern Venice', *Urban History* 49 (2022), 725–45.

Ågren, Maria, *Making and living, making a difference: gender and work in early modern European society* (Oxford: Oxford University Press, 2017).

Aikema, Bernard and Dulcia Meijers (eds), *Nel regno dei poveri: arte e storia dei grandi ospedali veneziani in età moderna 1474–1797* (Venice: Arsenale Editrice, 1989).

BIBLIOGRAPHY   189

Ajmar-Wollheim, Marta and Flora Dennis (eds), *At home in Renaissance Italy* (London: V&A Publications, 2006).

Alfani, Guido, *Calamities and the economy in Renaissance Italy: the Grand Tour of the Horsemen of the Apocalypse* (Basingstoke: Palgrave Macmillan, 2013).

Appuhn, Karl, *A forest on the sea: environmental expertise in Renaissance Venice* (Baltimore MD: Johns Hopkins University Press, 2009).

Appuhn, Karl, 'Ecologies of beef: eighteenth-century epizootics and the environmental history of early modern Europe', *Environmental History* 15:2 (2010), 268–87.

Arbel, Benjamin, The port towns of the Levant in sixteenth-century travel literature' in Alexander Cowan (ed.), *Mediterranean urban culture 1400–1700* (Exeter: University of Exeter Press, 2000), pp. 151–64.

Arbel, Benjamin, 'Venice's maritime empire in the early modern period' in Eric Dursteler (ed.), *A companion to Venetian History* 1400–1797 (Leiden: Brill, 2013), pp. 125–253.

Argenti, Philip, *The occupation of Chios by the Genoese and their administration of the island 1346–1566* (Cambridge: Cambridge University Press, 1958).

Arnade, Peter, Martha Howell, and Walter Simons, 'Fertile spaces: the productivity of urban space in northern Europe', *Journal of Interdisciplinary History* 32 (2002), 515–28.

Arnold, Ellen, 'Engineering miracles: water control, conversion and the creation of a religious landscape in the medieval Ardennes', *Environment and History* 13 (2007), 477–502.

Assereto, C. 'Porti e scali minori della Repubblica di Genova in età moderna', in Giorgio Doria and Paola Massa Piergiovanni (eds), *Il Sistema portuale*, pp. 221–58.

Assereto, Giovanni, *La metamorfosi della Repubblica. Saggi di storia genovese tra il XVI e il XIX secolo* (Savona: Daner, 1999).

Assereto, Giovanni, *'Per la comune salvezza dal morbo contagioso'. I controlli di sanità nella Repubblica di Genova* (Genoa: Città del silenzio, 2011).

Assereto, Giovanni, *Un giuoco così utile ai pubblici introiti: il lotto di Genova dal XVI al XVIII secolo* (Rome: Fondazione Benetton studi ricerche, 2013).

Assereto, Giovanni and Marco Doria (eds), *Storia della Liguria* (Rome: Gius Laterza et Figli Spa, 2007).

Bacci, Michele, 'Portolano sacro. Santuari e immagini sacre lungo le rotte di navigazione del Mediterraneo tra tardo Medioevo e prima età moderna' in Erik Thunø and Gerhard Wolf (eds), *The miraculous image in the Middle Ages and Renaissance* (Rome: 'L'Erma' di Bretschneider, 2004), pp. 223–48.

Bailey, Gauvin, Pamela Jones, Franco Mormando, and Thomas Worcester (eds), *Hope and healing: painting in Italy in a time of plague 1500–1800* (Worcester MA: Worcester Art Museum, 2005).

Bamji, Alexandra, 'Blowing smoke up your arse: drowning, resuscitation and public health in eighteenth-century Venice', *Bulletin for the History of Medicine* 94:1 (2020), 29–63.

Barker, Sheila, 'Miraculous images and the plagues of Italy, *c.*590–1656' in Sandra Cardarelli and Laura Fenelli (eds), *Saints, miracles and the image: healing saints and miraculous images in the Renaissance* (Turnhout: Brepols, 2017), pp. 29–52.

Barnett, Lydia, *After the flood: imagining the global environment in early modern Europe* (Baltimore MD: Johns Hopkins University Press, 2019).

Barzilay, Tzafrir, *Poisoned wells: accusations, persecution, and minorities in medieval Europe, 1321–1422* (Philadelphia PA: University of Pennsylvania Press, 2022).

Battaglini, Giuseppe M., *Cosmopolis: Portoferraio medicea storia urbana 1548–1737* (Rome: Multigrafica editrice, 1978).

190 BIBLIOGRAPHY

Bashford, Alison, David Armitage, and Sujit Sivasundaram (eds), *Oceanic histories* (Cambridge: Cambridge University Press, 2018).

Beaven, Brad, Karl Bell, and Robert James (eds), *Port towns and urban cultures: international histories of the waterfront c.1700–2000* (Basingstoke: Palgrave Macmillan, 2016).

Behringer, Wolfgang, *A cultural history of climate*, P. Camiller (trans) (Cambridge: Cambridge University Press, 2010).

Beltrami, Daniele, *Storia della popolazione di Venezia* (Padua: CEDAM, 1954).

Beneš, Carrie E. (ed.), *A companion to medieval Genoa* (Leiden: Brill, 2018).

Bergdolt, Klaus and Ingo F. Herrmann (eds), *Was ist Gesundheit? Antworten aus Jahrhunderten* (Stuttgart: Franz Steiner Verlag, 2011).

Bertelli, S., N. Rubinstein, and C. Hugh Smyth (eds), *Florence and Venice: comparisons and relations* (Florence: La nuova Italia, 1980).

Berveglieri, Roberto, *Inventori stranieri (1474–1788): importazione di tecnologiea e circolazione di tecnici artigiani inventori: repertorio* (Venice: Istituto Veneto di scienze, lettere ed arti, 1995).

Berveglieri, Roberto, *Le vie di Venezia: canali lagunari e rii a Venezia: inventori, brevetti, tecnologia e legislazione nei secoli XIII–XVIII* (Sommacampagna: Cierre, 1999).

Biow, Douglas, *The culture of cleanliness in Renaissance Italy* (Ithica NY: Cornell University Press, 2006).

Biow, Douglas, *On the importance of being an individual in Renaissance Italy: men, their professions, and their beards* (Philadelphia PA: University of Pennsylvania Press, 2015).

Bitossi, Carlo, *Il governo dei magnifici: patriziato e politica a Genova fra Cinque e Seicento* (Genoa: ECIG, 1990).

Boato, Anna, *Costruire 'alla moderna' materiali e tecniche a Genova tra XV e XVI secoli* (Genoa: All'Insegna del Giglio, 2005).

Boato, Anna and Anna Decri, 'Archive documents and building organisation: an example from the modern age' in S. Huerta (ed.), *Proceedings of the first international congress on construction history* (Madrid, 2003), pp. 383–90.

Bocchi, Francesca, 'Regulation of the urban environment by the Italian Communes from the twelfth to the fourteenth century', *Bulletin of the John Rylands Library* 72:3 (1990), 63–78.

Bontà, Giuseppe, *Storia della Madonna dell'Orto* (Genoa, 1847).

Boone, Marc and Heleni Porfyriou, 'Introduction' in Donatella Calabi and Stephen Turk Christensen (eds), *Cultural exchange in early modern Europe—Volume II: cities and cultural exchange in Europe, 1400–1700* (Cambridge: Cambridge University Press, 2007), pp. 59–65.

Boone, Marc and Martha Howell (eds), *The power of space in late medieval and early modern Europe: the cities of Italy, Northern France and the Low Countries* (Turnhout: Brepols, 2013).

Braddick, Michael J., *State formation in early modern England c.1550–1700* (Cambridge: Cambridge University Press, 2000).

Bradley, Mark, 'Approaches to pollution and propriety' in Mark Bradley (ed.), *Rome, pollution and propriety: dirt, disease and hygiene in the Eternal City from antiquity to modernity* (Cambridge: Cambridge University Press, 2012), pp. 11–40.

Bratchel, M. E., *Medieval Lucca and the evolution of the Renaissance state* (Oxford: Oxford University Press, 2008).

Brundin, Abigail, Deborah Howard, and Mary Laven, *The sacred home in Renaissance Italy* (Oxford: Oxford University Press, 2018).

BIBLIOGRAPHY 191

Bruzelius, Caroline, *Preaching, building, and burying: friars in the medieval city* (New Haven CT: Yale University Press, 2014).

Burke, Peter, *Popular culture in early modern Europe* (London: Temple Smith, 1994).

Burke, Peter, 'Cultural history as polyphonic history', *ARBOR Ciencia, Pensamiento y Cultura* CLXXXVI 743 (2010), 479–86.

Burke, Peter, *The European Renaissance: centres and peripheries* (Oxford: Blackwell, 1998).

Burke, Peter, 'Public and private spheres in late Renaissance Genoa', *Varieties of cultural history* (Cambridge: Cambridge University Press, 1997), pp. 111–23.

Butters, Humfrey and Gabriele Neher (eds), *Warfare and politics: cities and government in Renaissance Tuscany and Venice* (Amsterdam: Amsterdam University Press, 2019).

Buylaert, Frederik, Jelle de Rock, and Anne-Laure van Bruaene, 'City portrait, civic body, and commercial printing in sixteenth-century Ghent', *Renaissance Quarterly* 68:3 (2015), 803–39.

Cacciavillani, Ivone, *Le leggi ecologiche veneziane* (Padua: Invicta, 1990).

Calabi, Donatella, *The market and the city: square, street and architecture in early modern Europe* (Marlene Klein trans) (Aldershot: Ashgate, 2004).

Calabi, Donatella, 'The Jews and the city in the Mediterranean area' in Alexander Cowan (ed.), *Mediterranean urban culture 1400–1700* (Exeter: University of Exeter Press, 2000), pp. 56–68.

Calabi, Donatella and Stephen Turk Christensen (eds), *Cultural exchange in early modern Europe II: cities and cultural exchange in Europe, 1400–1700* (Cambridge: Cambridge University Press, 2006).

Calabi, Donatella and Paola Lanaro, *La città italiana e i luoghi degli stranieri XIV–XVIII sec* (Rome-Bari: Laterza, 1998).

Calabi, Donatella and Paolo Morachiello, *Rialto: le fabbriche e il Ponte 1514–91* (Turin: Einaudi, 1987).

Calaresu, Melissa and Danielle van den Heuvel (eds), *Food hawkers: selling in the streets from antiquity to the present* (London: Routledge, 2018).

Camuffo, Dario, 'Analysis of the sea surges at Venice from A.D. 782 to 1990', *Theoretical and Applied Climatology* 47:1 (1993), 1–14.

Camuffo, Dario, Chiara Bertolin, Alberto Craievich, Rossella Granziero, and Silvia Enzi, 'When the lagoon was frozen over in Venice', *Journal of Mediterranean Geography*, (2017) 1–59.

Camuffo, Dario, Caterina Secco, Peter Brimblecombe, and Javier Martin-Vide, 'Sea storms in the Adriatic Sea and the western Mediterranean during the last millennium', *Climatic Change* 46 (2000), 209–23.

Caniato, Giovanni and Renato della Venezia, *Il macello di San Giobbe: un'industria, un territorio* (Venice: Marsilio, 2006)

Caniato, Giovanni and Michela Dal Borgo, *Le arti edili a Venezia* (Rome: Edilstampa, 1990).

Cantor, David (ed.), *Reinventing Hippocrates* (Aldershot: Ashgate, 2002).

Cassen, Flora, *Marking the Jews in Renaissance Italy: politics, religion and the power of symbols* (Cambridge: Cambridge University Press, 2017).

Cavallo, Sandra and Tessa Storey, *Healthy living in late Renaissance Italy* (Oxford: Oxford University Press, 2014).

Cavallo, Sandra and Tessa Storey, (eds), *Conserving health in early modern culture: bodies and environments in Italy and England* (Manchester: Manchester University Press, 2017).

192 BIBLIOGRAPHY

Cecere, Domenico, Chiara De Caprio, Lorenza Gianfrancesco, and Pasquale Palmieri (eds), *Disaster narratives in early modern Naples: politics, communication and culture* (Rome: Viella, 2018).

Cesarani, David and Gemma Romain (eds), *Jews and port cities 1590–1990: commerce, community and cosmopolitanism* (London: Vallentine Mitchell, 2006).

Cessi, R. and N. Spada (eds), *Antichi scrittori d'idraulica Veneta* (Venice: Premiate Officine grafiche Carlo Ferrari, 1952).

Chambers, David and Brian Pullan, with Jennifer Fletcher, *Venice: a documentary history, 1450–1630* (Oxford: Blackwell, 1992).

Champion, Matthew S., *The fullness of time: temporalities of the fifteenth-century Low Countries* (Chicago IL: University of Chicago Press, 2017).

Cicogna, Emmanuele A., *Corpus delle iscrizioni di Venezia e delle isole della laguna veneta* (3 vols, Venice: Biblioteca Orafa di Sant'Antonio abate, 2001).

Cipolla, Carlo, *Public health and the medical profession in the Renaissance* (Cambridge: Cambridge University Press, 1976).

Ciriacono, Salvatore, 'Scrittori d'idraulica e politica delle acque' in Girolamo Arnaldi and Manlio Pastore Stocchi (eds), *Storia della cultura veneta. Dal primo Quattrocento al Concilio di Trento* vol 3/II (Vicenza: N. Pozza, 1980), pp. 491–512.

Ciriacono, Salvatore, *Building on water: Venice, Holland and the construction of the European landscape in early modern times* (Oxford: Berghahn Books, 2006).

Clarke, Georgia and Fabrizio Nevola (eds), 'The experience of the street in early modern Italy', *I Tatti Studies in the Italian Renaissance* 16:1/2 (2013), 47–55.

Clunas, Craig, 'Modernity global and local: consumption and the rise of the West', *The American Historical Review* 104:5 (1999), 1497–151.

Cohen, Simona, 'The early Renaissance personification of time and changing concepts of temporality', *Renaissance Studies* 14:3 (2000), 301–28.

Cohn Jr., Samuel K., *Cultures of plague: medical thinking at the end of the Renaissance* (Oxford: Oxford University Press, 2010).

Concina, Ennio, *Venezia nell'età moderna. Struttura e funzioni* (Venice: Marsilio, 1995).

Concina, Ennio, *Fondaci: architettura, arte e mercatura tra Levante, Venezia e Alemagna* (Venice: Marsilio, 1997).

Concina, Ennio, Ugo Camerino, and Donatella Calabi, *La città degli Ebrei. Il Ghetto di Venezia: architettura e urbanistica* (Venice: Albrizzi, 1991), pp. 211–16.

Conesa, Marc and Nicolas Poirier (eds), *Fumiers! Ordures! Gestion et usage des déchets dans les campagnes de l'Occident médiéval et moderne. Actes des XXXVIIIes Journées internationals d'histoire de l'abbaye de Flaran* (Toulouse: Presses universitaires du Midi, 2019).

Connell, William J. and Giles Constable, 'Sacrilege and redemption in Renaissance Florence: the case of Antonio Rinaldeschi', *Journal of the Warburg and Courtauld Institutes* 61 (1998), 53–92.

Constable, Olivia R., *Housing the stranger in the Mediterranean world: lodging, trade and travel in late Antiquity and the Middle Ages* (Cambridge: Cambridge University Press, 2003).

Coomans, Janna, *Community, urban health and the environment in the late medieval Low Countries* (Cambridge: Cambridge University Press, 2021).

Cooper, Tim, 'Recycling modernity: waste and environmental history', *History Compass* 8:9 (2010), 1114–25.

Corens, Liesbeth, Kate Peters, and Alexandra Walsham (eds), 'The social history of the archive: record-keeping in early modern Europe', *Past and Present* 230 suppl. 11 (2016).

BIBLIOGRAPHY 193

Corry, Maya, Deborah Howard, and Mary Laven (eds), *Madonnas and miracles: the holy home in Renaissance Italy* (London: Philip Wilson Publishers, 2017).

Costantini, Massimo, *L'acqua di Venezia: l'approvvigionamento idrico della Serenissima* (Venice: Arsenale Editrice, 1984).

Cowan, Alexander and Jill Steward, *The city and the senses: urban culture since 1500* (London: Routledge, 2016).

Cox, Rosie et al., *Dirt: the filthy reality of everyday life* (London: Profile Books, 2011).

Cozzi, Gaetano (ed.), *Gli ebrei a Venezia secoli XIV–XVIII* (Milan: Edizioni Comunità, 1987).

Craig, Heidi, 'Rags, ragpickers and early modern papermaking', *Literature Compass* 16:5 (2019), e12523.

Craik, Katherine A. (ed.), *Shakespeare and emotion* (Cambridge: Cambridge University Press, 2020).

Crouzet Pavan, Elizabeth, *'Sopra le acque salse': Espaces urbains, pouvoir et société à Venise à la fin du Moyen Age* (Rome: Istituto storico italiano per il Medio Evo, 1992).

Crovato, Giorgio and Maurizio Crovato, *Isole abbandonate della laguna veneziana: com'erano e come sono* (Venice: Patrocinio Associazione Settemari, 1978).

D'Amico, Stefano, *Spanish Milan: a city within the Empire, 1535–1706* (New York: Palgrave Macmillan, 2012).

Davids, Karel, 'On machines, self-organisation and the global traveling of knowledge, c.1500–1900', *Isis* 106:4 (2015), 866–74.

Davis, Kathleen, *Periodization and sovereignty: how ideas of feudalism and secularization govern the politics of time* (Philadelphia PA: University of Pennsylvania Press, 2008).

Davis, Robert C., *The war of the fists: popular culture and public violence in late Renaissance Venice* (Oxford: Oxford University Press, 1994).

Davis, Robert C., 'The trouble with bulls: the *cacce dei tori* in early modern Venice', *Histoire Sociale/Social History* 29:58 (1997), 275–90.

Davis, Robert C., 'Venetian shipbuilders and the fountain of wine', *Past and Present* 156 (1997), 55–87.

Davis, Robert C. and B. Ravid (eds), *The Jews of early modern Venice* (Baltimore MD: Johns Hopkins University Press, 2001).

Deagan, Kathleen (ed.), *Puerto real: the archaeology of a sixteenth-century Spanish town in Hispaniola* (Gainesville FL: University Press of Florida, 1995).

Dean, Trevor, 'Storm, suicide and miracle: Venice 1342' in Michael Knapton, John Law and Alison Smith (eds) *Venice and the Veneto during the Renaissance: the legacy of Benjamin Kohl* (Aldershot: Ashgate, 2000), pp. 309–22.

Dean, Trevor, 'Eight varieties of homicide in Renaissance Bologna' in Trevor Dean and K. J. P. Lowe (eds), *Murder in Renaissance Italy* (Cambridge: Cambridge University Press, 2017), pp. 83–105.

Decri, Anna, 'The historical aqueduct of Genoa: materials, techniques and history—a way to know' in Robert Carvais, André Guillerme, Valérie Nègre, and Joël Sakarovitch (eds), *Nuts and bolts of construction history* (Paris: Picard, 2012), vol 1, pp. 525–32.

de Vivo, Filippo, 'Walking in sixteenth-century Venice: mobilising the early modern city', *I Tatti Studies in the Italian Renaissance* 19:1 (2016), 115–41.

de Vivo, Filippo, Andrea Guidi, and Alessandro Silvestri (eds), 'Archival transformations in early modern Europe', *European History Quarterly* 46:3 (2016).

Dellerman, Rudolf, 'I mosaici della cappella di Sant'Isidoro nella basilica di San Marco a Venezia', *Arte veneta* 60 (2003), 6–29.

194 BIBLIOGRAPHY

Dobson, Mary, *The contours of death and disease in early modern England* (Cambridge: Cambridge University Press, 1997).

Dooley, Brendan, *A mattress maker's daughter: the Renaissance romance of Don Giovanni de'Medici and Livia Vernazza* (Cambridge MA: Harvard University Press, 2014).

Doria, Giorgio and Paola Massa Piergiovanni (eds), *Il Sistema portuale della Repubblica di Genova: profili organizzativi e politica gestionale (secc. XII–XVIII)* (Genoa: Nella sede della Società ligure di storia patria, 1988).

Douglas, Mary, *Purity and danger: an analysis of concepts of pollution and taboo* (London: Routledge, 2002).

Duden, Barbara, *The woman beneath the skin: a doctor's patients in eighteenth-century Germany* (Cambridge MA: Harvard University Press, 1998).

Eaton, R., *Ideal cities: utopianism and the (un)built environment* (London: Thames & Hudson, 2002).

Eckstein, Nicholas, 'Florence on foot: an eye-level mapping of the early modern city in time of plague', *Renaissance Studies* 30:2 (2015), 273–97.

Epstein, Stephen, *Genoa and the Genoese, 958–1528* (Chapel Hill NC: University of North Carolina Press, 1996).

Esser, Raingard, 'Fear of water and flood in the Low Countries' in William Naphy and Penny Roberts (eds), *Fear in early modern society* (Manchester: Manchester University Press, 1997), pp. 62–77.

Fane-Saunders, Peter, *Pliny the Elder and the emergence of Renaissance architecture* (Cambridge: Cambridge University Press, 2016).

Fara, Amelio, *Bernardo Buontalenti* (Milan: Electa, 1995).

Fasano Guarini, Elena, 'Regolamentazione delle acque e sistemazione del territorio' in G. Nudi (ed.), *Livorno e Pisa: due città e un territorio nella politica dei Medici* (Pisa: Nistri Lischi, 1980), pp. 43–75.

Ferguson, Dean, 'Nightsoil and the "great divergence": human waste, the urban economy and economic productivity, 1500–1900', *Journal of Global History* 9:3 (2014), 379–402.

Ferraro, Joanne, *Nefarious crimes, contested justice: illicit sex and infanticide in the Republic of Venice 1557–1789* (Baltimore MD: Johns Hopkins University Press, 2008).

Ferretti, Emanuela, *Acquedotti e fontane del Rinascimento in Toscana: acqua, architettura e città al tempo di Cosimo I dei Medici* (Florence: L. S. Olschki, 2016).

Finlay, Robert, *Politics in Renaissance Venice* (New Brunswick NJ: Rutgers University Press, 1980).

Finlay, Robert, 'The Immortal Republic: The myth of Venice during the Italian Wars (1494–1530)', *Sixteenth Century Journal* 30:4 (1999), 931–44.

Fissell, Mary, *Vernacular bodies: the politics of reproduction in early modern England* (Oxford: Oxford University Press, 2004).

Fleischer, Cornell, 'A Mediterranean apocalypse: prophecies of empire in the fifteenth and sixteenth centuries', *Journal of the Economic and Social History of the Orient* 61:1–2 (2018), 18–90.

Fontana, Gianjacopo, 'Sulla singolarità delle cisterne di Venezia', *Omnibus* (1854), 257–61.

Fortini Brown, Patricia, 'The Venetian casa', in Marta Ajmar-Wollheim and Flora Dennis (eds), *At home in Renaissance Italy* (London: V&A Publications, 2006), pp. 34–65.

Galassi, D., M. P. Rota, and A. Scrivano, *Popolazione e insediamento in Liguria secondo la testimonianza di Agostino Giustiniani* (Florence: L. S. Olschki, 1979).

Gallico, Sonia, *Guide to the ruins of Ostia* (Venice: ATS Italia, 1985).

Gamberini, Andrea and Isabella Lazzarini, *The Italian Renaissance state* (Cambridge: Cambridge University Press, 2012).

Gambi, Lucio, Antonio Pinelli et al., *La Galleria delle carte geografiche in Vaticano* (Modena: Panini, 1994).

Garnett, Jane and Gervase Rosser, *Spectacular miracles: transforming images in Italy from the Renaissance to the present* (London: Reaktion, 2013).

Gaston, R. W. (ed.), *Pirro Ligorio: artist and antiquarian* (Milan: Silvana, 1988).

Geltner, Guy, 'Healthscaping a medieval city: Lucca's *curia viarum* and the future of public health history', *Urban History* 40:3 (2013), 395–415.

Geltner, Guy, *The roads to health: infrastructure and urban wellbeing in medieval Italy* (Philadelphia PA: University of Pennsylvania Press, 2019).

Geltner, Guy, 'Urban viarii and the prosecution of public health offenders in late medieval Italy' in Carole Rawcliffe and Claire Weeda (eds), *Policing the urban environment in premodern Europe* (Amsterdam: Amsterdam University Press, 2019), pp. 97–119.

Geltner, Guy and Claire Weeda, 'Underground and over the sea: more community pro-phylactics in Europe, 1100–1600', *Journal of the History of Medicine and Allied Sciences* 76:2 (2021), 123–46.

Gentilcore, David, 'From "vilest beverage" to "universal medicine": drinking water in printed regimens and health guides 1450–1750', *Social History of Medicine* 33:3 (2020), 683–703.

Gentilcore, David, 'The cistern-system of early modern Venice: technology, politics and culture in a hydraulic society', *Water History* 13 (2021), 1–32.

Gerevini, Stefania, 'Inscribing history, (over)writing politics: word and image in the chapel of Sant'Isidoro at San Marco, Venice' in Wilfried E. Keil and Kristina Krüger (eds), *Sacred scripture sacred space: the interlacing of real places and conceptual spaces in medieval art and architecture* (Berlin: De Gruyter, 2019), pp. 323–49.

Ghirardo, Diane, 'The topography of prostitution in Renaissance Ferrara', *Journal of the Society of Architectural Historians* 60 (2001), 402–31.

Gianighian, Giorgio and Paola Pavanini, *Venezia come* (Venice: Gambier Keller, 2014).

Gorse, George, 'A classical stage for the old nobility: the Strada Nuova and sixteenth-century Genoa', *The Art Bulletin* 79:2 (1997), 301–26.

Gorse, George, 'Genova: repubblica dell'Impero' in Claudia Conforti and Richard J. Tuttle (eds), *Storia dell'architettura italiana: il secondo Cinquecento* (Milan: Electa, 2001), pp. 240–65.

Goy, Richard, *Venetian vernacular architecture: traditional housing in the Venetian lagoon* (Cambridge: Cambridge University Press, 1989).

Goy, Richard, *Building Renaissance Venice: patrons, architects, and builders, c.1430–1500* (New Haven CT: Yale University Press, 2006).

Grendi, Edoardo, *Il Cervo e la Repubblica. Il modello ligure di antico regime* (Turin: Einaudi, 1993).

Greif, Avner, 'Political organisations, social structure and institutional success: reflections from Genoa and Venice during the Commercial Revolution', *The Journal of Institutional and Theoretical Economics* 151:4 (1995), 734–40.

Guastoni, Claudio, *L'acquedotto civico di Genoa: un percorso al futuro* (Milan: Franco Angeli, 2004).

Hahn, Barbara, 'The social in the machine: how historians of technology look beyond the object', *Perspectives on History* 52:3 (2014), 30–1.

Handley, Sasha and John Morgan, 'Environment, emotion and early modernity', *Environment and History* 28:3 (2022), 355–61.

Hanke, Stephanie, 'Bathing all'antica: bathrooms in Genoese villas and palaces in the sixteenth century', *Renaissance Studies* 20:5 (2006), 674–700.

196 BIBLIOGRAPHY

Hanke, Stephanie, 'The splendour of bankers and merchants: Genoese garden grottoes of the sixteenth century', *Urban History* 37:3 (2010), 399–418.

Hebeisen, Erika (ed.), *Europe in the Renaissance: metamorphoses 1400–1600* (Zürich: Swiss National Museum, 2016).

Hellawell, Philippa, 'Diving engines, submarine knowledge and the 'wealth fetch'd out of the sea', *Renaissance Studies* 34:1 (2019), 78–94.

Hellawell, Philippa, ' "The best and most practical philosophers": seamen and the authority of experience in early modern science', *History of Science* 58:1 (2020), 28–50.

Henderson, John, ' "La schifezza, madre di corruzione": peste e società a Firenze nella prima epoca moderna', *Medicina e storia* 2 (2001), 23–56.

Henderson, John, *The Renaissance hospital: healing the body and healing the soul* (New Haven CT: Yale University Press, 2006).

Henderson, John, *Florence under siege: surviving plague in an early modern city* (New Haven CT: Yale University Press, 2019).

Hohti Erichsen, Paula, *Artisans, objects, and everyday life in Renaissance Italy: the material culture of the middling class* (Amsterdam: Amsterdam University Press, 2020).

Horden, Peregrine and Nicholas Purcell, *The corrupting sea: a study of Mediterranean history* (Oxford: Wiley-Blackwell, 2000).

Howard, Deborah, *The architectural history of Venice* (New Haven CT: Yale University Press, 2002).

Howard, Deborah, *Venice and the East: the impact of the Islamic world on Venetian architecture 1100–1500* (New Haven CT: Yale University Press, 2000).

Hughes, Diane, 'Kinsmen and neighbors in Medieval Genoa' in Harry A. Miskimin, David Herlihy, and Abraham L. Udovitch (eds), *The medieval city* (New Haven CT: Yale University Press, 1977), pp. 95–111.

Jain, Bhav, Simar S. Bajaj, and Fatima Cody Stanford, 'All infrastructure is health infrastructure', *American Journal of Public Health* 112:1 (2022), 24–6.

Jenner, Mark, 'Doctoring the environment without doctors? Public cleanliness and environmental governance in early modern London', *Storia urbana* 112 (2006), 17–37.

Judde de Larivière, Claire, 'The "public" and the "private" in sixteenth-century Venice: from medieval economy to early modern state', *Historical Social Research* 37:4 (2012), 76–94.

Jütte, Robert, 'Im Wunder vereint: eine spektakulaere Missgeburt im Ghetto 1575' in Uwe Israel, Robert Jütte, and Reinhold C. Mueller (eds), *Interstizi: culture ebraico-cristiane a Venezia e nei suoi domini dal medioevo all'eta moderna* (Rome: Edizioni di storia e letteratura, 2010), vol 5, pp. 517–40.

Kagan, R. L., 'Philip II and the art of the cityscape' in R. I. Rotberg and T. K. Rabb (eds), *Art and history: images and their meanings* (Cambridge: Cambridge University Press, 1986), pp. 115–37.

Kagan, R. L., *Urban images of the Hispanic world 1493–1793* (New Haven CT: Yale University Press, 2000).

Kane, Bronach C. and Simon Sandall, *The experience of neighbourhood in medieval and early modern Europe* (London: Routledge, 2022).

Kaplan, Debra, *Beyond expulsion: Jews, Christians and Reformation Strasbourg* (Stanford CA: Stanford University Press, 2011).

Katz, Dana E., ' "Clamber not you up to the casements": On ghetto views and viewing', *Jewish History* 24:2 (2010), 127–53.

Kaye, Joel, *A history of balance 1250–1375* (Cambridge: Cambridge University Press, 2014).

Kirk, Thomas A., *Genoa and the sea: policy and power in an early modern maritime republic, 1559–1684* (Baltimore MD: Johns Hopkins University Press, 2005).

BIBLIOGRAPHY 197

Kirk, Thomas A., 'Genoa and Livorno: sixteenth and seventeenth-century commercial rivalry as a stimulus to policy development', *The Historical Association* 86 (2001), 3–17.

Knoll, Martin, 'From "urban gap" to social metabolism: the early modern city in environmental history research' in Martin Knoll and Reinhold Reith (eds), *An environmental history of the early modern period: experiments and perspectives* (Zürich: Lit, 2014), pp. 45–50.

Konvitz, Josef, *Cities and the sea: port city planning in early modern Europe* (Baltimore MD: Johns Hopkins University Press, 2019).

Kostylo, Joanna, 'Pharmacy as a centre for Protestant reform in Renaissance Venice', *Renaissance Studies* 30:2 (2016), 236–53.

Kruft, Hanno-Walter, *Portali genovesi del Rinascimento* (Florence: Edam, 1971).

Kümin, Beat and Cornelie Usborne, 'At home and in the workplace: a historical introduction to the "spatial turn"', *History and Theory* 52 (2013), 305–18.

Lane, Frederic C. *Venice, a maritime republic* (Cambridge MA: Harvard University Press, 1973).

Lane, Frederic C., *Venice and History: the collected papers of Frederic C. Lane* (Baltimore MA: Johns Hopkins University Press, 2019).

Laughran, Michelle A., 'The body, public health and social control in sixteenth-century Venice' (unpublished PhD thesis, University of Connecticut, 1998).

Lee, Peter, Leonard Y. Andaya, Barbara Watson Andaya, Gael Newton, and Alan Chong, *Port cities: multicultural emporiums of Asia, 1500–1900* (Singapore: Asian Civilisations Museum, 2016).

Long, Pamela O., *Openness, secrecy, authorship: technical arts and the culture of knowledge from Antiquity to the Renaissance* (Baltimore MD: Johns Hopkins University Press, 2001).

Long, Pamela O., 'Hydraulic engineering and the study of Antiquity: Rome, 1557–70', *Renaissance Quarterly* 61:4 (2008), 1098–138.

Long, Pamela O., 'Trading zones in early modern Europe', *Isis* 106:4 (2015), 840–7.

Long, Pamela O., *Engineering the Eternal City: infrastructure, topography and the culture of knowledge in late sixteenth-century Rome* (Chicago IL: University of Chicago Press, 2018).

Magnusson, Roberta J., *Water technology in the Middle Ages: cities, monasteries and waterworks after the Roman Empire* (Baltimore MA: Johns Hopkins University Press, 2001).

Maier, Jessica, 'A "true likeness": the Renaissance city portrait', *Renaissance Quarterly* 65:3 (2012), 711–52.

Mallet, J. V. G., 'Tiled floors and court designers in Mantua and Northern Italy' in Cesare Mozzarelli, Robert Oresko, and Leandro Ventura (eds), *La corte di Mantova nell'età di Andrea Mantegna: 1450–1550* (Rome: Bulzoni, 1997), pp. 253–72.

Marani, E., *Sabbioneta e Vespasiano Gonzaga* (Sabbioneta: La Sabbionetana, 1977).

Marcocci, Giuseppe, *The globe on paper: writing histories of the world in Renaissance Europe and the Americas* (Oxford: Oxford University Press, 2020).

Marshall, Louise, 'Manipulating the sacred: image and plague in Renaissance Italy', *Renaissance Quarterly* 47:3 (1994), 485–532.

Martin, John Jeffries, *Venice's hidden enemies: Italian heretics in a Renaissance city* (Berkeley CA: University of California Press, 1993).

Martin, John Jeffries (ed.), *The Renaissance: Italy and abroad* (London: Routledge, 2003).

198 BIBLIOGRAPHY

Matheus, Michael, Gabriella Piccinni, Giuliano Pinto, and Gian Maria Varanini (eds), *Le calamità ambientali nel tardo medioevo europeo: realtà, percezioni, reazioni* (Florence: Firenze University Press, 2010).

Matteoni, Dario, *Livorno* (Bari: Edizioni Laterza, 1985).

Matthews-Grieco, Sara, 'Marriage and sexuality' in Marta Ajmar-Wollheim and Flora Dennis (eds), *At home in Renaissance Italy* (London: V&A Publications, 2006), pp. 104–19.

Mauch, Christof and Christian Pfister (eds), *Natural disasters, cultural responses: case studies towards a global environmental history* (Lanham MD: Lexington Books, 2009).

McGough, Laura, *Gender, sexuality and syphilis in early modern Venice: the disease that came to stay* (Basingstoke: Palgrave Macmillan, 2011).

Miglietti, Sara and John Morgan (eds), *Governing the environment in the early modern world: theory and practice* (London: Routledge, 2017).

Milner, Stephen, ' "Fanno bandire, notificare et expressamente comandare": town criers and the information economy of Renaissance Florence', *I Tatti Studies in the Italian Renaissance* 16:1/2 (2013), 107–51.

Molà, Luca, *The silk industry of Renaissance Venice* (Baltimore MD: Johns Hopkins University Press, 2000).

Mooney, Graham and Jonathan Reinarz (eds), *Permeable walls: historical perspectives on hospital and asylum visiting* (Amsterdam: Rodolpi, 2009).

Moore Jr, Barrington, 'Ethnic and religious hostilities in early modern port cities', *International Journal of Politics, Culture and Society* 14:4 (2001), 687–727.

Morgan, John, 'Understanding flooding in early modern England', *Journal of Historical Geography* 50 (2015), 37–50.

Morrison, Molly, 'Strange miracles: a study of the peculiar healings of St Maria Maddelena de'Pazzi', *Logos* 8 (2005), 129–44.

Mucciarelli, Roberta, 'Igiene, salute e pubblica decoro nel Medioevo' in Roberta Mucciarelli, Laura Vigni, and Donatella Fabbri (eds), *Vergognosa immunditia: igiene pubblica e privata a Siena dal medioevo all'età contemporanea* (Siena: NIE, 2000), pp. 15–84.

Muir, Edward, *Civic ritual in Renaissance Venice* (Princeton NJ: Princeton University Press, 1981).

Muir, Edward, 'The Virgin on the street corner: the place of the sacred in Italian cities' in Steven Ozment (ed.), *Religion and culture in the Renaissance and Reformation* (Kirksville MI: Sixteenth Century Journal Publishers, 1989), pp. 25–40.

Muir, Edward and Robert Weissman, 'Social and symbolic places in Renaissance Venice and Florence' in John Agnew and James Duncan (eds), *The power of place: bringing together geographical and sociological imaginations* (London: Unwin Hyman, 1992), pp. 81–103.

Muir, Edward, 'Was there Republicanism in the Renaissance Republics? Venice after Agnadello,' in John Martin and Dennis Romano (eds), *Venice Reconsidered: The History and Civilization of an Italian City-State, 1297–1797* (Baltimore MD: Johns Hopkins University Press, 2000), pp. 137–67.

Muir, Edwin, 'The Confirmation' in Gaby Morgan (ed.), *A Year of Scottish Poems* (London: Pan Macmillan, 2020).

Musacchio, Jacqueline, 'Lambs, coral, teeth and the intimate intersection of religion and magic' in Sally Cornelison and Scott Montgomery (eds), *Images, relics, and devotional practices in medieval and Renaissance Italy* (Temple AZ, 2006), pp. 139–56.

Nadalo, Stephanie, 'Negotiating slavery in a tolerant frontier: Livorno's Turkish *Bagno* (1547–1747), *Mediaevalia* 32 (2011), 275–324.

BIBLIOGRAPHY 199

Najemy, John M., 'The Republic's two bodies: body metaphors in Italian Renaissance political thought' in Alison Brown (ed.), *Language and images of Renaissance Italy* (Oxford: Oxford University Press, 1995), pp. 237–62.

Naser Eslami, Alireza and Marco Folin (eds), *La città multietnica nel mondo mediterraneo: porti, cantieri, minoranze* (Milan, 2019).

Nemser, Daniel, 'Triangulating blackness: Mexico City 1612', *Mexican Studies/Estudios Mexicanos* 33:3 (2017), 344–66.

Nevola, Fabrizio, 'Surveillance and control of the street in Renaissance Italy', in 'Experiences of the Street in Early Modern Italy', *I Tatti Studies in the Italian Renaissance* 16 (2013), 85–106.

Nevola, Fabrizio, *Street life in Renaissance Italy* (New Haven CT: Yale University Press, 2020).

Newton, Hannah, '"Nature concocts and expels": the agents and processes of recovery from disease in early modern England', *Social History of Medicine* 28:3 (2015), 465–86.

Nichols, Tom, *The art of poverty: irony and ideal in sixteenth-century beggar imagery* (Manchester: Manchester University Press, 2007).

Nichols, Tom, *Tintoretto: tradition and identity* (London: Reaktion, 2015).

North, Susan, *Sweet and clean? Bodies and clothes in early modern England* (Oxford: Oxford University Press, 2020).

Olgiati, Giustina (ed.), *Genova, porta del mondo. La città medievale e i suoi habitatores* (Genoa: Brigati, 2011).

Orlando, Ermanno, *Altre Venezie: Il dogado veneziano nei secoli XIII e XIV (giurisdizione, territorio, giustizia e amministrazione)* (Venice: Istituto veneto di scienze, lettere ed arti, 2008).

Pagliera, Nicola, 'Destri e cucine…' in Aurora Scotti Tosini (ed.), *Aspetti dell'abitare in Italia tra XV e XVI secolo: distribuzione, funzioni, impianti* (Milan: Unicopli, 2001), pp. 63–77.

Palmer, Richard, 'The control of plague in Venice and Northern Italy, 1348–1600' (unpublished PhD thesis, University of Kent, 1978).

Palmer, Richard, 'Nicolò Massa: his family and his fortune', *Medical History* 25 (1981), 395–410.

Pàstine, Onorato, 'L'arte dei corallieri nell'ordinamento delle corporazioni Genovesi (secoli XV–XVIII)', *Atti della Società Ligure di Storia Patria* 61 (1933), 277–415.

Pavanini, Paola, 'Venezia verso la pianificazione? Bonifiche urbane nel XVI secolo a Venezia' in *D'une ville à l'autre, Structures matérielles et organisatione de l'espace dans les villes européennes (XIIIe–XVIe siècle)* (Rome: École française de Rome, 1989), pp. 496–500.

Pérez-Mallaína Bueno, Pablo Emilio, *Spain's men of the sea: daily life on the Indies fleets in the sixteenth century* (Cambridge MA: Harvard University Press, 1998).

Perry, Mary Elizabeth, *Crime and society in early modern Seville* (Hanover NH University Press of New England, 1980).

Pessa, Loredana, *Le antiche spezierie degli ospedali genovesi di Pammatone e degli Incurabili* (Genoa: LOG, 2005).

Po-Chia Hsia, R., and H. Lehmann (eds), *In and out of the Ghetto: Jewish-Gentile relations in late medieval and early modern Germany* (Cambridge: Cambridge University Press, 1995).

Podestà, Francesco, *Il porto di Genova dalle origini fino alla caduta della Repubblica genovese* (Genoa: E. Spiotti, 1913).

200 BIBLIOGRAPHY

Podestà, Francesco, *Il porto di Genova 1128–2000* (Genoa: Consorzio Autonomo del Porto di Genova, 1971).

Poleggi, Ennio, *Strada nuova: una lottizzazione del '500 a Genova* (Genoa: Sagep, 1968).

Poleggi, Ennio, 'La topografía degli stranieri nella Genova di Antico Regime' in Donatella Calabi and Paola Lanaro (eds), *La città italiana e i luoghi degli stranieri XIV–XVIII secolo* (Rome-Bari: Laterza, 1998), pp.108–20.

Poleggi, Ennio and Paolo Cevini, *Genova* (Rome-Bari: Laterza, 2003).

Preto, Paolo, *I servizi segreti di Venezia* (Milan: Il Saggiatore, 1994).

Profumo, Luciana Müller, *Le pietre parlanti: L'ornamento nell'architettura genovese 1450–1600* (Genoa: Banca Carige, 1993).

Pullan, Brian, *Rich and poor in Renaissance Venice: the social institutions of a Catholic state, to 1620* (Oxford: Blackwells, 1971).

Quillien, Robin, and Solène Rivoal, 'Boatmen, fishermen and Venetian institutions: from negotiation to confrontation' in Maartje van Gelder and Claire Judde de Larivière (eds), *Popular politics in an aristocratic republic: political conflict and social contestation in late medieval and early modern Venice* (Routledge: London, 2020), pp. 197–216.

Raggio, Osvaldo, *Faide e parentele: lo stato genovese visto dalla Fontanabuona* (Turin: Einaudi, 1990).

Rapp, Richard, *Industry and economic decline in seventeenth-century Venice* (Cambridge MA: Harvard University Press, 1976).

Rawcliffe, Carole, 'A marginal occupation? The medieval laundress and her work', *Gender & History* 21:1 (2009), 147–69.

Rawcliffe, Carole, *Urban bodies: communal health in late medieval English towns and cities* (Woodbridge: The Boydell Press, 2013).

Rebora, Giovanni, 'I lavori di espurgazione della Darsena del porto di Genova nel 1545' in Giorgio Doria and Paola Massa Piergiovanni (eds), *Il Sistema portuale*, pp. 199–220.

Reeves, Peter, Frank Broeze, and Kenneth McPherson, 'Studying the Asian port city' in Frank Broeze (ed.), *Brides of the sea: port cities of Asia from the 16th–20th centuries* (Kensington N.S.W: New South Wales University Press, 1989), pp. 29–53.

Reid, Donald, *Paris sewers and sewermen: realities and representations* (Cambridge MA: Harvard University Press, 1991).

Reid, Elizabeth, 'Female representation, gender and violence in the ceremonial entries of the Italian Wars', *Renaissance Studies*, early view published online 6 May 2022.

Richards, Jennifer, *Voices and books in the English Renaissance: a new history of reading* (Oxford: Oxford University Press, 2019).

Rietbergen, Peter, 'Porto e citta o citta-porto? Qualche riflessione generale sul problema del rapporto fra porto e contesto urbano' in Simonetta Cavaciocchi (ed.), *I porti come impresa economica* (Florence: Le Monnier, 1988), pp. 615–6.

Rinne, Katherine, *The waters of Rome: aqueducts, fountains and the birth of the Baroque city* (New Haven CT: Yale University Press, 2010).

Rizzi, Alberto, *Vere di pozzo di Venezia* (Venice: Filippi, 2007).

Robinson, Michele, 'Dirty laundry: caring for clothing in early modern Italy', *Costume* 55:1 (2021), 3–23.

Romano, Dennis, 'Gender and the urban geography of Renaissance Venice', *Journal of Social History* 23:2 (1989), 339–53.

Romano, Dennis, *Markets and marketplaces in medieval Italy c.1100–1440* (New Haven CT: Yale University Press, 2015).

Rombough, Julia, 'Noisy soundscapes and women's institutions in early modern Florence', *The Sixteenth Century Journal* 50 (2019), 449–70.

BIBLIOGRAPHY 201

Roodenburg, Herman (ed.), *A cultural history of the senses in the Renaissance* (London: Bloomsbury Academic, 2016).

Rosand, David, *Myths of Venice: the figuration of a state* (Chapel Hill NC: University of North Carolina Press, 2001).

Rosenthal, Margaret, *The honest courtesan: Veronica Franco, citizen and writer in sixteenth-century Venice* (Chicago IL: University of Chicago Press, 1992).

Rota, Maria Pia, 'L'apparato portuale della Corsica "Genovese": una struttura in movimento' in Giorgio Doria and Paola Massa Piergiovanni (eds), *Il Sistema portuale*, pp. 297–328.

Rouse, Barbara, 'Nuisance neighbours and persistent polluters: the urban code of behaviour in late medieval London' in Andrew Brown and Jan Dumoly (eds), *Medieval urban culture* (Turnhout: Brepols, 2007), pp. 75–92.

Rubin, Miri, *Cities of strangers: making lives in medieval Europe* (Cambridge: Cambridge University Press, 2020).

Ruderman, David B., *Kabbalah, magic, and science: the cultural university of a sixteenth-century Jewish physician* (Cambridge MA: Harvard University Press, 1988).

Saccardo, P., *La cappella di S. Isidoro nella Basilica di San Marco* (Venice, 1987).

Salzberg, Rosa M., *Ephemeral city: cheap print and urban culture in Renaissance Venice* (Manchester: Manchester University Press, 2014).

Salzberg, Rosa M., 'The margins in the centre: working around Rialto in sixteenth-century Venice', in Andrew Spicer and Jane L. Stevens Crawshaw (eds), *The place of the social margins, 1350–1750* (London: Routledge, 2017), pp. 135–53.

Savelli, Rodolfo, 'Dalle confraternite allo stato: il Sistema assistenziale Genovese nel Cinquecento', *Atti della Società Ligure di Storia Patria* XXIV/1 (1984), pp. 171–216.

Schama, Simon, *The embarrassment of riches: an interpretation of Dutch culture in the Golden Age* (London: Fontana, 1987).

Schneider, Daniel, *Hybrid nature: sewage treatment and the contradictions of the industrial ecosystem* (Cambridge MA: MIT Press, 2011).

Schupbach, William, 'A Venetian "plague miracle" in 1464 and 1576', *Medical History* 20:3 (1976) 312–16.

Screpanti, Ernesto, *L'angelo della liberazione nel tumult di Ciompi: Firezne giugno–agosto 1378* (Siena: Protagon, 2008).

Shaw, Christine, 'Principles and practice in the civic government of fifteenth-century Genoa', *Renaissance Quarterly* 58 (2005), 45–90.

Shaw, Christine, 'Genoa' in Andrea Gamberini and Isabella Lazzarini (eds), *The Italian Renaissance state* (Cambridge: Cambridge University Press, 2012), pp. 220–36.

Siebenhüner, Kim 'Conversion, mobility and the Roman Inquisition in Italy around 1600', *Past and Present* 200 (2008), 5–35.

Siena, Kevin, *Rotten bodies: class and contagion in eighteenth-century Britain* (New Haven CT: Yale University Press, 2019).

Siraisi, Nancy G., *Medieval and Renaissance medicine: an introduction to knowledge and practice* (Chicago IL: University of Chicago Press, 1990).

Skelton, Kimberley (ed.), *Early modern spaces in motion: design, experience and rhetoric* (Amsterdam: Amsterdam University Press, 2020).

Sörlin, Sverker and Paul Warde (eds), *Nature's end: history and the environment* (Basingstoke: Palgrave Macmillan, 2009).

Spada, N., 'Leggi veneziane sulle industrie chimiche a tutela della salute pubblica dal secolo XIII al XVIII', *Archivio veneto* 5th series, 7 (1930), 126–56.

202 BIBLIOGRAPHY

Spicer, Andrew, 'Consecration and violation: preserving the sacred landscape in the (Arch) diocese of Cambrai, *c.*1550–1570' in Maarten Delbeke and Minou Schraven (eds), *Foundation, dedication and consecration in early modern Europe* 22 (Leiden: Brill, 2012), pp. 251–74.

Squatriti, Paolo, *Water and society in medieval Italy* (Cambridge: Cambridge University Press, 1998).

Stevens Crawshaw, Jane, *Plague hospitals: public health for the city in early modern Venice* (Aldershot: Ashgate, 2012).

Stevens Crawshaw, Jane, 'Families, medical secrets and public health in early modern Venice', *Renaissance Studies* 28:4 (2014), 597–618.

Stevens Crawshaw, Jane, 'Cleaning up the Renaissance city: the symbolic and physical place of the Genoese brothel in urban society' in Andrew Spicer and Jane Stevens Crawshaw (eds), *The place of the social margins 1350–1750* (London: Routledge, 2016), pp. 155–81.

Stevens Crawshaw, Jane, 'A sense of time: experiencing plague and quarantine in early modern Italy', *I Tatti Studies in the Italian Renaissance* 24:2 (2021), 269–90.

Stevenson, Jane, *The light of Italy: the life and times of Federico da Montefeltro* (London: Apollo, 2021).

Stilli, R., 'Un porto per Sanremo: difficoltà tecniche e problemi politico-finanziari' in in Giorgio Doria and Paola Massa Piergiovanni (eds), *Il Sistema portuale*, 259–96.

Stock, Paul (ed.), *The uses of space in early modern history* (Basingstoke: Palgrave Macmillan, 2015).

Stöger, Georg, 'Environmental perspectives on pre-modern European cities—difficulties and possibilities' in Martin Knoll and Reinhold Reith (eds), *An environmental history of the early modern period: experiments and perspectives* (Zürich: Lit, 2014), pp. 51–5.

Stringa, Paolo, *La strada dell'acque: l'acquedotto storico di Genova, tecnica ed architettura* (Genoa: Libreria Equilibri, 1980).

Stuart, Kathy, *Defiled trades and social outcasts: honor and ritual pollution in early modern Germany* (Cambridge: Cambridge University Press, 1999).

Subrahmanyam, Sanjay, 'Connected histories: notes towards a reconfiguration of early modern Eurasia', *Modern Asian Studies* 31:3 (1997), 735–62.

Syson, Luke and Dora Thornton, *Objects of virtue: art in Renaissance Italy* (London: British Museum, 2001).

Tassini, Giuseppe, *Curiosità veneziane* (Venice: M. Fontana, 1882).

Tazzara, Corey, *The free port of Livorno and the transformation of the Mediterranean World* (Oxford: Oxford University Press, 2017).

Terpstra, Nicholas, *Abandoned children of the Italian Renaissance: orphan care in Florence and Bologna* (Baltimore MD: Johns Hopkins University Press, 2005).

Thompson, Michael, *Rubbish theory: the creation and destruction of value* (London: Pluto Press, 2017).

Todeschini, Giacomo, *Il Prezzo della salvezza: lessici medievali del pensiero economico* (Rome: Nuova Italia scientifica, 1994).

Tomasi, Michele (ed.), 'Il culto di sant'Isidoro a Venezia', *Quaderni della Procuratoria* (2008).

van Bavel, Bas and Oscar Gelderblom, 'The economic origins of cleanliness in the Dutch Golden Age', *Past and Present* 205:1 (2009), 41–69.

van Dam, Petra J. E. M., Piet van Cruyningen, and Milja van Tielhof, 'A global comparison of pre-modern institutions for water management', *Environment and History* 23 (2017), 335–40.

BIBLIOGRAPHY 203

van de Pol, Lotte, *The burgher and the whore: prostitution in early modern Amsterdam* (Oxford: Oxford University Press, 2011).

van Gelder, Maartje and Claire Judde de Larivière (eds), *Popular politics in an aristocratic Republic: political conflict and social contestation in late medieval and early modern Venice* (London: Routledge, 2020).

van Gelder, Maartje and Filippo de Vivo, 'Papering over protest: contentious politics and archival suppression in early modern Venice', *Past and Present* 258:1 (2023), 44–78.

Venezia e la peste 1348–1797 (Venice: Marsilio, 1980).

Villa-Flores, Javier, *Dangerous speech: a social history of blasphemy in Colonial Mexico* (The University of Arizona Press, Tucson, 2006).

Walker, Jonathan, 'Gambling and Venetian noblemen c.1500–1700', *Past and Present* 162 (1999), 28–69.

Walker Bynum, Caroline, *Christian materiality: an essay on religion in late Medieval Europe* (New York: Zone Books, 2011).

Walsham, Alexandra, *The Reformation of the landscape: religion, identity and memory in early modern Britain and Ireland* (Oxford: Oxford University Press, 2011).

Warde, Paul, *The invention of sustainability: nature and destiny c.1500–1870* (Cambridge: Cambridge University Press, 2018).

Warner, Nicholas, *The true description of Cairo: a sixteenth-century Venetian view* (Oxford: Oxford University Press, 2006).

Wear, Andrew, *Knowledge and practice in early modern English medicine, 1550–1680* (Cambridge: Cambridge University Press, 2000).

Weddle, Saundra, 'Mobility and prostitution in early modern Venice', *Early Modern Women* 14:1 (2019), 95–108.

Weeda, Claire, 'Cleanliness, civility and the city in medieval ideals and scripts' in Carole Rawcliffe and Claire Weeda (eds), *Policing the environment in premodern Europe* (Amsterdam: Amsterdam University Press, 2019) pp. 39–68.

Welch, Evelyn, 'Lotteries in early modern Italy', *Past and Present* 199:1 (2008), 71–111.

Welch, Evelyn, *Shopping in the Renaissance consumer cultures in Italy, 1400–1600* (New Haven CT: Yale University Press, 2009).

Wheeler, Joseph, 'Stench in sixteenth-century Venice' in Alexander Cowan and Jill Steward (eds), *The city and the senses: urban culture since 1500* (Aldershot: Ashgate, 2007), pp. 25–38.

Wilson, Bronwen, *The world in Venice: print, the city and early modern identity* (Toronto: University of Toronto Press, 2005).

Wilson, Bronwen and Paul Yachnin (eds), *Making publics in early modern Europe: people, things, forms of knowledge* (London: Routledge, 2010).

Woodward, Donald, '"Swords into ploughshares": recycling in pre-industrial England', *The Economic History Review* 38:2 (1985), 175–91.

Zazzu, G. N., 'Prostituzione e moralità pubblica nella Genova del '400', *Studi genuensi* 5 (1987), 45–67.

Zemon Davis, Natalie, *Women on the margins: three seventeenth-century lives* (Cambridge MA: Harvard University Press, 2003).

Zemon Davis, Natalie, *A passion for history: conversations with Denis Crouzet* (Kirksville MI: Truman State University Press, 2010).

Zucchetta, Gianpietro, *Una fognatura per Venezia: storia di due secoli di progretti* (Venice: Istituto veneto di scienze, lettere ed arti, 1986).

Index

For the benefit of digital users, indexed terms that span two pages (e.g., 52–53) may, on occasion, appear on only one of those pages.

air see also *winds* 10–12, 15, 28–30, 36–7, 46–7, 52, 55, 60–1, 66, 70–1, 75, 80, 82, 84–5, 87, 100–2, 119, 121–2, 128, 134–5, 149–50, 170, 172–6
Alberti, Leon Battista [1404–72] 28–30, 35–6, 51, 111
Amalfi 34–5
animals 33, 53, 61–4, 66–7, 93–4, 128, 139–40, 161, 177
  hens 61–2, 89
  mules 153–4
  pigs 61–2, 103, 177
aqueduct 9, 20, 66, 78–83, 88–93, 100–1, 124–6, 136–7, 153
archival records 3–4, 20–2, 76–7, 107–8, 112–13, 118–19, 144, 171
Arsenals 29–30, 36–7, 42, 60, 109–10, 112–14, 117–18, 121–2, 126, 128, 138–41
Averlino, Antonio [c.1400–69], known as Filarete 29–33, 41–2

balance 10–12, 35–6, 47, 89–90, 129, 137, 172
ballast 137–9
bells 46–7, 72
boatmen 127–8, 137–8, 147–50, 153–6
boats 63, 95–6, 109–14, 120–2, 127–8, 137–9, 151–2, 154–6, 170–1, 178, 184
body 3, 10–11, 51, 65–6, 98, 168–9, 172–3
  metaphor of the 31, 35–6
breakwaters 29–31, 45–6, 68–9, 102, 110–11, 116–17, 119–20, 129, 136–9, 147, 153
bridges 12–13, 41, 54n.18, 63, 67–8, 71–2, 75, 95–8, 111–12, 123, 149n.108, 178–83
brothels see also *sex trade* 29–31, 40–1, 58–9, 80, 151, 177–8
building repairs see also *dilapidated buildings* 59, 176–7
building trades 9, 55, 120–1, 140
Buontalenti, Bernardo [c.1531–1608] 39–40, 42
butchers 43, 63–4

canals
  diggers (*cavacanali*) 127–8, 149–50, 155–7
  dredging 121–3
  Grand Canal (Venice) 20–1, 121–3

carts 31, 153–4
Catholic Reformation 1, 33–4
cavacanali see *canals, diggers*
charity 19, 24, 79–80, 82, 91, 123–4, 180
children 26, 38, 40–1, 54, 57, 85–6, 89, 99, 140, 142, 154, 162–3, 166, 172
cisterns 85, 88–9, 100
cleanliness 10–12, 56–7, 64, 66–7, 87, 94, 98, 119, 139–40, 158, 167–9, 171–2, 174–5
  historiography 8
  methodology 4, 7
community 17–18, 56, 70–1, 81, 85, 87, 103–4, 120–1, 123, 137–8, 161
  public health and tensions 65, 137
comparative history 5–6, 12–23, 184–5
courtesans 97

da Vinci, Leonardo [1452–1519] 26–8
denunciations 128, 138
di Giorgio Martini, Francesco [c.1439–1501] 28–30
dilapidated buildings 20–1, 57, 59
dishonourable trades 150–1
Douglas, Mary [1921–2007] 5–6, 134
drains 101–4, 152
dredging 119–26
  costs 123–4
  machines 115–19
  material 135, 144–6
  workforce 119–21
drought 92, 180–1
dye-houses 88–9, 91–2

earthquakes 158–60, 163–5
elements see also *air, water* 3, 10–11, 175–6

fires 10, 46–7, 78, 81, 96–7, 161–2, 164–5, 170, 174
fishermen 36–7, 43, 45, 111, 123, 141, 148
floods 1, 95, 146–7, 160, 180–3
  flood defences 105–6, 135
Florence 29, 33–4, 44–5, 67, 75, 96, 166
flow 10–12

206 INDEX

foodstuffs see also *street selling* 15–17, 28, 53, 64,
  70–1, 76–7
  waste 72, 142
foreign communities 17–20
  bagno or *seraglio* 39–40
  fondaci 20–2
fountains 27–8, 33, 39, 72, 79–80, 82–3, 92–5,
  100, 116–17, 141–2
  theft 93–4

gambling 165–7
gardens 33, 90–1, 95, 100, 122–3, 144, 152, 174,
  180–1
gateways 61, 68–70
Genoa 6–7, 12–23, 43–7
  alberghi 17–19
  aqueduct see *aqueduct*
  Casa di San Giorgio 19, 62–3
  citizenship 17–18
  districts 12
  fountains see *fountains*
  Health Office 20
  historiography 14
  Jewish community 18
  Padri del Comune 20, 22
  population 8, 17–18
  port 10, 15, 45
  renovatio genuae 46
  state 12–13, 15–17 see also *Liguria*
  Strada Nuova 52, 141
  topography 15, 37
Grassi, Cristoforo 20, 107–8
Gritti, Andrea (Doge of Venice)
  [1455–1538] 43–5
guilds 71, 82–3, 115, 155–6

health see also *public health*
  of the body 47, 52–3, 70–1
  of the soul 78–9, 158–70
Health Offices 6–7, 9, 20–1, 170–7
Hippocratic corpus 3, 7
hospitals 19, 44–5, 175
  Incurabili 55, 88–9, 129
  lazzaretti (plague hospitals) 19, 28–9, 170–1,
    175–7
  Pammatone 99, 102–3
humoural theory 3, 10–11

inns see *taverns*
inventions 83–5, 106, 110–11, 115–19

Jewish communities see also *Venice, Ghetto*
  18–20, 39, 56, 124, 133, 143–4, 162–5
judgement 1, 158–60, 163, 165, 179

land reclamation 115–16, 127–8, 157
latrines 33, 43, 80, 93, 102–4, 133–4, 150–1
laundry see *washing, cloth*
lighthouses 29–30, 34, 46, 136–8, 146–8
Liguria
  Camogli 166–7
  coastline 15
  Chiavari, Church of Nostra Signora
    dell'Orto 4, 174
  Gavi 64
  Rapallo 30, 137–8
  rivers 180, 182
  San Remo 119–20
  Savona 64, 66, 76, 85–7, 112–13, 117–18,
    154, 174
Little Ice Age 7–8
Livorno 39–42
lotteries 20–1, 124–6, 165

Mantua 63, 74–5
maps 16, 33–4, 43, 149
markets 43, 63, 72, 139–40, 142–3
materials
  coral 15–17, 161, 177
  glass 44–5, 112
  paving 52–3, 65–6, 162, 176–7
Milan 44–5, 69, 80–1, 116
miracles 139–40, 173
  miraculous images 160, 174
mulattieri (muleteers) 58, 137–8, 149–50,
  152–4, 181

Naples 45–7, 110–11, 165
natural disasters 8, 34–5, 84–5, 162–70 see also
  earthquakes, floods, plagues, storms
  portents 162–3
natural resources 9, 62–3, 112–13, 137–8
neighbours 7, 56, 65, 102–4, 172–3

Ostia 34–5, 46–7

parish 4, 56–7, 63, 82, 85, 87, 151–2,
  172–3, 185
Paschetti, Bartolomeo 11–12, 36–7,
  46–7, 98
petitions 80, 83–5, 96–7, 110–11, 115–19, 151
Pisa 28–9, 34–5, 42
plague 7–8, 29, 69–71, 103, 105–6, 124–5, 148–9,
  158–61, 169–78
pollution 80, 100–1, 133, 137, 151, 169
Ponzelli family of architects 98, 115
population growth 9
Porcacchi, Tommaso 16, 96
porters 75, 148–9, 176–7

INDEX 207

ports
 cosmopolitan society of 17–18, 37
 fortification 30, 33–4, 41–2, 44–5, 115
 historiography 28
 structures 30, 43, 45–6
poor, the 4, 11, 26, 56, 73, 79–80, 84–5, 92–4, 98,
  120–1, 123, 156, 171–4, 182
preaching 161–2
processions 76, 96, 169
proclamations 22, 53–4, 69–70, 136–8, 142
public health 5–7, 20–1, 25, 55, 87, 119, 170–1, 177

quarantine 170–3, 176–7

rainfall 53, 75, 80–1, 90–1, 96, 102–3, 140–1, 181–2
relics 167–8
religious institutions 55–7, 61, 67–8, 82–3, 85–7,
  91, 99, 126–7, 145–6, 173
Renaissance 6–9
rivers see also *Rome, Tiber*
 Bisagno 56, 67–8, 72–3, 77, 91, 99, 129
  146–50, 154, 180–3
 Brenta 82–3, 129, 135
 diversion 129
 Polcevera 129, 171, 182–3
 Rome 27–8, 31–2, 44–6, 52, 66, 78, 80, 106,
  160, 172
 Tiber 78, 95
rubble 52–3, 55, 74–6, 86–7, 115, 133, 137–8,
  140–1, 146–8, 153–5, 181
rubbish 22–3, 47, 52–3, 55–6, 61–2, 66–7, 73,
  75–6, 86–7, 89–90, 93, 95, 101–3, 127–8,
  133–57, 174–6, 185
 collection 57–8
 containers 27n.7, 124, 142–4

sacred space 56–7
sailors 28–30, 36–7, 112, 146–7, 180
saints
 St Isidore of Chios 167–9
 St Roch 158, 160, 162
 St Sebastian 125–6, 158, 160
 St Siro 168–9
salvage 109–14
Sanudo, Marin 41, 75, 164–5
seasonality 74–7, 92, 134–5, 147, 177–8
Seville 37
sex trade see also *brothel* 20, 40–1, 151
sewage 24n.130, 67, 93, 133–5
ships see *boats* 10, 15, 35–7, 46, 75, 83, 88, 93,
  107–14, 117, 175–6, 179–80
siltation 15, 29–30, 42, 45, 95, 101–2, 105–30,
  138–9, 143–4, 147, 149–50
stagnant water 30, 80, 84, 116–17

stench 27–8, 30, 55–6, 64–5, 72, 80, 105, 134–5,
  141–2, 144, 166–7, 177
storms 15, 34–5, 46–7, 75, 96–7, 107–10, 112–14,
  119, 126, 136–7, 146–7, 158–61, 169, 178–83
street food 76–7
streets
 cleaners 75, 149–52, 175
 disused 61
 paving 52–3, 65–70, 75–6, 80, 162, 176–7
 safety 59–61, 66–7, 77, 96–7, 154
 selling 70–4
 sweeping 53, 58, 66–7
 viability 52, 65–6, 71–2, 140–1
 washing 53, 66–7

tanning 36, 64, 100–1, 141–2
taverns and inns 30–1, 45, 71–2, 91–2, 165–6
Thompson, Michael 134
Tintoretto, Jacopo [c.1518–94] 1–2, 4
town criers 53–4
travel writing 34

vegetation 73, 89–90, 141–2
Venice
 Church of the Madonna dell'Orto 1–4
 citizenship 18
 comune marino 160
 fondamente 22–3, 61–2, 98, 121, 123, 126–7,
  136–7, 140, 178
 Ghetto 18, 39, 41, 53–4, 56, 124, 133, 143–4,
  150–1, 162–3
 Giudecca 64
 historiography 12–15
 islands 127, 145–6, 175–6, 179
 lagoon 1, 10, 20–1, 105, 109–10, 115–16,
  119–21, 123, 126, 128–30, 138, 141–2,
  144–6, 148, 154–5, 163, 178–9
 Murano 123, 148
  glass furnaces 44–7
 Piazza San Marco 43, 54, 65–6, 70–1, 139–40
 Provveditori alla Sanità (Health Office) 20–1,
  55, 70–1, 134–5, 139–40, 150–1, 170–3,
  175–7
 Provveditori di Comun 20–3, 57–9, 61–2,
  80–2, 84–5, 95–7, 101–2, 116–17, 122–3,
  126–7, 136–7, 140, 151–2, 155
 Punta di San Antonio 138, 145
 renovatio urbis 43
 Rialto 38–9, 43, 54, 60–1, 65–6, 70–1, 74,
  95–7, 142–3, 164–5, 175
 Savi ed Esecutori all Acque (Water
  Office) 20–1, 95–6, 116–17, 119, 126–8,
  143, 145, 155–6
 sottoportego di Corte Nova 160

208 INDEX

Virgin Mary 68–9, 112, 156–61, 172, 174
   Madonna del Boschetto 166–7
   Madonna de'Ricci 166

walls 26, 33, 39–41, 56, 60–1, 74, 140, 145, 160,
   164, 171–2, 175–7, 180–2
   city walls 27–8, 30, 41–2, 61, 68–9
   embankments 182–3
waste 9, 53–5, 61–3, 72–3, 133–57
   disposal 142–8
   removal 101–4
   reuse 135–6, 144–6
washing
   bodies 98
   cloth 98–101
   streets 67–8

water 78–104 see also *aqueduct, fountains,*
   washing, wells
   drinking 27–8, 34, 71, 79, 81–3, 88–91, 100
   moral associations 78, 80
   pollution 80, 100–1
   provision as act of charity 79–80, 83–5, 93–4,
   98, 100
wells 29–30, 72, 81–4, 100–1, 123–4, 136–7, 140
   cleaning 86–7, 149
   distribution 83–4
   form 82, 84–6
winds 36, 45, 146–7, 169, 171
windows 26, 55–6, 59–61, 80–1, 90, 102–3,
   141–2, 165, 174
women 11, 26, 37, 40–1, 54, 58–9, 71, 77–8, 99–100,
   103–4, 120–1, 142, 151, 161–2, 165, 168, 172